The Phantom Stethoscope

The Phantom Stethoscope

A Field Manual for Finding an Optimistic Future in Medicine

Stephen K. Klasko, M.D., M.B.A.
Gregory P. Shea, Ph.D.

HILLSBORO PRESS
Franklin, Tennessee

Printed in the United States of America

03   02   01   00   99   1   2   3   4   5

Library of Congress Catalog Card Number: 99-62184

ISBN: 1-57736-144-X

Cover by Gary Bozeman

Published by
HILLSBORO PRESS
an imprint of
PROVIDENCE HOUSE PUBLISHERS
238 Seaboard Lane • Franklin, Tennessee 37067
800-321-5692
www.providencehouse.com

*T*HROUGHOUT MY OWN SPACE TIME CONTINUUM, THERE HAVE BEEN PEOPLE WHO BELIEVED IN ME.

*T*O MY MOM & DAD, LEON & ESTELLE.

*T*O MY WIFE AND SPECIAL FRIENDS.

*M*OST IMPORTANTLY, TO LYNNE, DAVID, & JILL. MAY YOU HAVE AN OPTIMISTIC FUTURE AND BELIEVE IN YOURSELVES.

SKK

*T*O MY DAUGHTERS, WHO EXPRESS THE INCOMPREHENSIBLE NATURE OF WHAT I DO FOR A LIVING BY DECLARING THAT "DAD TEACHES MOSS ABOUT FUNGUS," BUT DO SEEM INTRIGUED WITH THE IDEA OF A BOOK, ANY BOOK, THAT WOULD HAVE MY NAME ON IT.

*T*O MY WIFE BECAUSE I AM BLESSED TO BE ABLE TO SAY THAT SHE IS MY WIFE.

GPS

CONTENTS

Preface   ix
Acknowledgments   xi

1. Of Bunn-o-matics and Basketballs   3
2. Of Computers and Cretins   8
3. Of Brothers and Blackouts   12
4. Of Abductions and Auntie Em   18
5. Of Mick Jagger and Managed Care   27
6. Of Prevention and Pain Relief   35
7. Of Orientation and Organized Care   43
8. Of Mind-sets and Metaphors   50
9. Of Alarm Clocks and Alphabet Soup   59
10. The History and Future of Managed Care   64
11. Of Risk Pools and Rolexes   80
12. Physicians as Negotiators: It's a Whole New Deal   89
13. Conflict Management: Negotiating Your Way to Resolution   95
14. Of Celebrities and Cesareans   103
15. Marketing and Strategic Planning in Health Care   109

16. Of Suits and Coats   119
17. The Challenge of Building Productive Alliances between
    Physicians and Administrators   123
18. Of Cat Scans and Customer Disservice   136
19. Market Forces and the Shape of Health Care Institutions   141
20. Of Caribbean Vacations and Contingency Fees   151
21. Law and Medicine   154
22. Of Pumpkins and Privilege   163
23. Information Systems in the Medical Environment   167
24. Total Quality Management and Clinical Pathways   174
25. Of French Toast and Friendly Interfaces   189
26. Physicians as Leaders: A Non-Physician Perspective   193
27. Of Genetic Selection and Jerry Springer   202
28. The Ethics of Medicine in the Twenty-First Century   205
29. Of Stress and Cinnamon Buns   221
30. Stress Management: The Personal and the Professional   224
31. Of Roberta and Revelations   229
32. Of Lattes and Lost (?) Opportunities   236

Glossary   243
About the Authors   257

PREFACE

THE PATH OF A CAREER IN MEDICINE USED TO BE PREDICTABLE. A student entered medical school, bought a stethoscope, and began a trek into a well-mapped world; a world established in its hierarchy and organization, understood by health care providers of all kinds, insurers and patients.

This is no longer true. The student, new stethoscope in hand—or the mid-career doc, for that matter—is now plunked into a landscape in flux. The old landmarks are gone, and new ones are yet to be found.

The Phantom Stethoscope (inspired by Norton Juster's classic *The Phantom Tollbooth*) is a field manual for survival in this chaos. It follows the story of Mila, who is abducted by aliens just before entering her residency in 1985, and who is returned fifteen years later with a pre-DRG understanding of how the system works. In alien-arranged tutorials by business school professors and health-care leaders, Mila is given a serious, clear analysis of the pitfalls that riddle this re-formed world of medicine; she—and we—are launched in the skills vital to success in this strange new environment.

This book is also best categorized as a medical business science fiction work. Why science fiction? When we first began this project of presenting an optimistic view of medicine over the next fifteen years, we were told by some that we were in a dream world. When we further explained that we would be starting the dialogue of what skill sets might be necessary for docs to understand the business world, many of our colleagues on both sides felt that was improbable, if not impossible. So, dream world? Art of the improbable? Sounded like a science fiction adventure to us. Most importantly, the fictional part of this book should help well established physicians understand more fully why they feel so frustrated about health care today. It should also help those who will be doing the bulk of their practice in the twenty-first century, from medical students to young physicians, understand why their older colleagues aren't having much fun nowadays. Hopefully after reading this book, you will move it from the fiction section of your library to the reference section and utilize the thoughts outlined here to feel more optimistic about the future of medicine.

In order to make the transition from fiction to reference easier, you will notice a few sanity saving tips:

- the fiction pages look very different from the nonfiction pages

- each fiction section is introduced by a small spaceship, each reference section by a small stethoscope

- and if you would care to do your browsing through the table of contents, it will quickly become apparent that the title to each fictional thread of the story begins with "Of."

- Since one of the premises in this book is that physicians take time to embrace change, we have made it easier to bridge that gap by allowing the readers to dip their feet into the cold water of reality instead of jumping right in. Chapter 8 bridges the story line with the skill sets by engaging Mila in a tutorial about . . . what else? . . . change. Our bias: the adaptation to rapid change is as real as it gets. Hopefully you will agree after reading this book.

In other words, if you would like to get to the "meat" of the book, that will be very easy.

So, enjoy the adventure. Remember that out of chaos can come creativity, and while these last few years might have convinced some providers to trade in their stethoscope for a briefcase, our ability to understand the clinical side, the social side, and now the business side will allow us to improve our own lives as well as those of our patients.

Stephen Klasko, M.D., M.B.A.
Gregory P. Shea, Ph.D.

Acknowledgments

SPECIAL THANK YOUS TO:

Beulah Trey . . . for her research and guidance and for understanding the true Mila.

The dozen physicians who consented to having their thoughts dissected by Beulah.

Karen Adelman . . . for editing . . . and editing . . . and editing.

Debbie Sims and Providence House Publishers for service above and beyond the call of at least contract and probably duty.

Richard Shel, Barbara Khan, Rob Burns, and Shel Rovin for lending the aliens their expertise.

Various Wharton faculty members consulted for various reasons.

Center For Applied Research, in particular Elizabeth Blaylock for conscientiousness extraordinaire; Jill Levan and Margaret Drubetsky for high quality, thorough researching and writing that is TRULY appreciated.

Robert Laskowski, M.D., M.B.A., for a graduation speech that made us proud to graduate.

Elliot Sussman, M.D., M.B.A., and Lehigh Valley Hospital for providing a vision of a medical system with an optimistic future.

Rose Haberacker for serving as the conscience of the book and making sure we got everything in on time or close enough.

Carol Varma for her creativity and brilliance.

Neil Berkowitz, M.D., who criticized this work as he does everything . . . honestly.

John Musich, M.D., M.B.A., who reminded me that the M.D. was much more important than the M.B.A.

Michael Patterson for unglossing the glossary.

Larry Stevens for being a father after mine was gone. (SKK)

The Phantom Stethoscope

CHAPTER 1

OF BUNN-O-MATICS
AND BASKETBALLS

PHILADELPHIA, PENNSYLVANIA, 1985

THIS WAS GOING TO BE A LONG, ROTTEN, HARD DAY. But if there was one thing that Mila had learned during her time at medical school, it was how to survive long, rotten, and hard days. You put your head down, you worked like a maniac, you followed the rules, you made it through.

What Mila had to survive at this moment was her daily 5:00 A.M. walk to work. The sun hadn't risen, and the sidewalks on Spruce Street were glazed with ice that had a menacing shine under the streetlights. Mila shoved her chapped hands deeper into her coat pockets. Just get to the deli, she thought. Caffeine will make it better.

The Spruce Street Deli was an oasis of warmth and light and good smells, although Mila could have done without hearing Olivia Newton John "getting physical" at this hour of the morning. Mila took her place in line, idly glancing at magazine covers. Half had headlines that used "Where's the beef?" in supposedly cute ways. Not that covers about the Woodstock fifteenth year reunion held a heck of a lot more appeal.

4   The Phantom Stethoscope

Stifling a yawn, Mila shifted around so she could see what was taking so long behind the counter. Well, that would explain it. Gladys, the large and cordial morning person, purveyor of the muddy coffee that sustained the Penn medical students, was making a new pot in the Bunn-o-matic. She was moving even more slowly than usual.

Tom Barrington, one of Mila's fellow med students from Penn, was first in line. He was an annoying guy, and Mila was glad to see that at the back of his blond head was a big, feathery cowlick he obviously knew nothing about.

"Hey, Big Gladys," Tom said, the cowlick flopping, "I'd like to get to my OB patient before she delivers."

Gladys continued to fit the filter into the machine. Didn't even turn to look at him. "You got a patient waiting on you in labor, and you're feeding your face? Shame on you, boy."

"She's not in labor, gorgeous Glads, she's only four months, but at the pace you're moving today, I still might miss the delivery."

Gladys shook her head, wiped her hands, and gave Tom a sharp assessing look. "Just to get you outta here, Doctor Tom, I'm going to stop what I'm doing and tell you about a real man. A real man who had me up all night, if you know what I mean."

"Thanks for sharing, Gladys. I feel a lot closer to you now. But I still don't have my coffee or donut."

"But Doctor Tom, you have to hear the details. We even left the Sixers-Bulls game early so my Moses Malone could win the bedroom scoring title. Man, he was good! With a capital G." Gladys let a slow smile cross her face, and Tom reddened. "Why Doctor Tom, you're awfully shy for a ladies' doc, aren't you? I just wanted you to know why I'm dragging today, wanted you to know it was worth it. If you had a social life, you'd have known without me telling you. As it is, I guess you could consider it part of your education."

Gladys turned back around and started in at the machine again. Slowly.

Mila, observing from the back of the line, bit back a laugh. Tom turned to her, as if in appeal, but Mila just shrugged. He cleared his throat. "Then again," he said to Gladys's broad back, "maybe I'll just skip coffee for today. Terrible for the cardiovascular system. Proven." As Tom left, the little bell on the door gave a merry jingle, and the cowlick seemed to dance to the tune.

"I do dearly love riling that boy," said Gladys. "You going to wait for the coffee, Mila?"

"Yup, although you've already started my day off right. There's really nothing like seeing Tom lose a round once in a while. Take your time."

Inwardly, though, Mila was cringing. The uncomfortable truth was that Tom wasn't the only one who did nothing but work. Nope, Mila thought, I can chalk up my social life as one of the sacrifices I've made for medicine. Maybe Gladys has the right idea. She works, goes home, has a life. It's a job, not a career. She has time for a love life.

Ah, yes, a love life. She thought about all the losers she had met—even gone out with once or twice—over the past six years. If you organized them properly, Mila thought, you'd need a whole category for the overconfident, overachieving, over-competitive Type A docs-to-be who were trying to overcome their lack of genital size by being overpowering in relationships. Yes, indeedy. All so hardworking, so ready to be deferred to by any and *every*body, that they could barely engage in civil conversation.

Then you'd need a category for the seemingly normal men who had grand mal seizures of insecurity when they found out she was a physician. All right, admittedly some of the disasters had been her fault. But only on the most insanely boring dates, and only because the guys always turned such a clinically interesting shade of vermillion when she managed to slip in a monologue about dissecting out the penis in anatomy lab.

The only person she knew who seemed to, well, "get it" about medicine and also have some kind of emotional groundedness and sense of humor was her med school classmate, Bill. He was clearly something special—smart as hell, but never preened himself about it; funny as hell, too, though he never shoved it down anyone's throat. In their sometimes childish med school gang, Bill was the grown-up, the one to trust. Of course, it didn't hurt that he was damn good-looking in a big boned, rambling way.

Yup, Bill would be on the short list if things were different, but things weren't different. He was her classmate and pal, and Mila was way too smart to mess with that.

If she'd learned anything from the people around her, it's that you don't mess with a friendship, and you don't start in on something that could screw up your work. When Mila was really honest about it she had to admit she simply did not have time or energy to pursue anybody or anything but getting the best grades she could. Maybe some day, but not now.

Mila knew all about combining medicine and relationships—she'd grown up with it. Mila's dad was a pediatrician in the old style. Respected and beloved, with pockets full of lollipops. There weren't too many kids in their town he didn't see pretty regularly. Well, OK, except his own. Medicine being more than just a job was one of the things Mila's dad had always loved. His patients loved it, too, and admired his being both a scientist and a caring physician.

Who knew if Dad realized what he'd given up of normal family life? When Mila was growing up, one of her mom's most constant refrains was reminding Mila's dad that he was home now, not at the hospital. That members of his family weren't patients who would hang on every word he said and treat him as if he were some all-knowing deity.

The bottom line, Mila thought, was that Dad was crazy about her and Matt and their mom; they always knew that, and they loved him back. But they also always knew that Daddy usually had to be at the clinic or at the hospital. Or on call. Or in his study. They shared him because they had to, and because he was a doctor. He knew things no one else, not even other grown-ups, knew, so only he could take sick people and make them well. Which in some potent way made him unlike other daddies. He was set apart and important. More important, in fact, than even the other important people whose kids he fixed.

There wasn't really ever a time that Mila didn't want all of that, too.

But she also wanted a sense of humor and the ability to look at life from the outside. That's what her mother had always had, and Mila was pretty sure that those qualities had kept their family together all these years. Her folks had actually beaten the national average for marriage longevity among physicians by more than twenty-four years, and her mom was rightly proud of that. Amazingly, her parents sometimes even still seemed to *like* each other.

"Honey, you meditating or ordering today?" Gladys's hands rested on her ample, aproned hips. "Egg hoagie, maybe? Give you some energy for saving all those lives?"

"Oh, shit!" Mila jolted out of her trance and saw her watch. "It's six!" She'd daydreamed her way to the front of the line, and now she was going to be late for morning rounds. "Just coffee, Gladys. A really, really big one."

"Mila, girl, life is short. You forget to enjoy it, baby, and it's gone just the same. You end up in the stars either way." She handed Mila a styrofoam cup with a smiley face, and a handful of change.

"In my next life, Gladys," Mila said as she zipped the coins into her purse, "I'll chug piña coladas and eat hoagies with mayo all day and all night. But now

I'm not stopping for anything." The door jingled as it swung shut behind her.

"That girl doesn't have time for anything," Gladys mused. "Everybody learns for their own selves, don't they?"

Nothing but stars. She slept. She woke. She had one of those dreams again—the one where she flew to bits in the end. What was a dream, what was real? She wasn't sure. Was it hours, or days, or years on the ship? She didn't know. "Going home soon," Quam thought into Mila's brain. But the concept of home had no meaning to her in this bewildered state.

Once again, the neural stimulator was fitted to her head. Before drifting off, she smiled back at her styrofoam coffee cup as she always did before she went back under. The contents, of course, were long since gone. Evaporated, every drop.

CHAPTER 2

OF COMPUTERS
AND CRETINS

MILA BUMPED INTO HER FRIENDS IN THE MEDICAL STUDENT LOUNGE. Literally bumped into them—at full speed—and sent Bill sprawling. He waved away her apologies and the hand she offered to help him up: "Gotta breathe again first," he gasped. She squatted next to him until he managed a smile. "I'm fine," he said. But then he cocked his shaggy head at her. "Are you OK, Mila? You look very strange."

She did feel a little peculiar. How had she gotten here?

Tom sauntered in, still sporting his cowlick, still coffeeless after his rout by Gladys, but otherwise seemingly recovered. "And he's down for the count! How you doing, Billy buddy? If you want to sue, I saw the whole thing!"

"Just an accident, Tom," Bill said as he got himself up.

Tom, however, had no intention of letting any opportunity pass. "Mila, I always dreamed of your astounding physical powers, but, whoa, baby . . ." He pressed a sarcastic hand to his heart, but then stopped. "Hey, wait a minute. How'd you get ahead of me, demon Mila? You teleport?"

"Hush, you," said Carla, who glanced from Bill to Mila. Carla's huge mass of frizzled hair seemed to swing independently of her head movements. There was a little line of concern between her eyes. "Mila may have astounding physical powers, but I have astounding *analytic* powers. And they tell me this is a good time for you to butt out. Mila? What's up?"

How *had* she gotten here? She tried to steady herself by studying the familiar surroundings. The brown vinyl couch, repaired with duct tape. The lingering smell of last night's anchovy pizza. The specimen cup full of aging daffodils. All the familiar, under-maintained details of the student lounge. But what was that dream, and where was her coffee?

"Mila? What's going on?"

Was she having a TIA or something? At that, Mila knew she was being absurd. "I'm sorry guys. Nothing. Zoning out, I guess," Over the last four years there was hardly a rare disease she hadn't convinced herself she had. Obviously, this was another. What a relief.

"Hey Mila," said Tom, "Could you bowl *me* over next time? But maybe in a cleaner place? I'm picturing sparkling white sheets—"

"Zip it," commanded Carla. "Didn't I make it clear that no one's in the mood today for your projectile idiocy?"

"Gotta love women, don't you think, Bill? So feisty when the moon is full. Thank God you're going into psych where you can't do anything irreparable when your hormones are up, Dr. Carla."

Bill brushed a gum wrapper off of his coat. He deposited it in the over-flowing wastebasket, from which it promptly fluttered back to the floor. He clapped one hand on Carla's shoulder, one hand on Tom's. "You know, guys, we're all a little tense about today. Why don't we all just relax and give each other a break."

Carla was having none of it. "At noon today, my misogynist friend," she said to Tom, "I will know at which prestigious university I will do my psychiatry residency. But I need no further education to handle insecure, genitally compromised males such as yourself. If the computer is so without conscience as to assign you to an OB-GYN residency *anywhere*, I will personally take on the responsibility of pounding the machine into little pieces. For the greater good of humanity."

"You are woman, hear you roar," sang Tom joyfully. He was always happy baiting Carla.

"Tom," said Bill, and put his arm around his shoulders, "you are a cretin. We're not in that frat of yours in Michigan. Knock it off. And Carla, don't worry. I injected the computer with 20 mg of Valium, and it assigned Tom to a family practice residency in South Dakota."

10   The Phantom Stethoscope

As the debate raged on, Mila slipped into the bathroom unnoticed. She was reeling again, but this time with the realization that she'd forgotten that this was one of the most important days of her career. Today was match day. At noon, exactly, she'd find out where she'd spend her residency, and what she'd be doing. Funny. With all the talk about the art of medicine, every medical student's future now depended on the output of a fancy box of electronics.

Mila splashed some water on her face. Maybe the looming of the match explained her lapses. Probably some sort of anxiety symptom.

Noon. She'd find out where she was going at noon. Would it be New York? The city didn't thrill her, but New York Eastside Hospital sure did. Boy, did that place have a great reputation.

She thought back to the interviews and all the things she wished she had said. But she didn't have a real secure feeling about getting Eastside, her first choice. It was all very well receiving that call from the residency director, and she'd gotten excited when he'd said she was a top pick. But then Mila'd realized he probably made that call to dozens of applicants, whether they'd ever be selected or not.

Out of paper towels, of course. How much effort would it take to keep this place minimally decent? She grabbed a stack of the waxy toilet paper and slapped it onto the ledge of the sink. OK, Mila, she thought, when you're taking it out on personal hygiene products, it's time to admit that you're nervous. She obviously needed this moment of privacy; she leaned on the tiled wall.

The whole process was a game. But, to tell the truth, it was a game she'd played, too. Her supposedly spontaneous "personal statement" had gone through many a draft. There were several attempts that made their way to the trash can. The first four had begun, "Ever since I was in the crib, I've wanted to be a physician." Ugh. Then she'd cleared her brain by writing a poem:

Cutting's what I want to do—
Couldn't bear to spend my days taking care of the flu.
I might want to strangle half the surgeons I meet
But getting those fees is sure gonna be sweet!

She'd tacked this opus on the wall over her typewriter next to one of her favorite Far Side cartoons. As often happened, her mind drifted for a few seconds, and the version she ended up using just spilled out. The first part was kind of hokey. A simile equating a surgical career to the care of a Mrs. Bonner, a particularly difficult patient she'd been assigned to help with in med school. Her last paragraph, however, had been a sincere attempt to predict the future that she would be inheriting five years hence at the end of her residency. She was proud of that last paragraph, and she could almost recite the last few sentences.

> I foresee a medical community more joined together by the academic and caring parts of medicine, and less by economics. As technology becomes less expensive and access to care more organized, physicians will gain stature not only as healers, but also as public health policy-makers. I look forward to being a part of that future in surgery. If progress continues at its current pace, my time in medicine will be the most exciting ever. It will resemble the strides in the sixties in space travel, with technology, organization, and government commitment working together for the good of all.

Pretty smooth for the daughter of a pediatrician. She ran her fingers through her hair, straightened up, and reality was gone.

CHAPTER 3

OF BROTHERS
AND BLACKOUTS

THE SPACESHIP SEEMED TO BE STANDING STILL. Mila, even semiconscious, could tell that Quam was really annoyed. He was yelling at Ajax and the other two Climarans standing next to him. Yelling was probably the wrong word, though, Mila thought dozily, since they communicated through telepathic brain waves. Climarans telegraphed a great deal through gill movement, too, but Mila was too far under to do more than peek out under heavy lids.

Quam was unhappy. Mila saw him motioning toward her with five of his six arms. Sleepy, sleepy. "Putting her back isn't working," he kept saying. Through the haze drifted the thought that they were having trouble returning her to earth where they had found her. And when they had found her. And that seemed important. Mmm. Back to sleep? Not yet. Sharp splinters of argument kept bothering her, keeping her awake.

"It is not close enough." Quam's thoughts needled her brain. "Fifteen years earth time is an unconscionable miss."

Down and down, their voice/thoughts a blur, ". . . standard memory erase . . ." great billowing clouds of black, ". . . new temporal zone . . ." and down and down and gone . . .

12

". . . Prostatectomy on Mr. Fenstermacher, Mila? Mila?" Thornton's voice was just sharp enough to break her daze. "Mila? Short interlude in outer space?"

Mila shook away the trance. Another dream. Another blank. Good God—she was on rounds with Dr. Thornton and didn't remember getting here. How could this be happening? "Excuse me Dr. Thornton. What was the question?"

"Lifestyle changes for Mr. Fenstermacher?" A strange looking orderly pushed an empty gurney past the knot of residents. "In the first months after prostatectomy?"

How could she have lost the thread of the case? What was that bizarre dream again?

"Well, one thing's for sure, sir," Tom grinned, "He can cancel his subscription to the Playboy channel."

"Barrington." Thornton was mildly annoyed, but Mila, for once, was grateful for Tom's blather. She couldn't quite focus; her glazed eyes kept straining at the retreating orderly with the gurney, trying to make sense of the image. The man's shape seemed to be arbitrarily lumpy, and the skin at the back of his neck seemed to be—greenish? She blinked several times. It was all so odd. "Barrington," Thornton was saying, "tell me you're not applying to Penn for your residency. Because if you are, I'll be forced to reevaluate my career options. Kamikaze pilot will suddenly look good."

"Don't worry, sir," Tom beamed. "I'm going to some nice community hospital where the women will reward my OB-GYN talents and winning personality with lots of gratitude. And money."

Dr. Thornton raised an eyebrow. "Ah, yes," he said, "patients—or at least their third party payers—will reward you richly for the sale of your soul. All you have to do is give up real, academic medicine. But, Barrington, it's debatable if women, or any humans for that matter, will appreciate your warped sense of humor in whatever town you end up in. Now, where were we? Of course. Mila was going to tell us about post-op expectations, then we'll go in and gently check our patient's incision. Mila?"

Mila's beeper went off with four sharp, loud tones. "Good timing, Mila," Carla whispered, leaning over. "Can you teach me to do that, too?"

Mila made her way down the hall to get her page. She was no wiser or happier about her strange blank, and she hated that she'd embarrassed herself in front of Dr. Thornton. He was the busiest surgeon at the University of Pennsylvania, and the one she admired the most. He'd forsaken most of the teaching and research aspects of his job in order to operate. "I didn't go into surgery to use my head," he often said. Despite that, he was great with his patients. He had an uncanny knack during rounds of leaving each patient smiling or laughing, sometimes clutching pillows over their incisions. "No more laughing for you," he'd say as he left.

By the time Mila got to the nursing station to pick up the phone, she felt much less discombobulated. She'd been under some strain and lost her concentration for a moment; that was all. And the orderly with "green" skin obviously just had a disorder she wasn't familiar with yet. As she tucked the battered receiver between shoulder and ear, a tour of expectant parents crowded the hall. Between the bulging bellies, Mila caught a glimpse of the poor orderly pushing what looked like the same gurney down the hall once again. What was it—the gurney soapbox relay from the dermatology department? She didn't have a clear enough view to guess at what could be wrong with him, but that could wait.

"Dr. Langston speaking," she said.

"So, sis, what surgical program will it be? At what hospital will you help medicine transcend its earthly bonds?" The pleasant normality of hearing her brother's voice caught Mila by surprise. Wow—she really was tightly wound.

"Thanks, Matt-o. Won't know 'til noon, but your calming influence is always appreciated. How's Liza?" Liza was Matt's incredibly sweet fiancee. The two of them were finishing pediatric residencies at the University of North Carolina and were preparing to start a practice together.

"She's great. I want to remind you to get July 18 off for the wedding." Mila smiled—this was at least the ninth unnecessary reminder. Matt didn't have any jitters about the impending marriage, but he sure did over the details of the wedding.

"Relax. Short of getting abducted by aliens, I'll be there. The way my love life is going, being maid of honor will be the closest I get to a wedding for a while."

Not that her brother's marriage or future progeny had a chance of being normal with two parents as pediatricians. Yes, yes, Matt kept saying he was going to be a different kind of physician than their dad. He'd even rebelled briefly against the medical career so thoroughly expected of him. He'd started out with a major in economics and gotten his MBA. But along the way he'd switched to a dual major with chemistry and had, eventually, made it to medical school. Then, to her father's pride, a pediatric residency. She always wondered whether her brother felt bad that he was, in essence, wasting his MBA. Realistically, how could that help him be a better doc in the future?

The future of medicine! That always seemed to be the major topic of Mila-Matt debates during school vacations. Matt held what Mila thought was an unrealistically pessimistic view. "Medicine's golden days are gone, Mila," he'd say. "An economic crisis is brewing, and it's going to be huge."

"I don't see why you have to be so cynical," Mila would say. "You've let yourself be perverted by those business types. They have no idea what we do."

Their father always ended up on her side. "If you take care of patients well, you will always be rewarded both professionally and economically. That will never change, and business people will never have a place in medicine." Matt would shrug and change the subject to one he had a chance of winning.

"What are you doing?" Somehow Mila managed to speak it aloud. Quam and Zolta turned to her, surprisingly unsurprised.

"We are trying to remember how we got into this mess," Zolta seemed to say. "This is the first Climaran borrowing that hasn't worked for millennia. It's been a disaster from the beginning. The time continuum has not cooperated. Does our specimen have no interest in the gain of knowledge?"

"Apparently not," said Quam.

Twenty minutes until match time. Funny, but it seemed as if everyone—including herself—had been on edge for weeks, and now there was an almost palpable calm. What could be done was done, their futures were determined and sitting on some hard disc, and all that was left was to find out.

Mercifully for patients and students alike, the med school gave them this hour off. Mila and her friends sat in the lounge, quiet. Carla and Tom sat next to each other on the worn couch. Each was intent on fiddling with tufts of stuffing poking out of the cracked cushions.

"Hey, Tom," Carla asked. She was almost whispering, her eyes turned away. "I was wondering. Why did you want to be a doctor? For real."

Tom took a moment, answering as quietly. "I wanted a career where nobody could tell me what to do. No matter what else changes about the world, doctors will always be their own boss."

Carla shook her head. She laughed softly. "Is that what you put in your personal statement?"

"Nah," murmured Tom, "I put the same bullshit as everyone else about wanting to be a healer since I've been a child." The intercom overhead clicked twice, then was silent.

"How about you, Bill?" Mila asked. Bill's big frame was stretched over the ancient, peeling captain's chair, and at her question he scrunched a smile at the ceiling. "I suppose I should be embarrassed. I really *have* had the dream of being a doctor ever since I was a kid. Even when my friends wanted to be singers and astronauts. I think it was because of our family doctor. I remember being sick at home and him stopping on his way from the office. He chatted with me and my mom and gave me a shot of penicillin. My folks had a lot of respect for him. He had a big farm house. Respect and a big farm, that was something for a kid to look up to in Iowa."

Chalk another one up for Bill, Mila thought, he really is something. Not cynical, yet not naive, either. She mulled that over, but only for a moment. Sentimental gush headed the list of Things She Had No Time for at the Moment. Wonder if she could get a custom Daytimer page for that? Great, the ultimate obsessive-compulsive—relegating my life to a to-do list. She shook the whole thing off. "Your turn, Carla," she said.

"Me?" Carla slid further down the cushion. "I actually had a lot of pressure not to go into medicine. My dad was a lawyer and both my brothers went to law school. But I was great at science and never liked writing those warm and fuzzy essays. It came down to doing what I was good at and making an impact. Law never made a whole lot of sense to me. I like black and white, right and wrong. There were too many gray areas in law."

"Hey," Tom said, "Three minutes till noon!"

Dr. Hughes, the dean of students, addressed the mob. "In a few minutes we will hand each of you a slip with your residency match printed on it. Please understand that this is a binding contract. It represents where you will spend the next three to five years of your life and career. I wish you all the best in your chosen disciplines."

When Mila got her envelope, she moved away from the crowd. While she enjoyed sharing experiences with her classmates, this was one that she wanted to be alone to appreciate—she headed toward the empty classroom next door.

At least she'd thought the room was empty. Just as she closed the door, she saw that same orderly, standing in the corner. He wore greens and a mask but, my God, how could she not have noticed? It wasn't a man but a . . . monster. Two heads, six arms, and six legs. She took a hurried step back.

"My name is Ajax," it said, "and I'll be your guide for the journey."

Climara, Mila learned, orbited around and between three suns. The possibilities for various degrees and qualities of "day" and "night," had the Climarans chosen to define them as such, were without end. The Climarans, however, did not divide time by the state of the sky. They worked until they tired, slept until they awoke. They were always amazed at how other planets saw time as something to chop apart, rather than the smooth, pliable, multidimensional unity it was.

Tom looked at the paper several times before he forced himself to believe it. He had not gotten into any of his first five choices. He was going to be spending the next four years doing OB-GYN at Presbyterian Samaritan Hospital in the heart of poverty in Chicago, damn the place.

Well. He'd make it into something good. If nothing else, he would appear to be that much more sophisticated in the eyes of his sweet suburban patients when he finally got to them. Sure. He could see it working.

But boy, Carla and Bill could be a little kinder than to celebrate right there in front of him.

"Where's Mila?" Bill said. He'd gotten his first choice, of course, Johns Hopkins. "I wish New York were closer to Baltimore. I'm sure she'll go to Eastside. But where is she?"

The crowd was dispersing. There were practical matters to attend to, such as finishing the last three months of medical school. But Mila was nowhere to be seen.

"That's strange," Bill said.

"Oh, well," said Tom, "Maybe she ended up someplace she didn't expect, too."

C H A P T E R 4

OF ABDUCTIONS
AND AUNTIE EM

THE ROOM, IF IT COULD BE CALLED A ROOM, WAS WHITE. But it couldn't be called a room, Mila thought. It was a Whiteness. The Whiteness was white. There was no up nor down, no here nor there. Only Mila and Not Mila. And Not Mila was white.

"Where would you prefer?" issued a thought into her brain.

"What?" Mila screamed, but she heard nothing of her voice.

"Not what. Where?" spoke the thought.

"Anywhere! A place. Any place."

"She requires corporeality. Of place and person, please. Use existing image."

Instantly Mila was in Dorothy's room in Auntie Em's house after the return from Oz. The walls, the light, Mila's own body, were the shades of grays and blacks from the beginning of the movie. Over her stood the farmhands, the three who'd been the Tin Man, the Lion, and the Scarecrow in Oz.

"What the hell is this?" asked Mila. "Where is my voice?"

"Auditory adjustments, Ajax,"

"What is this?" She screamed without sound, then suddenly, with sound. She promptly stopped. Mila was not a screamer.

18

"Thank you," she said. Talk about reflexive manners. "All right. Who are you? Where am I? I take it we're really not in Kansas anymore?"

"We extracted a comforting image from your emotion base," the Scarecrow/farmhand said. "I am Quam from the planet Climara. You are presently on our ship, but as it exists outside the space/time continuum with which you are familiar, it is without a physical presence you can perceive. Many beings dislike non-dimensionality, require corporeality for maximum comfort. Many, too, dislike direct essence-to-essence communication and require physical modes of discourse. We are happy to accommodate, as you can see."

"You are from another planet? You're aliens?"

"We are," said the Lion. "Would you prefer such an image? I think one exists in your psycho-emotional archive."

Instantly the scene around her changed, snapping into the cheesy colors of a mid-sixties B-movie. A sci-fi junker. She was in an alien spaceship, with curved walls rising around her covered with dials, levers, and tiny blinking lights. Mila lay strapped onto a gurney—the one the orderly had been pushing around, for God's sake.

She was in the room with aliens. Real, no-kidding, two-headed, six-armed little guys. Green.

"Are these surroundings more consistent with expectations?" The short one had spoken. "Your comfort is our pleasure."

"Who are you? And why are you quoting commercials?"

"I am Ajax, Mila, and I am considered an expert in many of the primitive cultures in your galaxy. I am most proud of my memorabilia and trivia knowledge about your planet. I would enjoy talking to you about twentieth-century earth. You might say that you and your planet are my 'hobby.'" Something beeped on the wall.

The hobby spoke, "Why have you kidnapped me?"

"Oh, Mila," said the tallest one reproachfully, "I am Quam. We do not kidnap, only borrow."

The middle-sized alien waved an arm significantly. "We Climarans are gatherers of knowledge, gainers of wisdom. Ajax brought you here so we may gain knowledge of your planet during your era. We've been borrowing you on and off for several of your weeks. Have you not noticed? You were semiconscious and were returned right where we found you. Almost. This is simply one of the few sessions we are conducting with you in a conscious state."

"Why me?" And why, wondered Mila, does this dream seem nothing like a dream?

"You were chosen because your medical system, while technologically of little interest, is at the cusp of major changes related to a confluence of clinical and economic factors. You are one of a group of physicians who will face that explosive change. Change is of interest to Climarans. We live in a nonlinear space/time continuum, hence sequentiality and consequentiality are concepts that intrigue us. Have no fear. We will extract the information painlessly and quickly, as we have done with you before, then return you to your time and place at the same moment we took you, again as we have done before. For your trouble, we will infuse you with some knowledge that will help you in your future career. Your residency placement, by the way, is New York Eastside Hospital."

Oh gee, thanks, Mila thought. Like I'm going to trust some B-movie dream character. Speaking of which, how could she have gone to sleep without getting the results of her match? Obviously she was going to wake up any minute and be back in her dorm, or back in another of those embarrassing situations that she'd been waking up to lately.

But wait. She'd never been aware during those "blackout" periods, of the actual "blackout." Or of reality. And why did this feel so persistently real? She tried to will herself to wake up. She blinked several times. The control panel lights, the creatures, all still there.

Mila started to panic. "I'm a hostage. Let me go!" Mila kicked at the restraints on the gurney, tore at them with her teeth.

"Certainly. They are not 'real' in any case," said the middle-sized alien. The straps disappeared, and so did Mila's fear. If it's a dream, it's a dream, she decided. And if not . . . well, never mind. "You're not going to dissect my brain or anything?" she asked.

"Oh, actually we're doing that now. Non-corporeally, of course. We've done it in every session. You don't mind, do you?"

A big, blue earth passed across the porthole.

"Do I mind?" Mila said, "Why, I must say I do."

"Then don't think of it as a brain dissection, Mila, think of it as downloading," said the alien. "I am Zorak."

Download this, thought Mila.

"A mildly obscene invective from the earth's twentieth century," trilled Ajax. "Oh, Quam, it really was! Do another, Mila!"

"No, thank you," said Mila, and did what she could to think nothing. There was a period in which there was no movement or sound but the fakey beeps and whirs of the ersatz spaceship equipment.

When Ajax spoke again, it was in a more respectful tone. "While the information is being 'downloaded,' Mila, might we talk?" Mila glared for a minute and then relented. What could it hurt, she thought. "What should we talk about?"

"There are a few things that have never made sense to me about your social arrangements. In your family structures, there seem to be only two main participants, correct?"

"Uh, ideally, yeah."

"But with an even number of mates, with no possible majority within a marriage, who casts the deciding vote? Who breaks ties?"

"Nobody breaks ties. We fight it out, Ajax. Usually one person wins and the other pouts about it for the next year or so." Mila paused. There had been something so—human about the question, she found herself feeling almost comfortable with him.

"See Mila, it's not so bad," Ajax said. "We are—now tell me how I'm doing with this—the hostess with the mostest, are we not?"

"Not bad, Ajax. But whether or not you're a hostess at all is somewhat dependent on the answer to my question for you. Do you advanced creatures not have sexes?"

"Our family units," broke in the Quam one, "are made up of three genders. Two are the equivalents of a male and a female in your world. The third is asexual but has an activated area in the brain for extra logic. Our marriages are comprised of a male, a female, and a logician. The logician gets the last word."

Now that would be some OB unit: Congratulations Ms. Climaran—it's a boy! No, a girl! No, a logician!

"That's not quite accurate, Mila. We are all born the same with the potential for male genitalia, female genitalia, or the extra logic lobe."

"Would you stop reading my mind? At least pretend to wait until I say things out loud, okay?"

"Okay," said Ajax. "Did you hear me? I got to say 'Okay.' Okay! This is very exciting for a student of primitive planets."

Quam proceeded, pointedly ignoring Ajax. "At the age of thirteen, we choose which lobe to activate. The decision is based on demographic need and our own preference. It actually works quite well. At that point we change our name. All female names start with a 'Z,' all male names with an 'A,' all logician names with a 'Q.' Very neat, very orderly, no need for conflict."

No room for fun either, Mila thought, forgetting that her thoughts were being read.

"Fun is very relative," Ajax said, maybe a bit miffed at being ignored in his "okay" transports. "On your planet, fun seems to be often at another's expense. Even sex seems to be used as a weapon. Our system accounts for disagreement with amiable third party resolution."

"And I," said Quam, "as attending logician, declare this discussion at an end. Mila, sleep."

Waking to the sight of flailing arms—especially when there are twelve arms and they belong to only two beings—is not pleasant. Nor is it pleasant to realize that waking has not dispelled a bad dream. Mila squeezed her eyes shut. OK, God, or whoever is up there without two heads: If I double-swear always to fold my clothes right out of the dryer, then could this dream please, please, be over?

"Mila." The name was thought into her mind. "There's a slight logistical problem. I advise you to clear your head of juvenilia and marshal your faculties. We have ceased administration of emotional or intellectual controls so you may participate in this discussion fully."

How about, thought Mila, how about, God, if I never check a chocolate, ever again! How about if I just always eat the first one I grab? And didn't we settle that you'd stay out of my brain and use voices to speak? Quam, didn't we?

"Mila."

Even if it's coconut. Even if it's marshmallow. Mila was back on the gurney. She turned face down and covered her head with her arms.

"Mila, there is an instability in the space/time continuum around your planet in 1985 and the time of your most recent departure. That this might account for the otherwise inexplicable popularity of someone named Kenny Rogers, of whom Ajax, it seems, is quite fond—"

Not happening. Not happening.

"—is interesting but insignificant. What is significant is that returning you to the precise moment of departure is not possible."

"Abduction, Quam," said Mila, twisting around to see him. It was impossible, but he was still there. Well, if this was to be her hallucination of choice, she would at least acquit herself with aplomb. "Abduction, not departure. If it'd been a departure I would've had my choice of peanuts or pretzels. I would've had my tray in the upright and locked position. And I . . ." She stopped. "What did you just say?"

"Each of several previous attempts at near-simultaneous return have resulted in your personal disintegration and in the subsequent overtaxing and failure of our human regeneration facilities. It falls to me to apologize and to inform you of these regrettable circumstances. We will therefore return you safely fifteen years into your future, in your year 2000."

Two thousand. This was absurd, obviously. This happened in really bad movies, yes. And in stupid dreams like the ones she'd been having in the last few days. Which made no sense. No sense. Nothing about this made sense.

Unless.

A bead of sweat ran down the side of her face, into the corner of her mouth.

Unless those dreams were the reentries Quam was talking about. The reentries that didn't work.

Unless this whole thing was completely impossible, but still, somehow, true.

But if it were true, it was bad. Very bad. She would leave earth at the age of twenty-seven, return at forty-two? Poof, just miss the prime of her life?

"No, no," spoke Quam into her mind, "these minutia have been accounted for. You will be returned at the physiological age at which you left. Moreover, information that will bring your clinical knowledge up to the minute will be infused into your brain. The clinical advances that have been made in your absence will be of interest to you, I trust, particularly as they will allow a smooth re-entry into your profession."

Ah, yes, Mila thought. I could strap on my personal futuristic jet-pack and zip on over to the nearest chief of surgery. Sorry, sir, those naughty aliens made me a little late, about fifteen years late. It'd go over big.

"We share your concern, Mila," said Zolta.

"Concern? This is not a concern. Concern is not getting honors or a high pass on a rotation. Concern is being fifteen minutes late for rounds, not fifteen years. This is a major, life-screwing-up, cataclysmic event." It would have taken all she had to keep Mila from flying at one of their throats if she could have figured out which throat to fly at.

"We have made the necessary arrangements, Mila," said Quam. "Your new residency plans are in place. Not only that, memories of your having been in a fifteen-year coma have been implanted in the minds of your friends, family, and colleagues, as has been a potent curiosity dampener which, as an added precaution, your body will involuntarily emit. An extended, unexplained coma with no deleterious effect on your health or career will seem unextraordinary to those with whom you interact."

"How handy," she said. "Forgive me if I seem unenthusiastic, but this little scheme cheats me of all those years I could have known my parents. And my brother. And my friends. She thought fleetingly of Bill. Have you thought of a way to 'arrange' that? Or were you planning to, hmm, inject us all with fifteen years of compressed memories? Maybe implant a nano-nostalgia-generation mechanism in my left nostril to make it all more comforting?"

There was a silence. "We should tell her," Mila heard Zolta thinking to Ajax. They seemed suddenly to forget she was there.

"Research indicates it would cause pain," thought Ajax. "Telling her is counter to the mandates of 1108a clause 19, paragraph B of the abduction—er—exchange code."

"Indeed," Quam thought. "And yet it is necessary."

Quam turned all four eyes upon Mila, one by one. "A recently developed technology allows us to follow strands of possibility along the space/time continuum. In order to assess the emotional loss to which you refer, we followed the strand representing the life you would have led had we not altered its course. We quantified the level of career satisfaction and interpersonal emotional charge you would have accumulated and found it, well, to be negligible. We factored in romantic love, familial affection, all possible affectors. Yet we found that in that undisturbed strand you would have become overwhelmed with the profound changes in the medical world and unable, as a result, to thrive in any aspect of your life. You would have become uninspired by your work, cynical, hopeless with your loved ones, stalled, and disappointed."

Ajax interrupted. "A real, ah, 'burnout case.' That, I believe, is the appropriate term."

"I guess I've just been called an intergalactic loser. You sure know how to flatter a gal." But let's remember, she thought, it's not like I have a choice about how to become a doc, or how to be one. The path is pretty damn straightforward. Not easy, but straightforward. And especially not easy for an "other gender surgeon." Though she'd never thought of herself as a woman undergraduate or woman medical student, it had been made thoroughly clear to her that what she was working to become was a woman surgeon. And that she'd have to put up with plenty of grief and use all of her determination to get there.

Nope, not easy. And the only thing in her control was whether she followed that straightforward path successfully or not. "Whatever these 'profound changes' are," Mila said fiercely, "they can't actually affect what it's like to be a physician. Not on the inside." You alien assholes, she added to herself.

"Mila," offered Ajax, "all my data about humanoids indicate that this will be difficult to accept."

"Could I possibly be allowed a private thought?"

"But Mila," he pressed, "the whole thing can really be seen as an extra-ordinarily fortuitous turn of events for you."

Zolta continued. "We will reimburse you for your relatively limited damages with a thorough education in the challenges and the opportunities in medicine at the turn of the century. You will be equipped, as you would not have been had we not borrowed you, to excel in this world and work to alter it as you think best. You will have the knowledge of what might have been to spur your efforts. You are being given a second chance, Mila. Not many are."

There was a silence, and as if by agreement, it was allowed to grow. A purple galactic cloud floated across a porthole. She didn't like it, but these beings were cracking her defenses. Stalled and disappointed? Minimal—what an expression—interpersonal emotional charge? Was that really where she'd been heading?

"We'll train you in areas in which, in your undisturbed strand, you were inadequately prepared: Negotiation, Strategic Planning, Marketing. One of us will even be available to you on site. Ajax, I think. He'd enjoy it the most."

Mila realized she was off the gurney and pacing. She stopped and turned to face the Climarans. Her shoes sank oddly into the floor. If there was one thing her medical training had taught her, it was the importance of moving on from what couldn't be controlled. She let out a long, slow breath.

"Well," she said, "when do we start?"

"Now," said Quam, and led her into a small, perfect study. Books lined the walls, although when Mila peered closely at them the titles seemed to blur. A beam of sunlight striped a neat wooden desk, on which lay a stack of rich vellum, quill pen, and ink.

"No," said Quam, and now arrayed on the desk was Mila's old school stuff: manual typewriter, small bottle of White-Out, chewed pencil with troll at the end, and all the other essentials of the 1970 junior-high homework crowd.

"I'll leave you now, if you like," said Quam.

"But what should I do?"

"Oh—everything you'll need you'll find in there. We thought it might be easier for you to start small." Now on the desk lay a wooden box, about a foot square, with a lid held on with a hook.

CHAPTER 5

OF MICK JAGGER
AND MANAGED CARE

MILA OPENED THE BOX AND FOUND HERSELF LOOKING DOWN ON SIX FINELY WROUGHT DOLLS IN LAB COATS. She took one out and almost yelped when she saw that it was a perfect little Tom. She dropped it. The Tom had winked.

"Jeez, Mila," said the little Tom, "some way to treat your pal. Simulations have feelings too, y'know." Simulation. Oh. Mila tried to calm her pulse. Climarans sure knew how to make learning fun, damn them.

"Steady as she goes, lil' filly," Tom flared his minuscule nostrils. "Isn't it good to know some things never change? It seems you're dependent, as usual, on old Tom for guidance. It's just too bad you had to travel so far for it, this time!"

Interesting. She wanted to kill even the six-inch Tom. Somehow, knowing that made her breathe more normally. She squinted at the figure—it was a Tom fifteen years older than the one she knew, a Tom with a little less hair and a paunch.

"I think I saw you in a biscuit ad, Tom. If I poke your belly, do you go 'Tee-Hee?'"

"Enjoy yourself, Mila, but you need to hear this." Something in his tone of voice was new and serious and almost eclipsed her annoyance. "In your absence, the medical profession has been spoiled."

"That strains credulity."

He shook his head. "I wanted to be a physician because of the independence, remember? Now doctors have lost the decision-making power in patient care. Ten years ago, if I wanted to admit a patient for a hysterectomy, I spoke to the patient, we picked a date, and that was it. *Now* I have to get a referral from the family doctor. I have to talk with the insurance company; I have to get three expert opinions; my nurse has to talk to his clerk; and I have to fight with a retired internist who tells me whether it is indicated or not and how long my patient can stay. By the time all that stuff is done, the patient and I have forgotten what we were going to do."

Mila must have looked as skeptical as she felt. Tom seemed to study her, then boosted himself onto a paperweight. He dangled his little feet.

"All right. I'll have to admit that the system had become bloated. We had a blank check to do as much as we wanted, to provide whatever care we thought appropriate. The more stuff we did, the better it was for us financially. Consumers weren't paying—someone else was. But now the 'someone else' has taken over entirely and the pendulum has swung too far. It's not a bad thing to worry about costs, but our first priority should always be quality. And the pressure from the insurance companies and managed care organizations is to put cost over quality. Mila, they tell our patients when they have to go home from the hospital. Some are ready, and some are not. I resent being told by some high school clerk in Minnesota what to do with my patient."

Mila sat back in her chair. These really were huge changes, and they didn't sound good.

"People forget that this country has enjoyed the best health care in the world. That costs money. I guess I'm not sure exactly how the decisions should be made, but now they're being made politically and financially. They come up with nice words for it, but rationing is rationing. You don't have to take it from me, Mila. Ask anyone. Ask them." Tom jerked a thumb toward the box.

The other dolls—Mila had entirely forgotten. No, it would not be a bad thing to see who else was in there. Someone cheerier, she hoped. This time she reached in gingerly and came up with a tiny white-haired man.

"Doc Abington!" She hadn't seen him for years and years, not since college. Their sweet old family doc who—how could this be?—except for his size, looked just the same. He used to seem old, and now he was old. No, she saw. Now he wore bifocals about the size of an unfolded staple.

"Mila," he grinned. "Mila Langston. You're all grown up."

"And up, and up," she said. "You're a simulation, too?"

"Oh, yes, Mila. Really just a kind of tactile animation. But I'm fully equipped to help you with your transition. I see you've already been speaking to our humorous young friend over there."

Tom saluted, and Mila rolled her eyes. "You know, this whole setup is about as real—and about as natural—as a high school slide show, but Tom, I'm going to enjoy this. Your every syllable is about to be contradicted. As contrived as this whole setup is, the real Doc Abington here has actual wisdom. If his simulation has gotten even a bit of that, no insurance company on this earth—or any other—could change him. Right, sir?"

"I don't know, Mila," said Dr. Abington. "Maybe we should respect that Tom's kept his sense of humor. It's rare enough, believe me. It's hard to laugh when you spend your day getting second-guessed by someone at the end of an 800 number."

"Told you so, Mila."

"Cork it."

Dr. Abington turned to Tom, "A clerk asked me how much of a drug I was going to give a patient. I made up some ridiculous number to see if she would know the difference."

"She didn't, did she?" asked Tom.

"She did not." Dr. Abington unfolded a soap-flake-sized handkerchief and dabbed at his brow. "Mila, bone marrow transplants are now reviewed by accountants, who analyze the cost-benefit ratio of the patient living longer. Women are given one day or three days to give birth, depending on what state they live in. It hasn't yet reached the point of managed care telling us when to stop feeding someone, or stop the ventilator, but I'm sure that's coming."

Tom hopped down from the paperweight. "Well, that's because medicine is now a big business. It used to be run by doctors who just got out of medical school and set up practices. They basically winged it. Pay some bills, talk to an accountant, take a loan—poof you're a doctor. They were running a few-hundred-thousand-dollar business without any training. Maybe this is more efficient, but it changes everything."

"Not the least of which is the doctor-patient relationship," agreed the old man. "Before, we could give the patient the care that she expected. Now, as so-called gatekeepers, we represent both the patient and the insurance company. The patient can't always get what she wants. Only what she needs."

"Like the Stones' song, huh? Yikes." My God, thought Mila, that'll be a golden oldie when I get back. Mick Jagger will be in his fifties. As if the complete upheaval of her profession weren't enough.

"I'm sorry," Dr. Abington said, "I know nothing of geology. I do, however, remember the 1940s and '50s, when insurance companies weren't important. People had nest eggs and hoped they wouldn't get sick. Obviously unsatisfactory. Then, two types of insurance developed: fee-for-service and Kaiser-type plans. Kaiser was really Health Maintenance Prevention. With indemnity plans, however, the medical world was at the fingertips of the patient. They could have everything done, and the cost didn't matter."

"Man, those golden olden days," said Tom. "A boob job, a liposuction—they could find someone to do it, and insurance would just hand over the moola."

"I might put it a bit differently, Tom," said Dr. Abington. To say the least, thought Mila. "But yes, the benefits always outweighed the costs. This was the system the baby boomers grew up with and learned to expect. And suddenly the companies are saying what will and will not be paid for. Oh, they talk very convincingly about customer service—they call patients 'customers' now." At this, Dr. Abington's mouth curled with distaste. "The customer service they tout is utterly superficial. In reality, patient expectations don't count. The corporate executives don't talk to the patients. We do. Patients are upset, and it's easy to see why.

"Let me give you an example," Dr. Abington continued. "Until just recently, many managed care patients were expected to be out of the hospital twenty-four hours after giving birth. It wasn't what patients wanted but what the managed care organizations needed to maintain their profits. They spent lots of marketing money trying to convince patients that twenty-four-hour discharges were in the patient's best interests. But patients aren't fooled by that kind of thing. They take it out on the doctors because the managed care organization is faceless to them.

"A female patient of mine was at a specialist's office and called for a referral. But according to her new insurance plan—the one her ex-husband switched her to by handing her the papers and saying 'sign'—she has to first come and see her family practice doctor. In this system, I can only make the referrals she needs, regardless of what she wants. She was angry, but she hadn't even bothered to read anything about the new insurance. I explained it to her, I told her to read the manual. She became confrontational. I told her, those are the rules of the game. If you feel you must find a new physician, well, do so. I can't bend the rules, even for patients who've been with me for years. The risk is too great. These confrontations are upsetting all around. They ruin relationships."

Mila grimaced. If even Doc Abington felt this way, things were in bad shape. "Maybe I will need Ajax around for a couple of weeks to explain this to me."

Tom snorted softly, "Ajax, Comet, nothing can clean up this mess we're in, Mila. But pay attention. This is going to be you."

Dr. Abington was on a roll. "Do you know what is happening in private practice? In the old days, patients would say they'd found out about my practice by hearing good things about me from so and so. Last Thursday night, I was working late—until 10:00—and I asked my patient how she'd heard about me. She said, 'my employer signed up for your insurance and you were the first name in the book.' There I am, still working at 10:00 P.M., but my patients aren't with me because I'm a wonderful doctor. They're coming because they 'get signed up' and my name happens to start with 'A.'"

"Yup," said Tom. "Mila, maybe you can change your name to AaaLangston. There's a practice hint for you, Mila. It really is that bad. Some docs even look at the insurance on the chart so they can determine how the patient will treat them and how they should treat the patient."

"Money is ruling medicine," agreed Dr. Abington. "CEOs, bonuses, and stock options. Medical schools going bankrupt and CEOs walking away with golden parachutes—leaving the patients, doctors, and students to clear the carnage. Shareholders making money. Not 'did I make my patients comfortable today?' but 'did I add value for the shareholders?' And doctors aren't immune. We used to compete to give the best care, the best paper, the best seminar. Now we have the competition of the parking lot: doctors competing with each other for who has the newest Lexus."

Dr. Abington plunged his balled fists into the pockets at the front of his coat. "Even the commitment of people in training and the faculty has changed. I'm not sure it is less, but it has changed. You know, all my attendings in the clinic always came for nothing. That was their citizenship. You gave your time to clinic and teaching. Friday nights as a resident, I'd spend in the emergency room. It didn't matter what rotation you were on. If you were in the emergency room, you could do things and get experience. If someone was going to have triplets, we would stay. If there was an unusual case, we would stay. Our students don't go to the emergency room anymore to get experience unless they are told to. It's almost as though young faculty and residents consider medicine a job, not a way of life like we did, and do. They turn it off at quitting time. The doctor-patient relationship just isn't as strong: 'OK, it's 5:00 P.M.; I'm gone and whoever is coming on will take over'; 'I can't stay to do that, I have to go to my daughter's soccer game.' I never heard that fifteen years ago. My wife still reminds me that when I say I'll be home in fifteen minutes it could be an hour, or two hours, but she understands that is just a part of what it is like as a physician. Now, when a physician says, 'I'll be home in fifteen minutes,' he or she comes home in fifteen minutes and hands the patient's care over to the next covering physician."

Well that part wasn't so bad, thought Mila. I don't think there was ever a school play my dad didn't have to miss. But there was no way she was saying that to Dr. Abington. He was going strong.

"I think about why it is that way. It's the intense focus on expenses, cost, value as opposed to the needs of the patient. It used to be that we wanted to know about our patient's background, about her perceptions. In 1985, when I made rounds with the residents, I'd make sure they understood the patient's needs and desires before deciding what would be the best medical course of action for her. Now, we need to get her out. The issue is cost effectiveness. We argue that we need outcomes data and the reason is mostly about finances. It's difficult trying to fit in what the patient wants. Outcomes are now defined as the number of times a patient is admitted, not whether her life is better now."

Mila put her chin on the desk as Dr. Abington, as tall as her eyebrows, continued: "Another factor is that the whole damn world is getting more complicated. Both partners work, women are delaying childbirth until they are older and more at risk. The divorce rate is so high. It's not the 'good old days' when everything seemed straightforward. Young physicians aren't immune from social problems. They compartmentalize their lives, they devote 'X' hours to the office, save the rest for the family. I think the patient-physician relationship loses, to the point that it has become adversarial. When you buy a toaster at Sears, you take it back and talk to the clerk in the complaint department. The clerk isn't polite but just goes by the book. I almost see patients getting into that mode."

"Exactly. Toasters!" Tom burst out of his silence. "Oh, except that when you buy a toaster, you have to pay. But physicians do the service, bill for it, and then get it denied.

"And, yes," Tom continued, "patients are being encouraged to take an adversarial approach with providers. It's fine that information is more readily available to patients, and that their expectations about delivery and quality of care are high, but they've got to keep in line with reality. It's ridiculous. Patients send us bills for their time spent waiting in our waiting room, saying their time is 'as valuable' as ours. They've been told to do this by the *Ladies Home Journal*, in the monthly feature 'Things You Should Expect from Your Physician.' They come in with articles from the internet . . ."

"The inter-what?" Mila was really confused.

The Tom simulation tried to remember what a 1985 understanding of the information superhighway might be. "Culture shock #52 for you, Mila. Let me continue. People negotiate their fees based on stories in *Redbook* like 'Here's How to Talk to Your Doctor.' I have to know what my patients are hearing—I end up spending more time reading those magazines than medical journals! The over-fifty physicians think, and I bet you do, Doc, 'who the hell do the patients think they are, telling me what tests to order.' Right?"

"Indeed."

"But guess what, Mila? If you're trying to build a practice, you have to be accommodating. So you order it, and that leaves you to argue with the insurance company as to why the test or procedure is necessary. But you play the game, because otherwise they'll go to the practice next door.

"And we haven't even begun to talk about malpractice. Remember when we were students, and it was a complete nonissue? I knew about malpractice because Pop was an OB and his estate was in probate over a case. But everyone else thought it was weird."

"No, Tom," Mila said, "we thought *you* were weird." It was a halfhearted barb. Tom was making too much scary sense to incite much real wit.

"Remember Carla?" Tom asked.

"Of course. What's she doing?"

"Private practice psychiatrist, dude."

"What? She was for research and university all the way. Something must really have changed."

"Help her, doc. Reality's sinking in. I ran into Carla a few months ago on a ski slope, of all places. I bet Doc Abington can guess what we talked about."

Dr. Abington cleared his throat, "I'll venture a guess: managed care, finances, what entity you were joining. What you were worried about. What the future had in store. What physicians always talk about these days when they get together."

"Bingo. Fees getting cut. Psychiatry as a carve out. Doctors begging to get onto care panels that they initially shunned but that now managed care companies are shutting them out of. And malpractice. Always malpractice. She said now everything revolves around the risk of malpractice cases. Not like when we were in school and mistakes were looked on as learning experiences. Nope. She said during her psych training she had an attending who did forensic consults. He started talking about how to write in charts, said it might be better not to keep notes of psychotherapy sessions. This way she wouldn't have notes to hand over as evidence in a suit. Get this, Mila. Carla also said she's thinking of going back and getting a law degree or an MBA."

"Pardon me while my brain explodes." Mila had to take a break. Her back ached from hunching; her eyes ached from squinting. Mercifully, it was at that moment that Quam opened the door and brought in some food on a tray. Mila reached for the sandwich. She gave Dr. Abington and Tom what was to them a bath-mat-sized potato chip, which they immediately started considering how to break apart. But when she snuck a glance at them from the easy chair across the room, they were frozen in place with their arms raised, in the middle of hacking at the chip with an immense thumbtack.

Like putting a Betamax on pause, Mila thought.

CHAPTER 6

OF PREVENTION
AND PAIN RELIEF

CONSIDERABLY REFRESHED BY A SELF-ADMINISTERED PEP TALK, NOT TO MENTION LUNCH, MILA WENT BACK TO THE DESK. Her simulated friends sat next to each other on the long space key of the typewriter, still talking and shaking their little heads in seeming dismay. Mila went straight for the box. As disconcerting as all these changes seemed, they were what she'd be living with. And they were the circumstances under which she'd been given a second chance by Quam. She wasn't about to waste opportunities, and she'd start by making damn sure she got all possible perspectives about the new system. "OK, little fellers, who's up next? Hey! Not a feller. Nurse Karen, welcome to my desktop."

Karen Bosman was a good friend and one of the few nurses who actually liked med students. She wore a rice-sized badge with impossibly small print: "Nurse Administrator Karen to you!" She grinned. "So I'm here to tell you about how managed care affects nursing?"

"Short story, right, Karen? Nursing must be pretty much the same?"

"No way. Managed care affects nursing more than anything else.

"Let's say we have a patient with insurance. Before we see him we have to call his insurance company to see what his particular managed care organization says about how many visits he can have. You know, it's nurses who see the living conditions and the anxiety of the patient. It can be difficult to separate the social problems from the medical problems—sometimes it's the social issues that land them in the hospital. But that doesn't matter from a business point of view. And the patient doesn't understand that we are limited by the insurance company. We end up calling those darn companies every day to see if we can give more visits. Even if they say we can't, we're nurses, so we provide the visits to make sure the patient is safe. But providing too many free visits can put us out of business. So it becomes an ethical issue—taking care of the patient versus taking care of the business.

"Oh, yes. There are definitely ethical costs. Financial ones, too, and some of them are hidden. There is pressure to keep people out of the hospital, but insurance companies aren't paying for social services. Someone has to watch over people the week after surgery whether the patient is in the hospital or not. Who does it? Women, usually. They continue to carry the burden for caring for people at home. That is what length-of-stay reduction means, and that isn't measured in any system.

"It's not always women, of course. One patient of mine went home with ovarian cancer, and her spouse was a practicing psychiatrist. He had to stop his practice while she was dying. Even though she had good insurance, we couldn't get respite care."

Karen stood for a moment, shaking her head with disbelief. "You know what else? It used to be that I would consult with the physician about what a patient needed. Now the physician is out of the loop. They're struggling, too. Patients end up back at the doctor's office for things that the visiting nurse used to do. Sometimes the physician's office will call the insurance company and come close to begging.

"I swear, some of the managed care organizations pay no attention what- ever to the patient as an individual. They have a person sitting there with a book, and they treat that book like the darn Bible. As if patients fit into tidy little categories and compartments. Yes, indeed. Pretty much everybody wants managed care, but pretty much everybody wants it for the rest of the popula- tion. When it comes to themselves, or their families, they want good, old-fashioned, unmanaged, nursing care."

This was not the fresh start that Mila wanted. "Karen, would you under- stand if we saved the rest of this depressing conversation for another time? Maybe over a beer with the non-animated you?"

"Microbrew?"

"As small a glass as you want, though I would think that by now you'd be sick of anything tiny. Meantime, though, I'm finding someone with a cheerier outlook. Maybe Dostoyevsky has a few minutes to spare. Hello? Anybody home? Oh, excuse me, Doctor, I didn't expect you."

Out of the box came Miles Reinhold, a family practitioner who'd just started a practice in town when Mila was moving out of her parents' house. He looked like he'd done all right for himself; he had the kind of suit that stayed smooth at the shoulder when he held out his hand to shake. Mila offered her giant pinkie; Dr. Reinhold took it without a blink. Now that's self-assurance, Mila thought.

"Mila Langston, is it? Miles Reinhold. You may not know that I'm now director of a PPO. I understand you're in need of some updating."

"Updating, upgrading, but mostly upsiding," Mila tried to sound chipper, but she was feeling increasingly glum. She didn't even know what a PPO was. "Please tell me you have something—anything—good to say about managed care."

Dr. Reinhold's right eyebrow shot up. "Managed care isn't a terrible, awful thing. In some ways it frees us to do our job better."

Hallelujah, thought Mila. "Tell me more!"

"Look. If something isn't paid for, you're reluctant to do it, right? Well, in the old system, prevention was never paid for, so it never got much attention. There was big energy put into, for instance, cardiac surgery—After-the-Fact Medicine. But little was done with diet, or cholesterol education, or keeping people's arteries free of disease in the first place. Medicine became disease-oriented, intervention-oriented. So in some respects, the incentives were all messed up. Our mission was to keep people healthy, but we were paid well to take care of severe disease." Dr. Reinhold folded his arms and went on.

"Incentives were skewed for patients, too. If insurance didn't cover something and patients needed to pay out of pocket, it usually didn't get done. Staying healthy fell into that noncovered category, and people weren't generally willing to pay for it themselves. One patient I remember was complaining about paying a two-hundred-dollar co-pay for the delivery of her baby. 'Doctors are getting greedy,' she said. In the next breath she was talking about her two-week Caribbean cruise and her three-thousand-dollar watch. Where were her priorities?"

Dr. Reinhold showed no sign of stopping, "No, no, it's not all doom and gloom. It really is, in some ways, a step forward. We have to get efficient. The demands on tracking patients—on their mammograms, blood pressure, cholesterol—forces us to keep in touch and provide better customer service. In the past, if the patient returned, fine. If not, he was lost to follow up. Now we can't afford for that to happen because we are responsible for maintaining the health of the individual. That's how we are paid. We're forced to look at wellness. We have an incentive to keep the health of our patients optimal."

"Hooey." It was Doc Abington calling out from the typewriter. He leaned heavily on the 'F' key and stood. "Forgive me, Miles, but hooey. How can you see this mess as an improvement? Yes, Mila, patients are tracked and physician practice patterns are tracked. All of this requires extensive documentation, which takes time out of seeing patients and decreases earnings. Reimbursements are decreased, and office practice costs more. Educate personnel! Generate data! Squeeze the bottom line! Balance the budget! At whose expense? I didn't talk like that in the old days. I don't want to talk like that now. No offense, Miles, but doctors should be doctors, not managers."

"No offense taken, Ab," said Dr. Reinhold. "In the old days, once you graduated, you got your horse and practiced medicine on your own. Physicians used to work with no oversight, but we're not in Dodge City anymore—now everybody is looking over our shoulders. Utilization review coordinators saying, 'are your patients still needing to be in the hospital?' Peer review organizations inspecting your charts with a fine-tooth comb after the tough decisions have been made. Cost containment councils looking at outcomes and saying your mortality-morbidity rate is higher or lower. Everybody has a piece of you. For plenty of physicians, it means depression, SSRIs, and longing for the good old days. Look, I've been able to handle this, but I know many of my colleagues really lament the loss of their independence—the loss of the old-west style. They get burnt out."

"That I am," said Dr. Abington.

Burnt out. Mila remembered Ajax using that term to describe her in the alternate future. This was all starting to make sense. Some things, however, still seemed like they were being spoken in a foreign language. SSRIs. Mila filed that with the 'internet' as words to look up when she finally landed in 2000 earth.

"But there really are advantages, Ab," Reinhold interrupted her daydreaming.

"Hmph."

"No, really. It used to be that if there were a hundred ways of doing some-thing, you chose one or invented your own and that was fine. Remember? Of course, some doctors did things better than others—worked more cost-effectively, got to diagnoses more quickly. Managed care lets us learn from them—it spreads that knowledge around."

"Miles," said Doc Abington, "there used to be only one question: Did your patient get better? Do you honestly think there's anything more important?"

"That question's still asked, but not only that question. How long did it take for your patient to get better, and how much did it cost? Could we have gotten better value another way? Could your patient have done even better? Is your patient educated in how to maintain a healthy status? That's the point of care management—getting the job done and also doing it cost efficiently and with the highest quality. Doing things not just the acceptable way, but the best way."

"You admit, don't you, that there's been a change in the way patients view doctors? Whatever happened to the love affair with physicians as scientists?"

"Oh, Ab, that Marcus Welby image—the doc in the white coat solving everything—was never an expectation or promise anyone could live up to. Mila, many older patients still hold the view that physicians should tell them what to do. When presented with options, they ask, 'why are you telling me this? Just tell me what I have to do—that's why I came here.' They need to be shown the importance of understanding the alternatives. Younger patients expect to make their own decisions. But they're often confused by the undif-ferentiated mass of information available. In general, communication is more important in medicine than at any time in the past. Mila, docs are even taking communications and public relations courses. That can't be bad."

"Can't it?" Dr. Abington shook his head.

"I think managed care has forced us to communicate better, and that's good. Modern medicine, you'll be happy to hear, Mila, is helping many more women survive cancer. But we've never really looked at the trade-offs involved. Sometimes people survive but are disfigured or unable to care for themselves. They don't consider it a life worth living. Ten years ago, we would have gone ahead with the surgery without much thought. Now we communi-cate with the patient. Patients usually choose life no matter what but have a much more realistic view of 'no matter what.' If patients know what they are facing, they can deal with it better."

"Excuse me, though." Tom had been unusually quiet for a long time. "Let's get back to this so-called 'value' issue because that's really the point, isn't it?"

He leaned forward, elbows on knees. "The payers have a distorted view of reality. They bank on our level of service, exceeding what would be reasonable to expect from an employee. But they insist on tight controls, too. There's supposed to be no limit to our commitment, but there sure is a limit on our freedom, resources, and reimbursement.

"In the old days, docs could be profitable with eighteen hundred patients. Now it's two thousand to twenty-five hundred per doctor. How are we supposed to do it? Either by not seeing patients, or by seeing a million of them per hour. On the other hand, managed care companies ask patients two questions to find out if they are satisfied with their care: 'did you see your doctor when you wanted, and did he spend enough time with you.' The emphasis, as far as I'm concerned, is not on real value. It's on perceived value."

"I don't deny that's a problem," said Reinhold reasonably, "but let's think it through instead of just throwing up our hands. There was a point when the insurance company was the only filter, deciding how much of what the patient wanted would be paid. That's different now because the employer is much more assertive about choosing insurance plans. Insurance companies need to make employers and patients happy—they don't need to worry about doctors because there are plenty of them to go around. So the insurance companies tell patients what they want to hear, and the doctors are forced to compete to provide it.

"Obviously the number of doctors had to come down, and companies started saying their role in the process was to thin the ranks by going for the best 'quality.' But they defined the 'best quality doctors' as the doctors who would charge them less. And besides, they were able to distort our side of the competition by controlling the number of patients. If a physician group is doing 90 percent managed care patients, and the managed care organization says 'we'll pull our patients away,' what choice does the group have than to say they'll do it for less? Quality becomes a catch phrase and a marketing tool."

Mila wondered if the holograms could read minds. She was thinking how pompous Reinhold sounded, but strangely, at the same time, he was the only one with any confidence about the future.

"What it comes down to," Reinhold continued, "is that the shareholders of large insurance companies too often determine how health care is managed.

The shareholders bought stock to increase the value of their portfolios, not for the improvement of health care for patients. It's not in their best interest to have an honest discussion about the financial ramifications of a program with actual high quality.

"But, really, what's the best response to this kind of situation? Hopelessness? I think not."

Reinhold folded his arms. For a moment, no one spoke. Mila could hear the muted whirring and popping noises that seemed always to emanate from the walls of the ship, even in the 'study.' Reinhold cleared his throat. "I guess it comes down to this. I spent a decade of the last fifteen years fighting managed care. I would collar anyone who would listen: 'This is a bad thing,' I'd tell them. 'It shouldn't happen. It's not good for anyone.'

"I finally realized, though, that like it or not, it was happening. And it was happening because business woke up and said, 'I'm not going to pay this bill anymore.' The forces were overwhelming.

"I had two choices, as do you, Tom and Ab, and as will you, Mila. Fight a battle I thought was already lost. Or jump in the thick of it and try to influence the outcome. It was a juggernaut, and I decided to jump on the wagon and try to steer it. Even if I couldn't determine how fast it was going.

"And guess what? I'm finding that I can have some influence. Yes, the forces are very powerful. But not so powerful as the doomsayers predict in the areas that are important, from my point of view, to change."

Finally! Finally someone had brought up the possibility of constructive, achievable change. Mila felt like throwing her arms around Reinhold, but didn't want to ruffle his composure. Or crush him, simulation or not. She restrained herself to a mental cheer. "What kind of changes are you talking about, Dr. Reinhold?"

"Well, for starters, an immediate priority is to encourage a new genera-tion of managed care. All right. Fee-for-service isn't going to work in the future. Let's just bury it and move on. The traditional HMOs that promote underutilization obviously aren't the answer, either, so let's save a grave for that one, too. If there's going to be a set amount of money to care for a partic-ular population, let's allow the insurance companies to do what they do best—insurance, administration, actuarial stuff. Then, if we can figure out ways to keep the population healthy, by reducing smoking, for example, we will have decreased the cost of health care and done a good thing. Unlike the old indemnity insurance, managed care gives an incentive for that sort of activity. Capitation moves the risk from the insurance company and employer to the physician and hospital. Risk has always been a dirty word to physicians, but it aligns our payment with our mission. We'll begin to look at populations in addition to individuals. And we have to look at ourselves, as physicians, honestly, too. What makes a doctor great is the ability to look at patients as individuals. By that definition, great doctors make poor allocators of resources."

At that moment, the door opened and in stuck one of Quam's heads. "Have you concluded your discussion?"

Mila felt buoyant for the first time in ages. Possibilities existed! "I think we have, Quam. It's been great." Out of curiosity, she looked at the little Dr. Abington. He was sunk deep into himself, obviously as unhappy as a simulation could be. Tom, though, actually looked like he was considering things. "You know," he said, "I hope my real self gives this all some thought."

"Are you sure, Tom?" Mila ribbed, "you have so little brain power to spare." Tom stuck out his tongue, and the two of them smiled. "Well, folks, back to the box. I know you're not real, but thank you so much."

One by one—Dr. Abington with some difficulty—the simulations climbed back into the box. Karen Bosman was last and stood, for a moment, with her head and shoulders poking over the side. "Hey, girlfriend," she said. "One last thing. About three years ago, a managed care organization was going to make patients pay for their own epidurals—because epidurals tend to prolong labor and make the whole shebang cost more. So they wanted patients to pay for their own pain relief, and they were going to let us be the ones to tell them.

"There were all men at this meeting, Mila, and I took a football out of my bag. I said, "I know! How about you guys take this football and insert it into your bums. After eight hours, just push it on out. Oh, and if anyone wants pain relief, why, you're welcome to cough up the dough. I think even the accountants got the picture."

Mila laughed. "Karen, that's a classic."

"Sometimes, Mila," she said, "sometimes you just gotta get their attention." And with that, she shut the lid and was gone.

C H A P T E R 7

OF ORIENTATION
AND ORGANIZED CARE

MILA WAS STILL SAVORING THE IMAGE OF EIGHT ACCOUN-
TANTS WITH FOOTBALLS SHOVED UP THEIR BUTTS WHEN SHE
REMEMBERED AJAX WAS WITH HER. She gave him a grin, "Gives a new
meaning to the word 'stuffy,' doesn't it?"

Ajax emanated a telepathic wave of discomfort. "On Climara, our logicians would settle such disputes without the necessity of such incivility." He
pressed an invisible button, and they were back in the rocket control room.

"Well, gee, Ajax, on Earth, abduction is considered a tad uncivil, too."

"Well, on Climara—"

"Ajax," thundered Quam telepathically, "I will reconsider the advisability
of sending you to Earth unless you demonstrate a measure of self-control in
the absence of a logician. End this squabble NOW."

Mila and Ajax stopped in mid-bicker, and Quam entered the room bodily.
"Much better," he said.

Ajax's gills quivered with embarrassment. "I'm ready, Quam. Don't worry.
You'll see."

"Show us, Ajax. Don't tell, show."

For a moment there was a bubble of silence—the kind Mila could never resist popping. "Let me guess, Quam," she said, "back home you're a high school principal, right? I can just see it. Motto: Think Loudly and Wave a Big Tentacle."

"This does not concern you, Mila," Quam said. But she could have sworn that Ajax shot her a look of thanks.

At this moment, Zorak stuck a head in the door. "Preparations are complete for the landing."

The landing. She hadn't even considered the logistics of being in outer space and getting back to earth. She'd been unconscious on the way up.

"Um, guys? Can I get a seat belt? Maybe a little Dramamine?"

"Just relax, Mila. As on the flight here, your body will be brought down to basic metabolic levels. We will start by playing you the discography of your fellow human, Barry Manilow. That is enough to reduce most Homo sapiens' consciousness by about 80 percent. We will then telepathically smooth any remaining brain waves.

"During the flight, we will download all the medical knowledge that you will need to be an effective first-year surgical resident in 2000. Your simulation, I believe, was instructive about other aspects of medical practice on your home world now. You are ready."

As ready as anyone in the middle of a good news-bad news joke can be, Mila thought. The bad news was that she'd been kidnapped by aliens and that everyone in the newly chaotic medical field was insecure and unsure about the future. The good news was that medicine was such a mess that being a fifteen-year hostage of aliens might—amazingly—turn out to be an advantage. She'd missed the turmoil that led to the insecurity and that might give her enough distance to see some opportunities she otherwise might not have seen.

"You know what, Quam? Weirdly enough, I think you're right. I'm as ready to graduate a residency in the year 2005 as anyone who was going to all along. Bring on the elevator Muzak." The first waves of Copacabana wafted through her headphones. They never did this on the Starship Enterprise, she thought dreamily as she began succumbing to the pull of semiconsciousness. Mila hoped they never went through with the threatened "new" Star Trek. It'd be like New Coke—a total fake. She sank into sleep smiling, thinking about how funny William Shatner would look now in those tight Starfleet uniforms.

All was White.

"It is not a good sign for a surgical resident to be sleeping on the first day of orientation. What's your name, Doctor?"

"Mila, Dr. Baskin." She was back! And she even knew the name of the attending in front of whom she'd just embarrassed herself! Thanks a bunch, Climarans, she thought. You're thorough little buggers, but your timing is for shit.

"I apologize, Dr. Baskin. With all the excitement, last night just flew by." Not to mention the last fifteen years. "I didn't get much sleep."

"Well, not getting sleep is something you'll all be getting used to. I'll try to be more stimulating so that Mila and the rest of you can stay awake."

Mila looked around. The conference room she and her fellow residents were in was pretty nice, especially for an urban hospital. It looked comfortingly like conference rooms used to look: gray laminate table, tubular chairs, big framed print of some paint splash of a modern picture. Except it's fifteen years less modern, now, she remembered. The residents around her looked the same as residents used to, thank God. So far, nothing she couldn't handle. Finally, she summoned up the courage to look at herself, at her own leg under the table.

This is the real proof of the pudding, guys, she thought.

She breathed a sigh of relief. She looked normal, the way she had in '85. Not bad considering she hadn't jogged for fifteen years, she thought. Of course, there'd been no Tasty Cakes for fifteen years, either.

Dr. Baskin, in the meantime, was finishing his talk. "We've reviewed the schedules, the safety procedures, medical records, and legal issues. I am now pleased to present our CEO, a man who has overseen our last two mergers and a billion-dollar construction project. And was a damned good doctor back when he actually took care of patients. This is Dr. Stuart Enos."

Dr. Enos, a white-haired man with the gaunt look of a runner, nodded to the applause. "I'd like to welcome you with a Woody Allen quote: 'We are at a crossroads. One path leads to total destruction, and the other leads to utter despair. Let's hope we pick the right path.'" There were a few knowing chuckles from the group.

"A number of you may think this applies rather neatly to medicine today." Dr. Enos scanned the room, eyebrows raised. "I, however, do not.

"As all of you doubtless know, medicine is currently incorporating ideas and perspectives from business. And as you will find out during your residencies, establishing clinical pathways, improving information technology, and adopting systems approaches are processes that are neither fun nor easy.

"But, my friends, because a transition is difficult does not mean it's not important and good. Case in point: Japanese car-makers in the seventies. They put us through the wringer for a while, if any of you are old enough to remember. But in the end they made us better automobile designers, did they not?

"We are indeed at a crossroads, but it is a crossroads that beckons with opportunity. Opportunity to improve medicine, opportunity to innovate, to help our society, our patients, ourselves.

"Now, a certain measure of pessimism and fear is natural during a time of major change, and if you look around, you will indeed find countless hand-wringers with visions of doctors as salaried automatons dancing in their heads. You may feel such leanings yourself.

"Consider this, however. Most of what we do as physicians every day is automatic; we're trained to respond in certain ways to certain situations, sometimes to respond even before thought, correct? As a result, I believe, we tend to become reflexive in our reactions, even when faced with situations that warrant thorough exploration. We tend to become automatically anti-innovation, anti-risk. It's a conservatism, my friends, that often keeps us from seeing opportunities that might yield a different, better future.

"My hope for you as you begin this residency program is that you will rebel against your own learned suspicion of change. That you will not spurn new ideas simply because they are new, or because they come from an unexpected source, nor succumb to easy cynicism or stubbornness because cynicism and stubbornness are comfortable.

"It helps no one—not ourselves, not our patients—if we physicians languish as victims to corporate medicine run amok. It's less obvious, but equally true, that we help no one if we do nothing but die noble deaths in fighting every possible change.

"The productive path at the crossroads, the path with the potential to improve medicine for everyone, is the path of learning and involvement. You must educate yourselves about the possibilities, about the new ideas that business brings to medicine, and that medicine brings to business.

Consider thoroughly how they might be used for the benefit of your patients and yourselves. Don't abandon your judgment, but allow yourselves to learn. Allow yourselves to change. Allow yourselves to take appropriate risks. Like it or not, Doctors, the future is in your hands. It's an historic moment for medicine, and it is your moment. Welcome, residents. I am eager to see where you take our world.

"Thank you for your attention, and as a reward for keeping my words under advisement, and for listening to me drone on, I believe we have some celebratory hors d'oeuvres and beverages for you across the hall."

The talk over, Mila found herself exhilarated. Dr. Enos was as optimistic as the simulated Dr. Reinhold on the ship, but Dr. Enos was real. And now Mila had an actual, flesh-and-blood chance to join in. The applause from the group around her, however, was merely polite. Don't they know what they just heard, Mila wondered? She joined the general shuffle to the reception room and joined the line at the bar.

"You went for that crap?" asked a sardonic voice behind her.

Mila spun around. "I beg your pardon?"

"Oh, sorry." It was a stocky, fortyish attending. "Not you. That was for our friendly full-time stiff over there." He nodded toward the less stocky, fortyish attending standing in front of her in the line for the bar.

"Hi, Mila—Surgery," he said. "You can see that I've mastered the art of name-tag reading. I'm Dennis—Family Practice, and the rude person in back of you is Nick—Orthopedics."

"I can't believe I'm walking into this one," said Mila, "but what the heck. What's a full-time stiff?"

Dennis grinned. "There's an icebreaker for you. That's great." He laughed. "Sorry. Look, you heard Dr. Enos's talk, right?"

"It was amazing, wasn't it?" Mila enthused. "If we could really use this business stuff to provide better care for the community and redesign medical care, this could be the golden age of medicine."

"Oh, my God, they've gotten to you already," Nick groaned. It was a joke, but there was genuine distaste behind it. "Full-time stiffs are the evil monsters who are out to get us, destroy private practice, and turn us all into lemmings. Stepford Docs. Don't be one."

Dennis shrugged. "Nick is one of those cavemen: 'Give me back the old days.' During the industrial revolution, he'd still be making horseshoes with molten iron and an anvil. I, personally—"

"Have sold out," Nick interrupted. "And why are you comparing medicine to making horseshoes? Maybe family practice is that banal, but orthopedics is still an art. And please don't start spouting about Enos. He got an MBA and took a few accounting courses. Wonderful. That doesn't mean I've got to kiss his ring and pledge loyalty like you traitors on the full-time staff."

"I'm not getting it," said Mila. "I thought being chosen by the hospital to be full time was more an academic than a political statement."

Dennis handed her a beer. "You're right, Mila. And we'll see where the woolly mammoth here stands academically when we reward the loyal people in the institution. He'll be lucky if all he has to kiss is Enos's ring."

The two attending physicians barely noticed Mila escape. She wasn't a big drinker but just now really needed a beer. Who wouldn't need a drink after she traveled ten thousand miles and fifteen years while listening to Barry Manilow . . . and now this!

Sure, she and her med school friends had teased each other pretty hard, but it had never been belligerent like this. Mila stared at the floor. It seemed there were hardened alliances already in place—and she wanted nothing to do with any of them.

"Very wise," said the person next to her. As she looked up she saw the starched white coat, then the name tag: Ajax, Climara.

"Ajax, my God!" It was he, being ignored in the middle of the reception in all his two-headed, six-armed glory. She grabbed him by an arm and started dragging him out of the room.

"Don't create a spectacle, Mila. No one can see me but you."

Mila spoke through clenched teeth: "Get out of here, Ajax. Get out of here now."

"As you like," he said, and Mila and he were in the White.

"Whatever happened to just sneaking off into a room someplace? Can't you find some place a little more . . . earthly?" she said without voice.

"Oh, of course." And then it was midday, they were together in a little rowboat, with no land in sight. Ajax sat across from her, wearing two sailor hats at opposite jaunty angles. "You were feeling at sea, right?" Ajax tittered.

"No, Ajax. You can't do this."

"Very well," said Ajax, and they were now in the calms of a wide river with the sound of rapids in the distance.

"That's *not* what I meant, and you know it. I feel like Darren in *Bewitched*. You cannot just whisk me away to some cute little metaphor. You can't just appear when I'm in public either, whether you're being green or being invisible. Hey, buddy, I saw the movie *Harvey*. I know that people with invisible friends get looked on as cute and eccentric, or get thrown in the loony bin. With the stories I'd tell under sodium pentothal about little aliens and their screwed-up genders, I'd be committed for life."

Ajax thought for a moment. "How about next time we try momentary semiconsciousness in *your* time/place while we interact in mine?"

It wasn't going to get any better than that. "Fine. But only when I really need you. And please, please try not to make me semiconscious in the middle of the OR. Or when someone is looking right at me."

Ajax sighed. "Agreed." They drifted for a moment, the boat rocking pleasantly in the sun.

"Ajax?"

"Yes?"

"Why am I here?"

"Oh, excuse me, Mila. Here." He handed her a lovely glossy travel brochure, entitled "Welcome to the land of Physician Adaptation to Change in an Uncertain Environment." She opened it to find it blank. "This is getting annoying. There's nothing there."

"That's exactly the point," said a strange voice. Mila looked up from the brochure. Ajax had disappeared, as had the brochure.

CHAPTER 8

OF MIND-SETS AND METAPHORS

ON THE SCULL SEAT OPPOSITE MILA WAS NOW SITTING AN AFFABLE LOOKING MAN WITH MORE BEARD THAN HAIR. He gave the sun a squint and a grin and began rolling up the sleeves of his white dress shirt, pausing for a moment to reach across the boat to shake hands. "I'm Greg Shea. I'm here about your mind-set."

"My mind-set?"

"Your paradigm. Heuristic. Operating metaphor. What lies behind your thought. The meta-organization of your thinking. The way you think about how you think."

"Silly me," said Mila as a duck paddled by, "here I was thinking that my problem had to do with someone else's damn metaphors."

"Mila," Greg said good-humoredly, "we both know we're not really here. However you might find it very helpful to listen before you judge. It may be difficult to believe that a business school professor or consultant can contribute to the practice of your craft, but that assumption is part of the psychic and emotional armor you were given in your training as a physician. I can help you learn something, but only if you set aside that armor."

"That's a lot to ask," said Mila.

"Too much for many," Greg agreed. A slight breeze rippled the water around the boat, and from the distance, again, Mila heard a rushing sound.

"I'll try," Mila said, "at least for a bit."

"Let's start with what you hear," said Greg, motioning with his head toward the roar of fast water somewhere beyond.

"I was noticing that before." Mila closed her eyes and listened. "It's getting louder. Are they rapids?"

"They are. Do you think they'll have an end, Mila?"

She opened her eyes. "Of course. All rapids end. At least in the real world."

"No, Mila, actually these rapids don't end; not here and not in your world—our world—either," Greg said, leaning forward in such a way as to off-balance the scull momentarily, "and that's important to know when you're guiding yourself and others in the midst of change. Many people contend that change is a process that moves us from flat, fairly placid waters—a steady state—through the temporary rapids of change, and then back to a steady state. The calm water has its challenges, but it's knowing how to meet them— with straight-ahead hard rowing. This doesn't work in white water, however. So when you start getting pummeled in rapids, you duck and cross your fingers until you reenter the flat stretch where the scull does well.

"This is a time-honored mind-set. It's seldom articulated explicitly, but it's at the heart of many of our tactics for coping, as individuals and as collectives." Greg paused to watch a dragonfly light on the edge of the boat.

"All right," said Mila as the creature aired its transparent wings. "What's the alternative?"

"In fact, we are in what Peter Vaill termed 'permanent white water.'[1] I don't have my files with me, but let me lay three sets of numbers on you. I'll work from memory, but they'll be pretty accurate. You tell me what they mean as we go along."

"First number: 30 percent." The dragonfly took off, and Greg continued. "That's the average tax burden of the average American tax payer today."

"Good grief! I thought the Republicans have been in office! I thought taxes had been cut!"

"They have been, and they were. The number still holds. Not only that, but keep the demographics fairly stable and hold Medicare, Medicaid, and Social Security in their current mode, and in thirty years the average American tax-payer will pay 66 percent of his or her income in taxes."

Mila coughed out a laugh and blurted, "Americans would never stand for it!"

"Exactly the point," Greg cried, throwing up his arms. Mila was afraid Greg would pitch them into the drink if he got any more emphatic. She covertly took hold of the sides of the boat as he continued. "The second number set begins with 14 percent. That's the percentage, roughly speaking, of the U.S. national product that goes to traditional health care (forget the rapidly growing amount that goes to so-called alternative health care)."

"What's wrong with that?" Mila spoke a little tentatively, both because she was feeling uncertain and so as not to incite her boatmate into further enthusiasm. "Sounds like a good use of money to me."

Much to Mila's relief, Greg's response was intense, but quietly so. "Statistics, like most other facts, have meaning only in context. Here, the economic context is that major international competing nations, like Germany and Japan, spend 7–9 percent of their national product on health care."

"So?"

"You tell me, Mila. Under what conditions would those numbers matter to a physician?"

Mila relaxed her grip on the boat; things seemed safe for the moment. "If I were a German or Japanese physician, I'd feel woefully undercompensated."

"That's one interpretation," Greg replied. "Here's another: we live in a globally competitive world. The way a nation spends its resources affects its people's employment prospects, affects the chance that its citizens will have jobs secure and lucrative enough to give them full lives and the belief that their children will have lives comparable to or better than their own. Is spending an extra 5–8 percent on health care a good use of those resources? Would that money more wisely be invested in breakfast programs, silicon chips, lasers, non-polluting fuels, or cleaner water?"

Mila thought for a moment before responding, "Caring for people who are alive today matters more than investment either for jobs or for the environment. Either for today or for the future."

"OK. Maybe we'll talk again if you have children. Here's another number in this set: 1/3. That's about how much of that 14 percent goes into administering the system."

"Ha!" This time it was Mila who set the scull rocking. "So the physicians aren't the problem after all? I'm beginning to like you."

Greg grinned, "That, too, shall pass. Why do you think the administration number is so big?"

Mila thought about what the tiny Doc Abington and Tom doll holograms had told her. "They're bloodsuckers. Incompetent to boot."

"Who?"

"The administrators, of course," Mila laughed.

"Funny," Greg said dryly, "they'd say the same thing about the physicians."

"Come on!"

"Administrators often complain that all doctors do is take, take, take. That they act like the world owes them riches because they spent a few extra years going to school. That doctors consider themselves "the talent" and everyone else qualifies as supporting cast or scut workers. That doctors believe no one else does real work."

Mila recoiled a bit. "That sounds a little harsh."

"Mila, fragmentation or balkanization is one of the classic signs of a system under stress. People retreat to various levels of tribalism when they're hurt or afraid. In extreme forms, they engage in cannibalism, real or metaphorical. If you would lead yourself, let alone others, through the stresses of permanent white water, then you cannot succumb to tribalism. Power lies at the boundaries, at the points between individuals and groups, the points of connection and healing or of disconnection and conflict. Get the mind-set clear and you can see across tribal lines; lose the view and you'll fall into tribal warfare."

"I just want to be a doctor," Mila moaned.

"I want you to be one too. The issue is figuring out what 'being a doctor' means. Let's go on to the third set of numbers."

"I feel like I'm about to be visited by the ghost of Christmas yet to come." Mila was joking, but she could hear the apprehension in her own voice.

"The third set of numbers begins with $3,600. That's about the average U.S. per capita expenditure on traditional health care per annum. Now, various wellness statistics and indexes appear from different sources at different times—numbers like life expectancy and infant mortality. Over the past few years, these statistics and indexes have generated increasing interest. Where do you suppose the U.S. comes out?"

"Oh, somewhere in the top ten."

"The U.S. generally does not make the top ten, and if so barely. It's more likely to rank in the teens."

"Some Scandinavian country with semi-socialized medicine probably comes out on top."

"Good guess, Mila, since they often do very well in such studies. However, places like Greece have shown up at or near the top."

"Greece?!" Mila exclaimed. "Why, you'd never catch me getting a CABG there!"

"Of course not. And that's the point or at least part of it. We're not talking clinical intervention here, not in any tertiary care center lexicon. How much money per capita per annum does Greece spend on health care?"

"Haven't the foggiest idea," Mila said, shaking her head.

"Not much over $300."

"OK, OK. I got it. It's economics AND it's health care," Mila continued to shake her head.

"Keep going," Greg encouraged.

"All right. How's this: people are paying a lot for health care in the U.S. They're paying a lot, whether you count it in absolute dollars or relative dollars, and whether you count it by person or by country. And it is not clear that we're taking the best overall care of our people despite spending all that money. Argh!"

"And?"

"And people will not just keep increasing their payments."

"And?"

"Oh, and all this pressure will continue to increase for the next thirty years or so . . . basically, for as long as I plan to practice medicine."

"You got it."

Mila buried her head in her hands and spoke from there. "Thanks for the mind-set change. Where's the exit? I hope Sartre is wrong."

Greg spoke gently, but insistently: "Virtually everyone in every sector of the economy is in or entering this condition of permanent white water. There are various ways in, but once you're in, there's always some combination of globalization, financial pressure, and technology that keeps you there. The key point in all of this is that we do not occupy a 'steady state-change-steady state world.' It is permanent white water. Believe it. Act accordingly."

"Look, I believe. Let's talk about what 'act accordingly' means. What do I do?"

"It's easier to say what not to do, Mila."

"Naturally. You enjoy this don't you?" Mila said in a slightly exasperated tone.

"Yes, actually. In a steady state-change-steady state world, people do well to lock in and pursue. But doggedly locking in while in rapids can get you undone just as easily as can mindless wandering. A permanent white water world demands you combine directionality and flexibility. What not to do? Don't hide at the bottom of the boat waiting for the rapids to end, because they won't. Don't paddle madly in the hope of overpowering the rapids, because you can't. Above all, forget about getting to the end of the rapids, because they won't end in your lifetime. You have to work the river.

"Good white water boaters have a wide variety of approaches. Sometimes they paddle with the current, sometimes against it, sometimes parallel to it, and sometimes not at all. No scull race, this. And to change analogies for a moment: you will fail if you think that this race is not for you, that you can avoid it if you don't enter it. You will also fail if you enter the race believing, perhaps hoping, that it's a sprint. Marathons are hard enough to run anyway—they're impossible to run as sprints."

"Greg, I think I'm getting this. There are the mind-sets themselves, the permanent white water, the 'don't do' mind-set, and the fact that the mind-set affects what one does."

"By?"

"By affecting what I see."

"By affecting how you see."

"Got it, professor."

"That's Herr Distinguished Doctor Professor to you. I think there's time for one more point before I fade to black. A different metaphor."

"What's *with* all these metaphors?"

"There are two answers to that, of course," Greg smiled.

Mila returned the smile. "Of course."

"The first answer is that metaphors are the language of leadership. They connect ideas. They link realities and thereby help us generalize and thereby create meaning—meaning that includes its own 'handles' for transportation from one circumstance to another. Leaders serve well who help others create meaning; the more transportable that meaning, and the more it helps people deal with varied and varying conditions (welcome to permanent white water), the better the leadership, the more able the follower."

Mila dipped her finger into the cold water. "And the second answer?"

"I'm of Irish extraction. I can't help but use metaphors." They chuckled. "One last metaphor?"

"One last metaphor."

"A friend of mine named Bob Keidel has worked extensively with metaphors and with what he calls triangular thinking. One expression of that work is he uses various types of sports as metaphors for types of organizations, hence for teamwork and leadership.[2] He makes an apparently simple, yet quite powerful point: know the game you're playing; it makes all the difference.

"Baseball, for example, involves highly independent individual players. The player is the star. Baseball is about as independent a team sport as one can find this side of a track, gymnastics, or swim meet. There are key points of interaction between the otherwise independent players (pitcher and catcher, for example), but in general, autonomy reigns. The team wins if each individual player concentrates on optimizing his individual performance. Good strategy in a stable, simple (without a drove of variables) business environment, especially if it's also fragmented and rich. Health care used to be such a game, especially as played by physicians. Everybody minded his own seam in the wall like in a coal mine, and the physician team did very, very well. But the game has changed; the seams have come together.

"In football (American style), a big brain calls the plays from the sidelines or the skybox or the blimp, and the players execute highly specialized roles. Regular timeouts (usually a de facto one after each play) allow time for the big brain to take stock and re-group. And there's a week between games. The coach or his surrogate (the quarterback) is the star. It's a good way to operate in a relatively stable but complex environment, especially with no or few competitors. Lots of time to think, relatively speaking, make this high-control model possible, even desirable due to its efficiency in that environment. This is the traditional American corporate model, the default model for administrators everywhere, in private sector and government and, of course, in hospitals.

"The most popular sports in the world, however, basketball, field hockey, ice hockey, and soccer, emphasize improvisational collaboration. Here, players receive general direction, but the game moves too quickly for the coaches or players alone to keep up. Players make the game up by drawing on subroutines ("plays") and retrofitting them on the field in real time, time and time again, *as the play unfolds*. There is very little off-line time. Team leaders are tremendously important, as are interpersonal and team chemistry. Baseball statistics for individual players allow one to predict about 80 percent of the variance in team records, while in basketball it's only about 20 percent. The unit in baseball is largely the individual, while in basketball it's the team, including the coach. It's a good approach in a dynamic, even turbulent, and yet fairly simple (limited number of variables) environment."

"So, Greg," said Mila, "you're saying that leadership looks different in different games. I should *not* try to impose my leadership first, but rather figure out what kind of game I'm in and work my leadership into that game."

"And in dynamic, complex environments like permanent white water?"

"I need to be able to play all three games. I also need to help others understand the game they're in at any moment."

"By Jove, I think she's got it. I also think I'm starting to melt away." Indeed, unlike the growing volume of the white water ahead, Greg's image did seem to Mila to be getting fainter.

"Two questions before I get on with the rest of my life, OK?" Mila asked.

"Fine by me," Greg responded.

"Why do you care about all of this anyway? You could practice your craft just about anywhere, I imagine. Why health care? Why clinicians? And especially why doctors?"

"Because I want the clinical voice alive and in fine form at the policy tables. That requires clinicians, and especially physicians, who can listen, understand, and address the other perspectives given voice at those tables: marketing, finance, strategy to name a few."

"That sounds noble," Mila said, loudly enough to be heard over the growing rush of the water and without hiding her skepticism.

"Nothing noble about it. I don't want my daughters, who today are all of eight and eleven, to bear *their* children in a system dominated by business interests. Present? By all means. Dominant? Not for *my* kids. If the gene pool that produces clearheaded clinical reasoning in this swirl of concerns isn't protected, isn't treated like an endangered species over the next handful of years, then it may simply die out. I don't want that, not for my kids, not for my grandkids. What's your second question, Mila?"

The sound of the white water was a roar now, and as the boat rounded a bend Mila could see she was almost into them. She shouted above the din: "Where the hell is my paddle?"

Cheshire Cat-like, Greg's image had gone but for mouth and beard. "Mind-set, Mila, mind-set."

She closed her eyes and was back at the new resident's reception.

Endnotes

1. Peter Vaill, *Management as a Performing Art* (San Francisco: Jossey-Bass Publishers, 1989): 2–3.

2. Robert Keidel, *Game Plans* (New York: E. P. Dutton, 1985); and Robert Keidel, *Seeing Organizational Patterns* (San Francisco: Berrett-Koehler, 1995).

OF ALARM CLOCKS
AND ALPHABET SOUP

WHEN MILA NOTICED IT AGAIN, HER COORS LIGHT WAS STILL HALF FULL, BUT IT WAS NOW HALF WARM, TOO. Fifteen years of innovation and still no way to keep beer cold during a simple, out-of-body alien tutorial.

Somehow she felt that downing a flat beer would do little for her mood, not to mention her general state of disorientation. She ditched it and headed out to see what kind of apartment the Climarans had arranged for her. She needed to review her schedule and reading material for tomorrow.

New York City, even in August is, well it's New York City. She walked downtown on First Avenue. In "her" day it would have been a scary walk, but now it seemed pretty gentrified and safe. And comfortingly un-Climaran. She dodged some spilling, steaming garbage to her left and passed a woman striding down the sidewalk in combat boots and a grass skirt. A young man sauntered by, his face prickling with what seemed to be surgical pins through his eyebrows and nose. Mila nodded to him. She was fresh enough from the hospital that she momentarily took his hardware to be some sort of post-op measure. Quickly she realized it was not, reddened, and looked away. But not before he stuck out his tongue at her, and she saw it, too, was studded with metal. Yuk, Mila thought, as if there isn't enough involuntary bodily mutilation. Oh, for the good old days, when kids settled for the simple elegance of green, spiked hair.

The phone was ringing as she let herself into the apartment, and she was almost overcome to hear her mother's voice. It will all seem unextraordinary to those with whom you interact, Quam had said. Well, she thought, here's the test of that.

"Oh, good, Mila. I'm glad I caught you, sweetie. How are you?"

You would have become uninspired by your work, cynical, hopeless with your loved ones, stalled, and disappointed.

"Are you settling in?" Her mother's voice sounded so normal, so matter-of-fact.

"Yes, Mom. And I'm eating my vegetables, too." It was her standard daughterly shrug-off, but she stopped. If she were really being given another chance, she wasn't going to waste it by dwelling on the past or by blindly sticking to old habits.

"Are you all right, dear?"

Mila thought for a moment, smiled, and said, "Yeah, Mom. I'm OK. I'm going to like it here."

Just then her dad got on the extension. "Hi, pumpkin. Did you hear Matt's news? He's taken the helm at a large multispecialty group, a place called The Health Center. That kid had foresight getting an MBA when he did. Isn't it great?"

Mila's mom chimed in. "He's looking forward to the management piece, Mila. It's very nice. He's been telling us for years that getting along in a large group requires the same kind of communication that being successful with patients requires."

Mila could almost hear her dad grinning. "Now all he has to do is persuade his old-fashioned doc of a Dad. Well, honey, I'll say goodnight. *ER*'s on in five minutes."

"You're going in again tonight, Dad?"

Her parents both chuckled. "You really have been working hard the last couple of years. The TV show, dear," said her mom.

"Enjoy your residency," her dad said. "Be sure to double glove."

"Don't worry Dad," said Mila, "they downloaded all that stuff about AIDS and universal precautions—" Whoops. Mila cringed. Don't let that openness go too far.

Luckily, they only laughed. Well done, Quam, thought Mila.

"Oh, Mila, that reminds me," said her mother, "Aunt Marie has a neighbor whose son is a medical resident at Columbia—"

"Goodnight, Mom." There were limits, even if she was going to lose some of her old assumptions. Mila had not traveled ten thousand miles to hear about another loser blind date. Although, after spending all that time with the Climarans, perhaps her physical standards had lessened a bit.

"Notorious BIG to wake you up this morning."

Ugh. The last thing she needed at 5:15 A.M. was an assault from her radio. She slapped the snooze button so hard her hand stung, but at least the noise stopped. As far as I'm concerned, Mila thought, that could have as easily been Climaran as Earth music. Then she shook her head. I've turned into a twenty-seven-year-old Old Fart. I guess they didn't update my culture sensors. I'll just have to do that myself.

After a Pop-Tart and a quick shower, Mila arrived at the hospital at 5:45 and got her assignments. Eight patients for whom she'd be primarily responsible. That was a light load compared to 1985 standards, but nowadays patients were shunted into and out of the hospital so quickly that by the time you wrote their name on the index card, their inpatient insurance days had run out. I'd better start earlier, Mila thought, if I need to finish pre-rounds, meet with the attending, and be on time for OR prep at 7:20. Fortunately for Mila, sleep was something she could do without. She just needed to find a radio station that would wake her up a bit more gently than that BIG guy. She'd save her acculturation for afternoons.

All the reading and talking about the business of health care had made her almost forget the joy of actually taking care of patients. And joy it was. She was actually able to pay attention to nothing but patients for a whole hour. Electrolyte values and wound incisions were just what the doctor ordered to get her back into a clinical mode. Hey, this is great, Mila thought. If I can play real doc all day, I can convince Ajax that I don't need him, and he can hop the first time-space commuter out of here.

Just then she caught sight of her attending down the hall. In the excitement of yesterday she'd barely noticed him, but now she did. Thumbs up on the strong-featured face that seemed always to be appreciating some irony. Big time thumbs down on the nasal voice, always a little too loud, and the large cufflinks. On the whole, Mila decided, he looked like the kind of guy who'd bought himself a Porsche when he began to lose his hair.

"Dr. Baskin," Mila said, meeting him. "Whenever it's a good time I can run down the patients with you."

"Forget them," Dr. Baskin said, his eyes on his clipboard. "We'll see them after surgery. I want to make the first half of the IDS meeting."

Mila quickly ransacked her brain for something—anything—about IDS. A new type of grand rounds, maybe? As she opened her mouth to frame a question that would keep her from looking too stupid, however, she found herself in the White.

"What the hell am I doing here? I was just about to learn something, for Pete's sake. I'm supposed to be a doctor!" Maybe the worst part was she was getting used to yelling with no voice. "And get me out of this White, damn it!"

"Mila!" said Ajax. "You're angry, aren't you! It's really wonderfully exciting to observe."

"Ajax. Physical. Reality. NOW."

Mila and Ajax were suddenly sitting in the front row of an empty, arena-type classroom. Ajax leaned over to her conspiratorially and whispered, "How do you like it? Awfully nice reproduction of your Bio 2 lecture room, don't you think?"

Mila found herself whispering, too. "Ajax. I don't need to retake Bio 2. If I've forgotten this—what is it?—IDS from that class, I'll remember it soon or I'll look it up in my regular old textbook."

"Be quiet and pay attention," Ajax said. "An IDS is not biology or medicine, and you are actually quite ignorant about it, as are many of your colleagues. I picked this setting because you experienced being plunged into new material here. And if you wish to practice medicine, you will need to learn new material once again. We do not wish you to appear the fool."

A carefully and conservatively dressed man entered, acknowledged them with a nod, and took his place at the podium.

"Who is he?" whispered Mila.

"An expert on managed care and IDS—Integrated Delivery Systems. He'll explain IDS, PHO, IPA, and their interrelations."

"Well," Mila said begrudgingly, "he'd better make the alphabet lesson quick."

The distinguished professor looked down at Mila. "Is there a problem here?"

Mila looked at Ajax. He shrugged a shoulder.

"Well, sir," she said, "I've got patients to see. Could you just explain IDS and let me get back to them?"

The professor raised an eyebrow. "Certainly. I'll summarize. An IDS is a vehicle to organize a response to managed care. Response is necessary because payers have already organized in order to exert power over physicians, known in the new order as providers. There is an array of options for physicians. The options vary in their intrusiveness and in their ability to deliver patients—the trade-off is between autonomy and economic security. The trick, you see, is to get the right mix for you as a physician at your stage of your career. After all, physicians vary in their personalities, and a physician's practice has a business life cycle to it. For instance, the younger a practice, the more significant a factor is economic security. My overall message is that you'd better organize. Do something. Get bigger."

Mila felt a knot at the pit of her stomach. "How did this happen? Where will it lead?"

"Well, young lady, I'll be happy to give you details about where we've been and where we might be going in managed care. I should be able to help you with the alphabet soup of IPA and PHO, as well as IDS, if you can spare the time."

Mila leaned back unhappily. "OK, it sounds like I'd better hear it. All of it."

"My pleasure." He smiled smoothly and returned to the podium.

CHAPTER 10

THE HISTORY AND FUTURE
OF MANAGED CARE

Background

UNTIL RECENTLY, MEDI-cine in the United States was dominated by small group and individual providers. According to an article by Bruce A. Barron in the *American Jewish Committee Commentary*, physicians acted as entrepreneurs and made most decisions concerning the medical care provided to their patients. Similar in many ways to a retail service business, medical care differed from most such businesses in the crucial aspect of payment. Instead of the patient paying the bill, insurance companies took on much of that responsibility. As "third-party payers," the insurance companies learned how much to remit to doctors only upon receipt of claims. Eventually, the insurance providers used unmediated aggregates of claims to determine what premiums to charge. Then the patient still did not directly pay the premiums as medical insurance was frequently paid, at least in part, by employers.

This arrangement kept physician and patient at a financial distance. The beneficiaries of the service, the patients, didn't do the paying. Those who did do the paying, employers and insurers, had no say in the service provided, and therefore no way to influence cost. With no direct relationship between buyer and seller, the system was not affected by natural market forces, in a kind of fiscal freefall.

Eventually, insurance carriers took steps to control costs by establishing a range of "reasonable and customary fees" for specific services.[1] Physicians, however, could choose whether or not to accept these fees as complete payments. This weakened the market pressures which the limits might have otherwise brought. That system was the structure of fee-for-service medicine which was put into place during a period—about the last half-century—when the overall use of health care increased tremendously, turning the practice of medicine into big business. "At $900 billion a year, that business is now the largest single sector of the American economy, and the costs associated with it are staggering."[2]

These costs are commonly credited with the rethinking of the relationship of physician and patient, physician and hospital, and physician and payer. However, Barron contends that the direction of the rethinking was greatly influenced by another factor—the financial crumbling of the academic medical center, long the foundation of the industry.

Federal programs initiated after World War II caused the university schools of medicine to grow to sizes never before imagined. The schools developed into huge and intricate organizations motivated by research, education, and patient care. Private and government funding drastically increased, and academic institutions and their physicians became rich.

Not surprisingly, more and more hospitals sought medical school affiliation, and existing medical school hospitals grew still larger. A typical academic medical center became a behemoth including a medical school, a dental school, a nursing school, training programs for paramedical specialists like physical and occupational therapists, research institutes for particular diseases such as cancer or heart disease, special units for the clinical care of certain groups of patients—women's hospitals, children's hospitals, eye institutes. And, not least, it contained a hospital. One example Barron provides is Presbyterian Hospital in New York City, the clinical arm of the Columbia Presbyterian Medical Center, which has an annual budget in excess of $1 billion, and is not, Barron claims, an atypical medical center.

"The finances of these centers in their heyday were very complicated, with revenues coming from different sources and few if any fiscal controls."[3] Physicians who taught at the medical school and practiced medicine only at that school's affiliated hospital were considered full-time clinical faculty members and received income both from research grants and from patient fees. For the privilege of involvement in the center's educational and research activities, as well as a challenging and diverse practice, these faculty members taught medical students and staff, helped to care for the impoverished people served by the hospital, and yielded part of their practice income to their clinical department.

The hospital and medical school administrations also received great rewards. Patients were drawn by the clinical faculty, and funds from various government agencies were drawn by the research. Additional monies came as a result of the medical schools' not-for-profit status; the faculty's earnings were passed through university accounts and any net profits were not taxed. On top of that, every research grant included an amount to be paid directly to the institution for overhead costs. In the 1960s, "the overhead charged by medical schools ran at about 20 percent of the total award, and constituted no small part of the operating budgets of most medical schools."[4]

By the mid-seventies, however, government research funds were difficult to find. Medical schools were forced to increase the institutional "tax" on the faculty's income from patient care. Barron points out that the move from dependence on research revenue to dependence on practice revenue was only the first of many changes. Doctors once treated

indigent patients on a voluntary basis, but the Medicaid program began paying for this service; monies collected in the physician's name were often kept by the medical school. However, when this change was still unable to provide enough funds, the charge added to grant applications for indirect costs was increased yet again. At many centers, "it now exceeds 100 percent."[5]

While this occurred in the medical school components of the centers, Barron explains that the problem did not stop there. The hospital components were also experiencing decreasing revenue. More and more surgical procedures could be done on an outpatient basis, greatly reducing hospitalization stays.

As subspecialties grew, an even more profound change occurred. The medical centers trained and sent out many high-tech specialists, who, in turn, transformed many community hospitals into medical complexes competing for the same, limited number of patients needing such high-tech care. Intense competition exists to attract patients from outside the centers' usual base area. For instance, Barron relates that even the prestigious Johns Hopkins Medical Center in Baltimore now advertises for patients in New York City.

In the late 1980s, the government began requiring precertification for services to Medicare and Medicaid patients, again reducing the number of patients and length of stay and again decreasing revenue. Soon, insurance company policies began requiring the same qualifications. "The ensuing shortfall severely reduced the ability of hospitals to repay the huge sums of money they had borrowed from the federal government for capital investment in growth."[6]

The centers were unable to respond immediately to their budgetary problems. Many did not have accurate accounting measures. For example, a chief financial officer, while aware of what the hospital *charged* for certain procedures, was unaware of how much those services actually *cost* the hospital to provide. Barron compares this lack of knowledge to a restaurateur listing prices on a menu without knowing his own cost to serve the food.

Hospitals, as a result, fell victim to American corporate managers in the 1990s. These executives knew the deficient balance sheets of even the most prestigious teaching institutions, and they seized the opportunity. The centers were in such financial straits that the upper hand was held both by the large employers, who controlled the patients upon whom hospitals depended, and by the insurance companies, who easily determined how much would be paid for the services. Some hospitals sought survival through hastily arranged partnerships with managed care

companies, but the overall result was drastically reduced independence for all centers. "So began the wholesale overhaul of what had been, until then, the best medical-care service in the world."[7]

MANAGED CARE

Of the 160 million insured Americans, 120 million are in managed care arrangements. These arrangements vary in detail but are all, as put by the Health Insurance Association of America, ". . . systems that integrate the financing and delivery of appropriate health-care services to covered individuals . . ."[8] They are all, too, spurred on by the need to contain costs and by the duty to provide appropriate health care.

Health benefits, in one way or another, have enjoyed tax-free status for years. Michael Sachs, in an article in *Frontiers of Health Service Management*, explains that, at first, medical care was paid with after-tax dollars by patients. Then, insurers paid for medical care costs but were themselves paid by employers using tax-free dollars. Because it was (and is) in any employer's best interest to have healthy employees satisfied with their benefits, and to achieve that health and satisfaction at the lowest reasonable costs, the employer-financed health care system grew.

Utilization of health care and the resulting expenditures greatly increased for several reasons. First, patients were no longer confronted with medical bills. Second, high-tech breakthroughs, such as open heart surgery and CT scans, although expensive, had obvious benefits and perhaps created the trend away from lower-cost, traditional therapies. Additionally, monetary incentives (fee-for-service arrangements) were provided for physicians to utilize the costly technology even if resulting in only marginal benefit.[9] Finally, an aging population and a steady supply of funds from Medicare, Medicaid, and private insurance companies also added to health care expenditures.

In 1973, the federal government passed the Health Maintenance Organization Act requiring companies with twenty-five or more employees to offer a health maintenance option to employees. At first, HMOs were more expensive than traditional insurance (except in union plans) because federal statute required them to cover more services.

In 1982, in an effort to decrease health care costs, the federal government changed from a cost-plus payment system to a flat payment-per-admission system, reducing medical spending in the Medicare program. However, hospitals responded by increasing rates in the private sector, and corporate America had to compensate for the government's decreased payments.

By the late eighties, big business grew weary of large premiums and further increases. This situation provided managed care companies the opportunity to enter and negotiate payments with physicians, hospitals, and insurance providers, reducing the payment gap between the public and private sectors. In fact, by the early 1990s, "hospitals had begun to reduce absolute operating costs to the point that Medicare and Medicaid once again became the better payer."[10]

THE MEDICAL CARE DELIVERY MODEL

Two views of medical care are the economically driven care model and the medical care delivery model. Critics of the former argue that the quality of care suffers with this model because its two objectives—good care and good profits—conflict. Others, however, suggest the free choice of the consumer resolves the problem. An article in *Time* magazine (January 22, 1996) made the following statement:

No one disputes that managed care has at last put the brakes on medical spending, or that it has proved an effective vehicle for rationing health care. . . . At issue, rather, are the costs of the process itself—the effort and delay inherent in acquiring care and the extent to which considerations other than mere health are brought to bear by corporate managers. . . .[11]

According to Sachs, however, the belief that managed care companies are efficient operators is inaccurate when statistics of medical-loss and administrative cost ratios are considered. As a result, such economic model plans, with the goal of increasing efficiencies, can be more expensive than the previously mentioned medical care delivery model.

In the medical care delivery model, quality comes first. Physicians and providers work together and, as with all HMOs, hire a medical director. The HMO "handles payer contract negotiations and administrative, utilization, and outcome review functions. The prepaid nature of this plan focuses attention on participant wellness."[12]

The California Kaiser network is one example Sachs gives of the medical care delivery model. The network applies fully 96.5 percent of funds to patient care and only 3.0 percent to administrative overhead. Kaiser assigns between 11.9 percent and 16.4 percent more of each dollar to direct patient care than economically driven managed care groups.[13]

When considering administrative costs, Kaiser is the only plan in single digits. "All economically driven managed care groups spend at least three-and-a-half times that amount, from

Aetna-U.S. Healthcare on the low end with an 11.8 percent administrative cost ratio, to Oxford Health Plan on the high end, with 15.7 percent of each dollar covering administrative expenses."[14]

A HIGHLY CRITICAL VIEW OF MANAGED CARE

There is a good deal of cynicism about the value of managed care for patients and for society. It is argued that managed care is used to manage costs instead of care. Bruce A. Barron suggests three ways in which managed care attempts to limit the amount of spending on medical care. These are to reduce the number of "units" of medical care, reduce the cost per unit, or place restrictions on certain units of care, such as organ transplantation or infertility treatment.[15]

Insurance carriers argue that reduced costs are not reducing quality and that the actual problems—overuse, fraud, and abuse—when brought under control, "will be sufficient to rein in the normal rate of increase in the cost of care."[16] Yet, Barron disagrees that eliminating these bad habits could actually achieve the goal of managing costs. He further states that managed care, in fact, limits services, reduces payments to providers, and restricts choices.

The effects of managed care on medical service has been seen in several areas, explains Barron. First, the amount of time physicians spend with patients has been greatly reduced. Second, the level of training required for certain tasks has been reduced. Additionally, surgeons and other hospital staff members must be cost-conscious, refraining from promoting longer hospital stays and/or ordering expensive tests.

The clinical effects can be seen in the fact that a nursing degree is all that is required for the person interpreting the guidelines for managed care programs, decisions once made by physicians. Physicians, then, are under threat of removal if they deviate from the guidelines. In addition, when the physicians are compensated a fixed amount per patient (capitation or risk-sharing), they are further encouraged to follow the guidelines. On top of this, managed care programs claim no liability in malpractice cases, stating that they are only agents of the purchaser.

Barron provides the following example of how this directly affects the patient. Five years ago, an elderly woman in need of surgery would be admitted to a hospital the day before her operation. She could be completely evaluated for any complications and receive any necessary intravenous fluids. She would meet those who were taking care of her, and they would all become familiar with her history and current condition. All relevant information would be recorded for the surgeon and would greatly reduce the chance that some critical information could be missed.

Today, contrasts Barron, that same patient will arrive only three hours before the scheduled surgery, change her clothes, and go directly to the operating room. Her physician will have previously received approval by answering computer-generated questions asked by a managed care company staff member, usually a nurse without relevant training or experience. In some instances, the physician's request will be denied at which point the doctor may pursue the issue further, taking much time and making many telephone calls, with the final decision still being made by "an insurance-company employee whose credentials would likely not be acceptable for appointment to a major medical center."[17]

The results of managed care, which has come about because of the self-induced financial collapse of academic medical centers, may be evident both short term and long-term. According to Barron, fiscal results may be seen soon in the decreased diagnosis and care of those who are ill. However, long-term results may only become clear with a review in the future of age and disease-specific mortality rates and life expectancy.

While Barron concedes that the academic medical center model may be gone forever, he suggests that solutions exist to reduce costs of medical care without reducing the quality of care. The solutions, Barron continues, would require making medical insurance more accessible, as well as reinstating consumer choice and responsibility. Barron's conclusion is a grim one, questioning the possibility of fresh thinking in an era of managed care and advising Americans to make every effort to stay well.[18]

A MORE SELECTIVELY CRITICAL VIEW OF MANAGED CARE

The highly critical view many hold of managed care mistakenly assumes that the system is static. In reality, the organization of health care in this country is still finding its most efficient form.

Many employers question the contributions of health plans to reducing costs and voice considerable dissatisfaction with the lack of cost and outcomes data they generate. J. Daniel Beckham, in his article in *The Healthcare Forum*, suggests that the HMO model has been flawed from the beginning because it involves an unnecessary middleman who simply increases cost.

Here's an easy test for value-added in the healthcare industry. Ask: "What percentage of an organization's employees put hands on patients vs. those who never touch a patient?" In most HMOs (with the exception of staff-model HMOs, which again, like Kaiser, are really prepaid group practices), the ratio is probably somewhere below 1 percent.[19]

When evidence of value is demanded by buyers of health care and delivered by providers, Beckham predicts that HMOs will be pushed out.

Additionally, HMOs don't hold up well in court. HMOs' goals—such as the use of money to influence utilization—make sense to economists, but "jurors tend to find abhorrent the notion that somebody might receive a bonus for 'withholding care' or for punishing a physician who delivered 'too much care.'"[20]

The fact is that sick people don't need a health plan; they need a doctor. Consumers are seeking the value of some type of health care service. Beckham comments, "It is evidence of continuing myopia in the healthcare industry that health plans and financing have received the level of attention and power they've been afforded. This will change."[21]

THE FUTURE OF
MANAGED CARE

Until recently (mid–1998), many analysts and observers believed that managed care would continue to grow and would drive the health care industry toward greater integration. Large-scale, corporate, and publicly traded organizations would deliver an increasing share of health care services.

For example, in a 1996 publication, *The Rising Tide*, the Advisory Board, a premier health care consulting company and think tank, argues that the national economy as a whole is moving from privately owned, sub-scale organizations to investor-owned, highly organized corporations, which operate on a national scale.[22] Evidence for this is the large share of national income accounted for by publicly traded companies (59 percent in 1993), the rise of publicly traded companies (6,432 in 1984 to 8,296 in 1994) and the growth of publicly traded shares, (40 billion in 1986 to 152 billion in 1994).[23]

The health care industry, they argue, is still on the frontier but will not be for long. Hospitals and physicians, both in mostly nonprofit situations, are still, for the most part, unorganized.[24] According to a Wall Street analyst, this segment of the economy is ready for a change. The number of securities analysts covering health care did rise from 75 in 1991 to 381 in 1996. The number of publicly traded health care companies has also grown from 33 in 1992 to 144 in 1996. In California, the changes that began in 1985 had, in 1995, resulted in the majority of health care being provided by statewide or national, investor-owned HMOs.[25] This is now the trend on the national level.

The Advisory Board points to the rise of physician practice management companies (PPMCs) as a part of this trend. The largest of these companies, like PhyCor, Inc., and MedPartners/ Mullikin, have become truly national companies although they still only accounted for a very small portion (2 percent) of the number of physicians in practice in the United States.[26]

Perhaps the greatest illustration of the trend is the example of Columbia/HCA. In the six years from 1990 to 1996, Columbia's revenue grew from $0.29 billion to $22.00 billion. By 1996, Columbia operated over 350 hospitals, 130 surgery centers, and 200 home health agencies. It significantly outperformed the S&P 500 on annual revenue growth, EPS, and shareholder return.[27]

However, by the middle of 1998, doubts were being raised about the effectiveness of the large scale, fully integrated corporate model. Leaders in health care continue to appreciate the potential for clinical integration, for example, making radiology results available more systematically to all of the providers involved in the care for a single patient.[28] However, many of the major corporate health care power-houses have encountered hard times and are moving away from direct ownership of large numbers of health care facilities. Columbia/HCA's revenues and earnings have shrunk, and in 1998 it sold a number of hospitals and its home health operations. It is now working toward "becoming a smaller, more focused company."[29] MedPartners announced in November 1998 that it would divest its physician practice management operations and focus instead on its pharmacy benefits management and therapeutic services businesses.[30]

Columbia's example provides lessons for others in the industry. In 1996, when Columbia was concerned with internal growth, profits from then current operations rose to 43.7 percent. They remained competitive, achieving their low cost position in part through scale. According to the Advisory Board, they had great purchasing leverage and large economies of scale.[31] In addition, they focused management attention relentlessly on key operating indicators, such as total admissions, average length of stay, and operating expenses/adjusted admission.[32]

ORGANIZATIONAL FORMS FOR ADJUSTING TO MANAGED CARE: IDS, IPA, PHO

Medical care providers, having grown weary of battling insurers, have found strength in joining together in provider networks. According to *Medical Utilization Management*, physicians and hospitals working alone have become rare. The book relates the findings of the American Association of PHOs (physician-hospital organizations) and IDSs (Integrated Delivery Systems) that at least one thousand PHOs exist. Also reported is that of the six hundred HMOs analyzed by InterStudy, a research organization, eighty of them are "provider-owned." Further, provider networks are in the works (from contemplation to implementation) for at least twenty-two of the country's state medical societies. In addition, Provider-Sponsored Networks (PSNs) are quickly growing in Medicare HMOs.[33]

Two reasons providers are networking together are to achieve economies of scale in all areas and to gain greater influence in contract negotiations with payers. *Medical Utilization Management* also claims that "PSNs' latest and potentially most powerful tactic is the assumption of risk, which will enable them to enjoy the financial payoff from their cost control and eventually may eliminate the middle man."[34] The book refers to a survey done by Lincoln National Insurance, along with the American Association of PHOs and the National Association of Managed Care Physicians, which found that at least half of all PHOs in the market have at-risk contracts.[35]

Providers, while perhaps breaking free from third-party payers, are discovering new challenges. Three barriers discussed are capital requirements, the difficulty of reaching agreements, and a twisted regulatory environment. However, one of the most significant challenges in these networks is the relationship between physicians and hospitals, according to Stephen Shortell, professor of health services management at the J. L. Kellogg Graduate School of Management at Northwestern University. "The issues of control, of the financial incentives involved, can pose real challenges when trying to find common ground for cooperation," Shortell says. "That's why capitation is so important; if you capitate the delivery of care in total then you begin to finally align the incentives for everyone."[36]

Stephen Melek, in an article in *Managed Behavioral Health News*, states that it makes sense for the occurrence of financial integration and risk-sharing between the behavioral and medical components of health care to exist. He suggests that risk-sharing promotes lower-cost alternatives and high-quality health care.[37] Melek provides the following explanation:

> An HMO or insurer capitates a physician-hospital organization or other integrated delivery system to provide health care services. The PHO then uses the capitation revenue to fund a risk-sharing arrangement among its medical providers that includes an institutional/facility risk pool, a specialty physician risk pool and primary care physician capitation.

> The risk-sharing occurs when the risk pool balances are identified and assessed to the affected provider groups. The surpluses and deficits in the facility risk pool are typically split among the facilities, specialists and primary care physicians. The surpluses and deficits in the physician specialty pool are typically split between the specialists and primary care physicians. That is designed to financially motivate the various groups to work together to control costs and to promote wellness . . . to get people healthy and keep them healthy. In turn the PHO will be able to take larger numbers of members into its delivery system and

provide high-quality care to a larger number of covered lives. Poor or low-quality care could result in covered members re-entering the health care delivery system in need of more care and incurring extra costs, perhaps with greater intensity.[38]

THE TYPES OF INTEGRATION

For small group practices, integration provides the means to reach their desired goals. However, it is often more difficult for these small groups to develop successful unity than for larger practices. Many physicians are in small group practices precisely because they want to avoid complex business relationships with large numbers of providers. Yet integration is likely to be the critical ingredient in their success.

According to Bruce A. Johnson and Darrell L. Schryver in an article in *Healthcare Financial Management*, three integration strategies are commonly pursued by small group practices. The strategy with the least integrated form of organization avoids any full-fledged merger in favor of the creation of horizontally integrated networks: strategic alliances are formed among separate providers for managed care contracting.

A second integration strategy, also along the horizontal continuum, is groups-without-walls, which includes more traditional group practices. The groups-without-walls strategy is often developed in such a way as to encourage more individual physician independence. In fact, Johnson and Schryver point out that "some of the benefits enjoyed by a small group practice are preserved through the group's income and expense distribution and governance systems."[39]

Finally, the third integration strategy they describe is vertical integration. This strategy uses management, organizations, PHOs, IDSs, and other models to join physician group practices to health care organizations and third-party investors.

VIRTUAL INTEGRATION

Mention should now be made of another form of integration—virtual integration. Discussed in the book, *Remaking Health Care in America*, the process of virtual integration can include contracts, strategic alliances, and direct ownership. Virtual integration builds an organized delivery system, which is "a network of organizations that provides, or arranges to provide a coordinated continuum of services to a defined population and is willing to be held clinically and fiscally accountable for the outcomes and the health status of the population served."[40] Organized delivery systems may also be built around physician groups (e.g., Mayo Clinic), around insurance companies (e.g., Aetna and Cigna), or around hybrids of the above (e.g., Kaiser-Permanente, and Cigna-Lovelace Clinic).

THE INTEGRATION PROCESS

Bruce A. Johnson and Darrell L. Schryver (previously mentioned) explain the process of integration in small group practices. The process usually begins "with physician members of the group examining the market in which they practice, assessing the practice's current and potential position in that market, then identifying the form of integration that would best suit their needs."[41] They describe the first phase as consisting of discussions, initially informal and then becoming more focused and formal and involving other health care entities. Johnson and Schryver suggest that integrations resulting from the initiative of physicians, as opposed to outside forces (such as the arrival of a managed care plan in their community), are often the most successful.

The second phase, then, is the time where the prospective partners focus on compatibility in areas such as mission, vision, strengths and weaknesses, as well as their goals regarding the integration itself. Personal meetings are vital at this point, and an evaluation of the varying cultural, professional, and interpersonal styles occurs. The presence of an objective third party is also important to determine goals and needs. The results of this phase are whether or not integration will take place, and, if so, who the future partners will be.

One guideline for initial small group practice integration, says Johnson and Schryver, is to take it slow and build on preexisting relationships.[42] Most prospective partners are found locally and through established relationships, whether business or casual. Of course, the marketplace demands and needs of the area will also affect the final mix.

RENTAL NETWORKS

Allison Bell, in an article in *National Underwriter Life and Health*, writes about rental networks in which physicians join with networks which rent their (the doctors') services to health plans. Some of those networks include physician/hospital organizations and independent practice associations. Bell reports that the trade group representing integrated delivery systems would not provide statistics on the size of this industry. However, Mark Hopkins, a health care consultant at Watson Wyatt & Co. in Washington, D.C., estimates that as many as nine thousand provider rental networks and a few dozen national rental networks exist.

Bell further records Hopkins's reports that preferred provider organizations and health maintenance organizations may also rent their networks; but in the purest form, these networks do not accept insurance risk. Primary care providers usually join primary care networks that rent services to many of the managed care plans in a community. Also according to Hopkins, "a specialist tries to gain access to as many managed care plan patients as possible by joining several specialty care networks."[43]

ANTITRUST CONCERNS

When considering these partnerships, however, one must be aware of the legal ramifications. Regardless of the model used for joint venture—integrated delivery system, individual practice association, physician-hospital organization, etc.—hospitals, physicians, and other health care providers must be cautious of violating antitrust laws.[44]

Additionally, due to state constitutional constraints, public hospitals may not be able to participate in physician-hospital organizations, integrated delivery systems, other

managed care risk-sharing arrangements with doctors, or multihospital linkages. In fact, in an article by Monte Dube in *Healthcare Financial Management*, even programs designed to draw physicians and allied health practitioners to "medically underserved communities may be outlawed by constitutional prohibitions against the pledging of public credit or wrongful use of municipal funds."[45]

ADVANTAGES AND DISADVANTAGES

From the patient's perspective, each of the many types of insurance plans available—standard health insurance, PPOs, IPA, HMOs, second opinion programs, et al.—offers advantages and disadvantages. In general, patients face a choice between convenience and cost (higher premiums). HMO plans, for example, cost members less than comparable full-coverage "standard" insurance, but are somewhat inconvenient since care can only come from the HMO staff. IPAs and PPOs come in between HMOs and fee-for-service plans. According to Charles E. Phelps in *Health Economics*, many options now exist in health care that were not previously available. In addition, since people's preferences vary, "we can expect that no single form of such plans will dominate the market, and a pluralistic system will persist."[46]

There are advantages and disadvantages to each arrangement from the physician's standpoint, too, and each option must be carefully studied. The only constant for all physicians, regardless of other differences, is the reality of change. Physicians must learn about and consider the new possibilities with the same attention they bring to their practices. When they use care, diligence, and intelligence, physicians can take hold of their futures.

Endnotes

1. Bruce A. Barron, "The price of managed care," *American Jewish Committee Commentary* 103 (May 1997): 49.

2. Ibid.

3. Ibid.

4. Ibid.

5. Ibid.

6. Ibid.

7. Ibid.

8. Michael A. Sachs, "Managed care: The next generation," *Frontiers of Health Service Management* 14 (Fall 1997): 3–26.

9. Ibid.

10. Ibid.

11. Michael A. Sachs, "Managed care."

12. Michael A. Sachs, "Managed care."

13. Ibid.

14. Ibid.

15. Bruce A. Barron, "The price of managed care."

16. Ibid.

17. Ibid.

18. Ibid.

19. J. Daniel Beckham, "The beginning of the end for HMOs—Part 1: The awakening market," *The Health Care Forum* (November/December 1997).

20. Ibid.

21. Ibid.

22. The Advisory Board, *The Rising Tide* (Washington, D.C.: The Governance Committee, 1996): 5, 8–9.

23. Ibid.

24. Ibid., 16–17.

25. Ibid., 18–21.

26. Ibid., 28–29.

27. Ibid., 35–37.

28. Example given in a talk by Harris Berman, CEO of the Tufts Health Plan, at Harvard, November 24, 1998.

29. November 1997 press release, Columbia/HCA.

30. November 11, 1998 press release, MedPartners.

31. *The Rising Tide*, 90.

32. Ibid.

33. "Provider-Sponsored Networks: An Evaluation," *Medical Utilization Management* 24 (December 5, 1996).

34. Ibid.

35. Ibid.

36. Quoted in "Provider-Sponsored Networks."

37. Stephen Melek, "Risk Overlap Models Bridge Gaps Between Behavioral Health, Medical Care," *Managed Behavioral Health News* 2 (August 29, 1996; © 1999 Dow Jones & Company, Inc;

© 1996 Information Access Company). (Melek serves as consulting actuary for Milliman & Robertson, Inc.).

38. Ibid.

39. Bruce A. Johnson and Darrell L. Schryver, "Integration from the small group practice perspective," *Healthcare Financial Management* 50 (July 1996): 80–82.

40. Stephen M. Shortell et al., *Remaking Health Care in America: Building Organized Delivery Systems* (San Francisco: Jossey-Bass Publishers, 1993): 7–8.

41. Bruce A. Johnson and Darrell L. Schryver, "Integration from the small group practice perspective."

42. Ibid.

43. Allison Bell, "Rental networks reshape health care: renting of hospitals and doctors to health plans," *National Underwriter Life & Health—Financial Services Edition* 101 (October 27, 1997): 40.

44. Paul L. Grimaldi, "Network formation made easier," *Nursing Management* 27 (December 1996): 9–10.

45. Monte Dube , "Restructuring public hospitals to meet marketplace demands," *Healthcare Financial Management* 50 (February 1996): 38.

46. Charles Phelps E., *Health Economics*, Second Edition (Reading, Massachusetts: Addison-Wesley, 1997): 399.

CHAPTER 1

OF RISK POOLS
AND ROLEXES

". . . DON'T THINK SO?" ASKED DR. BASKIN, WAVING MILA AHEAD OF HIM OUT THE CONFERENCE ROOM DOOR. Apparently, the IDS meeting was over, and it was as if Mila had never been away, as if she hadn't just reentered reality in mid-sentence.

They started down the hall, passing illegible scrawls of graffiti at regular five-step intervals. They wove around three elderly men in wheelchairs. "You know, Mila," Dr. Baskin said, "I can tell you were paying attention at that meeting because you look a little ill."

Ajax must have sent a hologram of her to the meeting. Mila gave Dr. Baskin her best, blank smile, which seemed to content him perfectly.

"We have time to make lightning rounds before surgery," he said. "Now you can tell me how my patients are doing."

Out the elevator doors, over to the pile of charts, and on to Mrs. Klay's room. "Post-op, day 2, gallbladder," reported Mila. She looked up to continue, then stopped.

"Dr. Baskin?" She was talking to a damn fire extinguisher. "Hello?" Where was he? Mila's heart clutched—what was going on? Were Climarans snatching them one by one?

"Ajax?" she said loudly, and a passing visitor widened his arc around her. "Show yourself, Ajax!"

"Doctor, can I help you find something?" The nurse, a sharp-faced woman of about forty, sounded less than thrilled to be helping a first-day resident. "Are we lost?"

Mila felt like a seven year old in a doctor suit. "I, uh . . . Dr. Baskin. Where could he be?" The nurse looked over her glasses and pointed with her pen to the desk where Dr. Baskin stood. Normal, corporeal, earthbound, and uttering curses at a computer screen.

"Yeah," said Mila, her heart still thumping. "Yeah, there he is, all right. Not taken by aliens after all."

"To be sure," said the nurse. She adjusted the chain holding the halves of her cardigan together and turned on her soundless, rubber heel. Well, she's about as comforting as a catheter, thought Mila. Woe be to the patient who depends on her TLC.

Mila circled around a mop, a pail, and a pool of unidentifiable-but-smelly liquid on the floor and asked Dr. Baskin about seeing the patients. He didn't even look up. "I can see everything I need right here on this screen. It's great! I used to have to come to the hospital, round on every patient, listen to the nurse tell me how each one was doing. Then the patient would talk. And talk. It would take me an hour to get through twenty patients.

"Now we can do all that on-line! All I have to do is to sign on at a computer terminal. I can get access to data about how my patients are doing, including their lab results, from anywhere. I can find out what hospital services are overcrowded and discharge patients early in units where beds are tight, all by e-mail. I can even do all this from home! I can find out what I need to know and not waste my life on what I don't need to know.

One thing I'm not doing, thought Mila, is violating the grand surgical pecking order on day one. I'm not going to say a word about this. But then Mila remembered Dr. Thornton's patients laughing as he left their rooms, and the words came tumbling out: "What about doctor-patient interaction, bedside manner, that sort of thing?" She braced herself for a curt reminder of her ignorance—what she didn't expect was Baskin's loud snort.

He turned to the nurse with the cardigan, who was trying hard to ignore the conversation. "Penny, tell Mila about the paperwork revolution." Without giving the nurse a chance to speak, he continued. "Records, records, records. Fifteen years ago the paperwork was manageable. Back then we had time to worry about bedside manner. You, Mila, were skinning your knees and playing hopscotch in those days."

Actually not, thought Mila, but for once she shut up. Dr. Baskin went on. "Nowadays everyone is tracking, and they all need data to do it. We document everything for everyone. We live in a world where documenting is more important than doing. I spend an awful lot of my time justifying what I am doing to a list of people, most of them not even doctors. Am I right, Penny? Tell Mila I'm right."

Penny pursed her lips. "Of course you're right, Dr. Baskin," she said, and returned to her screen.

"No, Penny. Tell her for real."

Penny let out a small sigh and crossed her arms. "Even with so-called patient-centered care, doctors and nurses are paper-focused, documentation-focused." Something in her tone seemed to give, and suddenly she sounded more wistful than sour. Mila realized with a start that she herself would have now been Penny's age if she'd stayed on earth. "When I walked the floor in the old days, I'd see everyone doing things for and around the patients. We now live in a world where a nurse could stay at her desk, make the paperwork look good, and be considered to be doing a fine job. It sure ain't what I bought into when I went to nursing school."

Is Penny stalled and disappointed? Mila wondered. She met Penny's eyes and started to speak, but Dr. Baskin wasn't done. "This is what a morning of rounding is like: you're always thinking you're going to do medicine, but really you end up using your time getting the computer to work, talking to different committees, collecting data. Everything but seeing patients. They don't teach you this stuff in medical school, do they? Welcome to the real world of managed care surgery." The phone trilled. Penny picked it up, then paged someone over the intercom. It was odd hearing her voice both in person and over the scratchy system overhead.

"You know," Dr. Baskin mused, "they should have new rotations for you guys. Forget vascular surgery, colo-rectal. First years should get paperwork 101, second years should get advanced documentation. If you make it through those two rigorous courses, we sign you up for specialty work—filling out referral forms, or speaking to primary care doctors."

"Let him go on like that, you'll miss a whole day of surgery." It was Robert Goodner, another physician, a youngish, slightly soft-looking man with wire-frame glasses too small for his face.

"Dr. Goodner," nodded Penny as she went off to answer a patient call. Mila saw her stop on the way to warn a ragged, ageless, homeless man not to light the cigarette he had in his mouth.

"Meet Bob Goodner, Mila," said Baskin. "Chief of OB-GYN. One of the guys that couldn't make it in general surgery. Mila here is our first-year resident. She's going to be a real surgeon when she grows up."

Goodner gave Baskin a conciliatory pat on the shoulder. "If it makes you feel good to say that, go ahead. Hey—we know what we're doing. This year we've decided to be primary care doctors." Goodner's voice was light, but patronizing. "So, you do the real surgery while we primary care doctors go ahead and rule the system."

Mila was not at all in the mood to be in the middle of another fight, so she was relieved when Dr. Goodner began to speak more earnestly, "It really is a mess when you're acting both as specialist and caretaker of well patients, Mila. With a lot of managed care companies, patients can come to me for a yearly exam. But if I find a problem, I have to call the primary care doctor to get authorization. Some are reasonable; some are assholes. I had a couple of doctors send a patient for bleeding. We say she needs a D&C; they say they won't authorize it. We have to call the managed care company for authorization. So that takes an hour of our time, she's bleeding, and I'm blown away for the rest of the day. It is so aggravating. So unnecessary."

Dr. Goodner took off his glasses and polished them on his coat, shaking his head. The image on the computer converted to an aquarium screensaver that alone would have taken up most of the computing power of Mila's '84 Apple Mac Classic. "Each managed care company has its own lab, its own guidelines, and its own ideas of when they will pay you and for what. If I'm seeing a patient who may need to come to the emergency room, I have to ask her what kind of insurance she has. I hate the perception of that. I'm asking so I know whether I have to call her family doctor, but she thinks it's about the care I am going to give her."

Dr. Baskin looked at his Rolex. He really was a bit of a midlife crisis poster boy, just a tad too conscious of his masculine accouterments for Mila's taste. "Hey, Bob, don't forget about that negotiation session for the IPA risk pool allocation this afternoon. Maybe I'll bring Mila. That should be a real learning experience."

Dr. Goodner grabbed a cookie from an open tin behind the desk and took a bite. He spoke as he chewed. "Yeah, she'll learn that doctors have no idea

how to negotiate, especially when it comes to finances. It will be truly ugly."
He gave her a slightly crumb-filled smile and left.

Mila knew already that she didn't want to go to this meeting, but the way
her day was going, it seemed unlikely that she would miss it. She tried to
calculate what percentage of her day was actually being spent on clinical
medicine, but it was too depressing.

"Hey—sleeping yesterday, daydreaming today?" Dr. Baskin took a cookie,
too, and began to stride off. "We'll be late for the OR. I don't want to get
reported to the OR abuse committee. I'll lose that great 7:30 block time."

Mila got through the gallbladder, hernia repair, and fem-pop and only
thought about the business side of medicine when the matronly OR nurse told
her she was leaving too much residual suture after tying knots. The nurse
said, only half-kidding, "those extra sutures come directly from our paycheck,
dear." Apparently the entire OR staff now had financial incentives for 'operations improvement,' also known as cutting costs. Presumably without
decreasing quality.

Despite that, she was happy to see that nothing else had changed about
the surgical theater. The same bad jokes, the familiar pecking order: the chief
resident was first assistant, Mila was second assistant. She even got her hand
slapped once for not holding the retractor at the right angle. It amazed her
how good that slap felt. It felt like the old days.

After surgery, as promised, Mila was given the "opportunity" to join the
IPA risk allocation meeting at which Dr. Baskin represented the general
surgeons. It was in the same conference room that the orientation had been
in, but now around the table sat serious-looking senior physicians shuffling
papers. They were all there, according to Dr. Baskin, to argue that their own
particular specialties were the most deserving of the lion's share of the risk
pool. Empty seats waited for the insurance people against whom the docs
would be negotiating.

Mila could hear Dr. Goodner talking to a distinguished-looking woman
across the table. "Hey this IPA negotiation stuff is nothing. Try telling your
sixteen-year-old daughter that she can't have the car for the weekend—that's
real negotiation. I guarantee you that whatever logic she uses has more basis
in reality than these ophthalmologists trying to convince us that they are really
primary care providers." Mila wondered if things had changed enough that the
female physician would feel as comfortable as Goodner referring to her own
daughter in a work situation. Probably not. But she did have to admit that it

was pretty damn amazing just how taken-for-granted female docs were in this era—even female surgeons. It was amusing, actually. Of all the wrenching changes that she hadn't anticipated, the single change she had seen coming and had girded herself for—the inevitable breaking into surgery by women—was the single change that in reality turned out to have been relatively painless. So much for her predictive powers.

Just then, the chief of colo-rectal surgery came into the room, apologizing for being late. Dr. Goodner continued, "There's another primary care provider. He just enters the discipline from the back end."

"Hilarious, Bob," said the doctor. "Never heard a joke like that before."

"We should start the meeting," said the silver-haired Dr. Waltner, taking the empty seat next to Goodner. "I have a session in forty-five minutes." He was a psychiatrist.

"Boy, Stan," said Goodner, "if I could charge what you do for listening to someone tell you how screwed up they are, it would solve my daughter's car-sharing problem. I'd just have a Jag for every member of the family."

The psychiatrist sat back in his chair. "Well, Bob," he said, "it hardly matters what I charge because the insurance companies have decided that having a bunch of untreated depressed patients around is really OK in the world of managed care."

"Uh-oh," said Dr. Goodner. "Sounds like something new happened."

"It's just that I got a letter from Blue Cross. A certified letter. I hate getting certified letters. They are taking me off the panel. Was it quality oriented? Was it based on objective parameters? No. They are going to reduce the individual players in the panel and just use large groups. I hate this! I haven't seen a patient from them in a while—it's not about them or the money. I'd be happy if all I could do is deal with patients again."

Amen, Mila thought.

Dr. Waltner's serious tone was unmistakably infused with distress. The docs around the table all turned to him. "It's amazing," he said. "I've been practicing for twenty-five years. When I first started, docs who had physical or psychiatric disabilities would do anything they could to keep working. Insurance companies used to say that the safest insurance they could write was physician disability insurance. Nobody wanted to stop working. Now, a physician stubs a toe or needs to go on Prozac for a mild case of depression, and it's disability benefits time. It's become so high risk you can't even get a good policy. All in fifteen years."

There was a silence around the table. "Stan," someone said at the end of the table, "it sounds like it may be time for you to look into renovating that house in Hilton Head that you've been saving for your retirement."

"I *will* be in Hilton Head in a minute if this factory mentality gets worse. I have friends in full-time groups with productivity minimums they have to meet each week. Thirty-seven pap smears, twenty depressed people. Plus there are the increased demands from patients."

"Here's an idea," said Dr. Goodner, tapping a slightly chubby finger on the table. "Maybe we should learn from the airlines—when you pay coach, you go coach. Right now these people on supersaver medicine expect legroom and lobster. Hey, if you want to go first class, you have to pay a premium."

The woman at the head of the table cleared her throat and looked around authoritatively. There was a dull pencil stuck through her chignon and a sharpened one in her hand.

"That's Jill Reston, a family doc," nudged Baskin privately to Mila. "What Bob Goodner calls an 'undisputed primary care provider.'"

"Let's get started. I'm sure we can agree that if stress were a disability, we'd all be able to cash in on our insurance policies. But we in this room have chosen to stay, and we have to determine how to allocate the risk pool dollars."

Dr. Reston looked around the table, and she seemed to find evidence that everyone was ready. "Let me review the system. For our capitated patients, we get the money up front to provide the service. If we keep patients healthier than predicted, we'll have some money left over."

Everyone nodded, and Dr. Reston tapped the table with her pencil eraser once, then went on. "We spent six months negotiating with the PHO and the hospital so that doctors would get 60 percent of those dollars. If you'll remember, at the time, we were all on the same team. Of course, that was before Goodner decided that OB-GYNs weren't specialists anymore."

Ten annoyed faces turned to Dr. Goodner, who took a small, defiant bow.

Dr. Reston put her hands flat on the table, the pencil rolled a few inches, and stopped. "Now, the hard part. We have to determine the relative value of each of us in this risk system." A dissatisfied murmur passed through the room. "I would like to avoid name calling and conflicting agendas, doctors, and get down to where our interests are in common. Now I know that physicians have taken a bad rap as negotiators, and I know that these discussions can get pretty ugly. I am determined to keep this on a high level and not get entrenched in positions."

"Well now, Jill," Dr. Baskin had been leaning forward over the table, but now he tilted his chair back, deliberately casual. "That's easy for you to say. You're a family practice doc who's been bought out by the hospital. For us private practice surgeons, though, the only way we'll survive is to damn well entrench in a position and stick to it. We want to make sure we get our piece of the pie."

"Mark, I sympathize" said Dr. Goodner, "but if we don't get this resolved, none of this will matter because none of us will get any dessert. We've got to negotiate like businesspeople. In a few minutes the executive director of the PHO and the chief negotiator for the managed care organization will be here. I, for one, don't want to confirm their vision of us as spoiled brats who only play if we get our own way. So I agree with Jill. Let's try to keep this on a reasonably high level."

Mila didn't like at all what she was seeing. She had learned enough to know that risk pools would greatly affect her practice and her pay. And these prominent physicians were clearly unprepared for negotiations that began in five minutes. Her colleagues could not agree, did not understand what was at stake, and had remarkable faith in the exclusive importance of their own disciplines. She winced to think how vulnerable they must seem to the negotiators representing the other side.

The problem was that although she knew this was bad, she didn't know what *good* looked like. She made a little show of looking on the floor for an unidentified object, then bent underneath the table. She thought as loudly as she could, "AJAX," and it was White.

"You rang?" Ajax said in a bass voice, dressed as a giant butler.

"Ajax, you're not allowed to make an Addams Family *reference ever again. And besides, you look more like Uncle Fester than Lerch. Now, can we get out of here?"*

They were back in Mila's apartment, she was on her new used couch with a bowl of popcorn at her elbow.

"OK, Ajax, what's the hokey connection between my apartment and negotiation?"

"Actually, Mila, there isn't one. I just wanted to give you a comfortable place to learn and do some rethinking. After all, there should be some reward for your beginning to accept assistance when you need it, should there not?" He went over to the TV and switched it on. "Welcome to the Negotiating Zone.

A land where doctors are prepared and have acquired the skills to become collaborative negotiators." On the screen were two docs with the words "empathy," "respect," and "problem solving" emblazoned on their white coats. The taller one spoke, but soundlessly.

"Why aren't there any words coming out?" Mila asked.

"Well," said Ajax, "it could be because doctors have not learned the most important skill needed to negotiate . . . listening. Or it could be that you haven't turned up the volume control."

Mila stopped short, shot Ajax a grin, and turned up the sound.

One of the TV professors began. "Shall we start, Mila? When negotiating, you must always assume there's a better solution than the one that comes to mind first . . ."

CHAPTER 12

PHYSICIANS AS NEGOTIATORS: IT'S A WHOLE NEW DEAL

WHEN NEGOTIATING, YOU must always assume there's a better solution than the one that comes to mind first.

There is no shortage of "how-to" books for physicians extolling the virtues of some quick-fix mechanism to allow them to be more effective in a changing health care schema. While these mechanisms can shape a short-term strategy for a given physician in a given situation, those in the medical field have lamented that after the consultants leave, the results do not appear to be as stellar. Much as the experience of ordering an item by mail order only to find that its appeal has been significantly magnified in the catalog, physicians are left frustrated and even more confused by their inability to apply these business concepts to their own experience.

Nowhere is this more evident than in the realm of effective negotiating. In fact, physicians often do not even realize a basic truth in negotiation, namely that there is almost always a better and more creative solution than the one which comes to mind first. The way to discover that solution is to ask questions—lots of them—before forming strong judgements. In the present health care system, the success of an individual physician is often related to the success of the health organization with which he or she is associated. Conversely, the success of the organization often depends on having the individual physician's behavior aligned with its organizational goals. The common denominator for these behaviors is collaborative negotiation.

Collaborative efforts which concentrate on recognizing shared needs, and principled negotiations in which participants forego entrenched positions are, therefore, in everyone's interests. The effort must be on creatively enlarging the pie for everyone, rather than nabbing the largest slice of a shrinking pie. If it is a collaborative solution, multiple interests will be served; in other words all parties will feel that they have been dealt with fairly. This is a basic tenet of negotiation, but one which seems to be particularly difficult for physicians. Why?

Many factors in a physician's background and disposition work against this kind of creative negotiating. Hard won skills that serve us well in training and throughout our clinical careers are sharply counterproductive in negotiation. Only by deprogramming these destructive biases which physicians bring to the table can we become the effective negotiators we need to be.

1. THE COMPETITIVE BIAS

Begin with the oft-repeated scene of an auditorium filled with eager pre-med students being told, "Look to the right, look to the left. Only one of every three of you will make it into med school." Right from the beginning, we as physicians are encouraged to see colleagues not as potential collaborators, but as competitors. The pattern is set—almost every educational exercise in medical training is distributive, with someone winning and someone losing.

This emphasis on competition became particularly sharp when baby boom-age physicians were entering med school. At that time, for example, many six-year pre-med/medical school programs were being formed. Most of these programs routinely accepted five or ten times more students at the wide, pre-medical end of the funnel than they could accommodate at the narrow medical school end. In such circumstances, students quickly learned that anything they might do that resulted in a win-win or collaborative solution might damage their chances of being in the elite few.

Indeed, medical schools' standards of selection favored (and still do favor) students who would thrive in the competitive fray. Despite long-standing lip service to the value of "humanism" in the selection process, few medical schools have ever been willing to "take a chance" on an applicant who, despite average grades or modest standardized test scores, has demonstrated dedication to "helping others" or has markedly collaborative qualities. At best, character issues might aid an already qualified (by traditional parameters) applicant. Nor, once admitted, are medical students or residents judged by measures that value these qualities.

As pre-meds, then, most physicians were forced by necessity to adopt the prevailing winner-takes-all philosophy. At the time, they may have considered it a temporary attitude they would slip out of once they had "made it into medical school." When the time came, though, few could shrug off their distributive thinking. Survival in medical school, residencies, and fellowships required the same bared teeth. Even at med schools that specifically set out to encourage team thinking, students found themselves suspicious that pass-fail grading was a trap; they couldn't transcend the assumption that eventually they would be judged in comparison to their peers. As senior physicians they eventually completed the cycle by assuming places in the hierarchy that placed them in the "abuser" role.

A good general education broadens and deepens one's human understanding and encourages exploration and connection—all qualities vital, among other places, at the negotiation table. The system of medical training, however, denied especially baby boom physicians the advantages of such an education. Pre-med and medical students became imbued with

the belief that there was only one worthwhile use of time—taking courses that sharpened their edge in med school. Forget the humanities; forget the arts. Those were "cake" courses unworthy of those on the fast track to the academic medicine of the seventies and eighties.

Even now, when medical school and residency curricula include an increasing number of "humanistic" studies, such endeavors are often undermined by more traditional professors and are the first to be "sacrificed" when conflicts occur.

The not so subtle message: The old way of doing business in medical education—non-collaborative, distributive, and numbers-based—still prevails.

This de facto indoctrination results in a psychological framework built of suspicion. Peering out is a physician-negotiator wary of those sitting across the table, ill equipped to engage in the collaboration and understanding of mutual needs that is necessary for successful negotiation.[1]

2. THE AUTONOMY BIAS

Physicians, studies confirm, are driven by a potent need for independence. They often feel that the high emotional, financial and physical price paid in training can be compensated only by subsequent freedom from the dictates of others. This fierce desire for autonomy, clearly works against physicians entering into effective collaborations and, therefore, negotiations.

Equally significant is that physicians often see this autonomy as a flat entitlement. In the normal business equation, autonomy is a privilege for which one pays in assumption of risk: an employee trades autonomy for security; an entrepreneur trades security for autonomy. Many physicians, by contrast, consider both professional independence and job security as separate and equally inviolable rights. These hardened assumptions, when combined with a general risk aversion, a competitive mind-set, and an "abused/abuser" history, serve as virtual shackles for physicians in business in general, and as negotiators in particular.

Physicians often interpret negotiations as personal interactions, a perception that puts them at an immediate disadvantage. A lowball opening offer is seen as a personal affront to a physician's worth, rather than the strategic maneuver it is, and often drives him/her from the table. Physicians, more than other negotiators, too often become entangled in the bottom line and worry about "winning the game." It is difficult for the medical mind to recognize that the skillful negotiator is not necessarily the one who gets his needs met without taking the other's needs into account, but rather the one who meets the other's needs at the cheapest cost to oneself.[2]

3. THE HIERARCHY BIAS

How many times is a young physician told that there is a "pecking order" in medical training? In medicine, more than in most other professions, a position entitles its holder to specific treatment. Age, merit, and value often take a back seat to professorship status and academic title. It is almost a militaristic approach; one's future is as much dependent on proper interactions within the hierarchy as it is to clinical skills or any merit inherent in one's research ideas.

This hierarchy is a necessity in many research and clinical arenas. In high acuity specialties and in surgery, nonambiguous relationships can mean the difference between life and death. Surgical teams are valued for their precision and consistency; these qualities are based on an unspoken understanding of the exact boundaries within which each member of the team is able and allowed to contribute.

What is a valuable approach in clinical and research settings, however, is a straightjacket at the negotiating table. Many physicians dislike the ambiguity and lack of structure of negotiations; more than members of other professions, perhaps, they are unaccustomed to making contributions in areas outside their expertise, in handling matters at which they are not already adept.

The formative negotiation experience for most physicians is between parties of vastly different statures, for instance young faculty members negotiating with deans, in which the junior member is without power. The "new" type of negotiation, however, requires an even playing field for all. This means that participants must temporarily work outside the context of titles, a condition unfamiliar and unpleasant for many physicians.

A study that shows the mechanics of physician biases at work was conducted by Drs. Richard Shell and Stephen Klasko of the Wharton School. A business situation was presented to a group of medical students, residents, and attendings.[3] Solving the given problem successfully required abandoning distributive strategy and initiating creative negotiations that would allow all the parties to return as winners.

The results were compared to those of nonphysician students in an executive MBA course. While over 80 percent of the MBA students were able to conclude the exercise with a win-win scenario, less than one in five of the physicians was able to do so. They were unable to break through the traditional "piece of the pie" negotiating strategy, and consequently, most came out of the exercise as losers. Even in the groups in which a physician or two made a successful grab at the given resources, it was at the expense of hard feelings from the other participants.

It became clear in the subsequent discussions about the exercise that the physicians felt that they were either going to win it all or lose it all. Many admitted that they would rather bring the whole group down and lose together rather than risk the "other side" winning (competitive bias). They also felt that this exercise was going to be won or lost by their individual actions and seldom even considered a collaborative alternative (autonomy bias). The physicians were much more content than the business students to follow blindly the given rules; they were much less able to see possibilities outside the given structure (hierarchical bias). Moreover, groups that included physicians of differing status (medical students, attendings, and residents) were the least able to cooperate and the least able to come up with equitable results. In these groups, the individual with the highest status consistently won the lion's share of resources, regardless of whether this was the best solution for the group as a whole (hierarchical bias again).

A patient does or does not do well. That is the basis of clinical outcomes. In negotiation, however, such dichotomizing is counterproductive. Physicians must learn to recognize this and the other barriers to collaboration they might have formed during their training. Only then will they be able to conduct themselves successfully in collaboration, in negotiation, in what is, after all, the cornerstone of success in the modern medical context. In many business schools, grading is largely dependent on combined efforts of study groups. Therefore, the individuals in those groups soon learn that collaboration and utilizing the talents of others becomes the key to their individual success. Unless we incorporate some of those educational techniques into medical education, physicians have no one to blame but themselves when doctors view themselves as independent contractors as opposed to collaborative negotiating groups.

Endnotes

1.   G. R. Shell, J.D., and Stephen K. Klasko, M.D, M.B.A., "Biases Physicians Bring to the Table," *The Physician Executive* 22 (December 19, 1996): 4–7.

2.   Ibid.

3.   The original simulation called "The Commodity Purchase" was written by Professor Leonard Greenhalgh of the Tuck School at Dartmouth College. The case was modified by Professor Richard Shell and is called "The Pheasant Egg Deal."

CHAPTER 13

CONFLICT MANAGEMENT: NEGOTIATING YOUR WAY TO RESOLUTION

THE RELATED SUBJECTS of negotiation and conflict management have been thoroughly dissected and systematized in recent years. This is a welcome development for health care professionals, who need, suddenly, to be able to collaborate and negotiate with people of different backgrounds, as well as partners with different interests and values than their own. Gregory Shea suggests framing conflict within a more familiar and more general concept of problem solving.[1]

According to Jeffrey T. Polzer and Margaret A. Neale in the book *Essentials of Health Care Management*, competition and conflict, from which can spring the need for negotiation, both arise over the distribution of limited resources. In an organization, members might struggle over power, money, information, advice, or praise— none of which can ever be abundant enough.[2]

While similar in some aspects, Polzer and Neale express the importance of noting the differences between conflict and competition. Both are characterized by the tension between opponents with incompatible goals. In a competition, each side tries to triumph by outdoing the other; the sides vie, but on independent tracks, with mutual noninterference. In a conflict, on the other hand, there is interaction between the parties.

Conflicts, then, occur when one party is unable to reach their goal because of another party.

Competition, of course, and indeed a moderate amount of certain kinds of conflict, are tolerable—even desirable—within an organization. The price of avoiding all friction can be high—second-best consensus solutions. Disagreements over how to achieve a goal can generate ideas and yield discovery of the best way. Clearly, however, too much, or the wrong kind of conflict is destructive and should be addressed.

Sources of conflict can be many; some may be subtle and intangible. Examples of such intangible causes of conflict include one employee feeling that his coworker is receiving more praise, even if that is not the case; two managers may disagree on a dress code policy for employees; and a doctor and an administrator may have different opinions about the need for a particular treatment for a patient.[3] Given this complexity, analyzing the level and type of a particular conflict can be a useful first step in managing it.

The *level* at which a conflict occurs refers to its participants. Polzer and Neale suggest that "conflict can occur within an individual (*intrapersonal conflict*), between individuals (*interpersonal conflict*), within a group (*intragroup conflict*), and

between groups (*intergroup conflict*)."[4]

Karen Jehn (as recorded by Polzer and Neale) defines the *types* of conflict. *Emotional conflicts* are interpersonal incompatibilities among people working together. Those involved in such conflicts generally dislike and are angry with one another.

Administrative conflicts are over the distribution of tasks and responsibilities within a group. Members of a group practice might have an administrative conflict over who among them should work with the ad agency they all agreed should be hired.

Task content conflicts are disagreements about how a particular task can best be performed. The same group, for instance, might have such a conflict over whether their ads should run on television or radio.[5]

In either a conflict or a negotiation, comparing the degree of concern about an individual's outcome and that of his opponent can help shape strategy. Kenneth Thomas, who has studied and written about conflict, has created a model of conflict management techniques that shows how, depending on these two dimensions of concern, a negotiator might select one of four different strategies for handling a conflict.[6] If you care about your outcome but not your opponents' outcome, pursuing a competing, or pressing, strategy makes sense. If a low concern for your own outcome is coupled with a high concern for the other's, accommodation, or capitulation, would be the best strategy. If you care greatly about the outcome for both sides, collaborate. Finally, if an immediate decision needs to be made and the concern is high again for both sides, then compromise is the fitting strategy.[7]

Negotiation includes both collaboration and compromise. "Negotiation is a process of potentially opportunistic interaction in which two or more parties with some conflicting interests seek to do better by jointly decided action than they could otherwise."[8] Negotiations can be split into two broad categories: distributive negotiation and integrative negotiation. Single issue negotiations, according to Polzer and Neale, are the most common example of *distributive negotiations*.[9] The resources available are limited, and the gain of one party always means the loss of the other. Polzer and Neale explain that amicable resolution in distributive negotiations usually includes reciprocal compromise, with each party giving a little at a time until agreement is reached. In such negotiations, the most useful strategies are ones that help negotiators claim as large a share of the resources as possible.[10]

By contrast, the most basic assumption underlying *integrative negotiation* is that mutual benefit is possible; that each party can gain without the other having to lose. Integrative negotiation relies on a problem-solving, cooperative approach rather than the competitive approach of distributive negotiations. The parties in this kind of negotiation concentrate together on creating value; they try to expand the pie rather than split it up. The success of integrative negotiation depends on mutual trust.[11] Creating value by finding integrative solutions requires primarily cooperative behavior, while claiming value in distributive negotiation requires primarily competitive behavior.

Polzer and Neale point out that many people mistakenly plan to enlarge the pie with integrative negotiation, then divvy it up with distributive negotiation. Not only is it very unlikely for these techniques to work well sequentially, but in an integrative negotiation the process of integration and distribution occur simultaneously.

Skillful integrative negotiators simultaneously balance cooperative and competitive behavior—they enlarge the pie *and* claim huge chunks. This fundamental tension between cooperation and competition is at the core of negotiation. "The way that the value is created affects the way it is divided; the process of creating value is entwined with the process of claiming it."[12] The truth in the statement is most clearly seen when the motives and behavior of the other party are not apparent.

One of the best ways to ensure the success of any kind of negotiation is to plan for its failure. Before anything else, establish a fall-back plan—a Best Alternative To a Negotiated Agreement (BATNA).[13] Polzer and Neale suggest that knowing the best alternative allows a comparison of the BATNA to the possible agreements; that, in turn, provides an opportunity to see which agreements are desirable and should be accepted, and which are worse than the BATNA and should be rejected. Additionally, the ability to "walk away from the negotiation if a satisfactory agreement does not appear to be forthcoming can be a valuable negotiating tool . . . it is also important to know when you actually should walk away."[14]

According to Polzer and Neale, a BATNA is put into place in conjunction with a reservation price and an aspiration level. The reservation price is the point at which an impasse and an agreement would be of equal value. It is one's bottom line, and is stated in terms of whatever units are under negotiation, often dollars. A car buyer might have a reservation price—a price above which he will not buy a car.[15] An aspiration level is the target, or goal. It's what the negotiator would ideally like to achieve. They recommend that an aspiration level should be challenging but attainable.

In general, "executives and lawyers from outside the U.S. tend to devote more time and attention to the prenegotiation phase than do Americans," because Americans tend to want to just get down to business.[16] However, preparation for a negotiation often proves as critical to success as the negotiation itself. Unfortunately, physicians often begin negotiations with little or no preparation. Nothing takes higher priority than developing a BATNA and a reservation price, but a thorough preparation encompasses much else, too. Some negotiation preparation guidelines by Polzer and Neale follow.

1. Consider all issues that have been raised, or are likely to be raised, by the other party and build a reserve of issues you yourself might need or want to raise.

2. Prepare objective standards that might be acceptable to the other party.

3. Find out what you can about the negotiators the other party will use and adjust your own team accordingly.

4. Consider, before a negotiation, how important your post-negotiation relationship with the other side is likely to be—and how important the other side will consider it. If you'll be relying on the other party to implement part of the deal, for instance, it won't be wise to have them unhappy with the agreement, or with you.

5. Find out, if you can, if the other side is working under a time constraint. The side with more time before it needs to reach an agreement has an advantage, but only if both parties know about the time constraints of the other.

6. Plan your opening and your ending. An initial offer should not be too extreme, but it should prevent the other party from "anchoring" the negotiation. At the conclusion, you may want to keep some information confidential.[17]

The party able to glean the greater amount of information about the other side's interests, both before and during a negotiation, has an advantage. Knowing how far the other side can be pushed, for example, and having a sense of the other side's commitment to an integrative solution is extremely useful. In addition, according to W. Zartman and M. Berman in *The Practical Negotiator,* if we

come to the bargaining table knowing something about our counterpart—what motivates him, what his basic needs are, how he views the negotiation situation, what he expects to do—we will be in an improved position to predict his choice of strategy and prepared to deal with him and reach an early and favorable agreement.[18]

Gathering specific, accurate information—and sharing it—are core behaviors of negotiation. Polzer and Neale stress that sharing information is not the same as talking. The side that talks more may actually be revealing less of value about its interests. (The talkative side *may* also be more persuasive, which may be to its advantage, but that is a separate issue from information sharing.)

Polzer and Neale recommend several strategies that can be used to get more information from the other party. Some of them are simple but often overlooked.

Ask questions.

Build trust between the parties so that information is more likely to be shared.

Give away some information unilaterally to encourage the other party to do the same.

Present multiple offers and infer the other party's interests from the acceptability of each offer.

Search for postsettlement settlements ("agreements that occur based on an extended search after an initial agreement is reached").[19]

Before and during negotiations, try to understand what you can about the biases of the other side. According to Polzer and Neale, many negotiators have a fixed-pie bias, assuming their task in negotiation is distributive. Others are inhibited by an incompatibility bias, which leads them to assume that the two sides' preferences must necessarily be in direct conflict and that there are no common interests. These biases can keep negotiators from recognizing agreement when they see it and result in unnecessarily compromised results for everyone.

Negotiators often try to support their views using the concept of fairness. "Fairness is not a unidimensional concept, however, and the application of different norms of fairness can lead to different outcomes."[20] The most prevalent view of fairness in our society is equality, by which each party gets an identical share of resources. A different fairness norm, often used to determine compensation, is equity. In this situation, each person receives resources according to his or her value to the organization. Allocating resources according to need is a third "fair" way of doing things. Polzer and Neale emphasize that negotiators should consider which of these is relevant when they or one of their opponents desire the outcome to be "fair."

Unethical behavior carries its own consequences even in negotiations. The rewards it can bring are generally short-term, while the harm to one's reputation is permanent. As with the idea of fairness, however, ethical standards can vary. Polzer and Neale suggest that each party think through their ideals prior to negotiations—before being confronted with difficult situations. One should never assume that the other side shares the same ideals or that they will behave (or restrict their behavior) according to the same morals.

By no means are all negotiations dyadic, involving only two sides. In health care, multiparty negotiations are common—among state or federal payment agencies, hospitals, and physicians, for example. While many of the concepts of negotiation can be applied to both dyadic and multiparty negotiation, multiparty negotiations are infinitely more difficult to conduct.

The essential negotiating task of building trust is much more arduous when there are multiple parties involved—especially if coalitions form within groups of negotiators. There may even be parties who would prefer that no agreement be reached. In fact, reveals Polzer and Neale, their purpose at the negotiation table (whether disguised or not) may be to hinder negotiation.

In a negotiation among three or more parties, it is useful to identify a bargaining zone. The bargaining zone is "the set of agreements that exceed every party's reservation price."[21] Multiparty negotiations can be so complex that it can be hard to determine whether a bargaining zone exists, much less gauge its size, and yet it should be done.

If those involved in a negotiation are unable to resolve their conflict, uninvolved third party interventions can help. Arbitrators, or even the court system, can resolve differences between parties if necessary. Shea offers the following checklist for negotiations.

1. Know your BATNA.
2. Be willing to own 51 percent of the responsibility for effective communications.
3. Remember
   • our inherent tendency to blame problems on other *people* (as opposed to the *situation* in which they found themselves).
   • you may need this person tomorrow.
   • replacing this person may cost you money.
4. Remain calm and make sure that the discussion is private.
5. Take the time necessary for a full discussion of the situation.
6. Move through the problem-solving steps.
7. Encourage the other person to elaborate his or her point of view.
8. Listen carefully to what the other person says and state your understanding of it.
9. State your opinion calmly and clearly and ask the other person to state his or her understanding of your point of view.
10. Concentrate on specific events or actions.
11. If an assumption or inference appears, check its validity.
12. Attempt to reach an agreement, where possible, on what happened.
13. Clarify disagreements in as specific terms as possible.
14. Exchange ideas on what to do next about what was agreed upon.
15. Exchange ideas on what to do next about what was not agreed upon.
16. Draft a follow-up plan.
17. Monitor implementations of the plan.[22]

Endnotes

1. Gregory P. Shea, "Negotiation as Problem Solving," *Managing Hospitals,* eds. Sheldon Rovin, Lois Ginsberg. (San Francisco: Jossey-Bass Publishers, 1991): 232.

2. Jeffrey T. Polzer, and Margaret A. Neale, "Conflict Management and Negotiation," *Essentials of Health Care Management,* eds. Stephen M. Shortell and Arnold D. Kaluzny (Albany: Delmar Publishers, 1997): 136.

3. Ibid., 137.

4. Ibid., 139; see also Gregory P. Shea, "The Study of Bargaining and Conflict Behavior: Broadening the Conceptual Arena," *Journal of Conflict Resolution* (Sage Publications, Inc., 1980): 732–40, for a consideration of the implication of the level of analysis on handling conflict.

5. Ibid., 137–38.

6. Model and information from Kenneth Thomas found in ibid., 142–43.

7. Jeffrey T. Polzer and Margaret A. Neale, "Conflict Management and Negotiation," 142.

8. David. A. Lax and James K. Sebenius, "Interests: The Measure of Negotiation," *Negotiation Theory and Practice,* eds. J. William Breslin and Jeffrey Z. Rubin (Cambridge: Pon Books, 1991): 179.

9. Jeffrey T. Polzer and Margaret A. Neale, "Conflict Management and Negotiation," 147.

10. See also Gregory P. Shea, "The Study of Bargaining and Conflict Behavior," 712–13.

11. Ibid., 147–48.

12. Ibid., 148–49.

13. R. Fisher and W. Ury, *Getting to Yes* (Boston: Houghton-Mifflin, 1981): 145.

14. Jeffrey T. Polzer and Margaret A. Neale, "Conflict Management and Negotiation," 145–46.

15. Ibid.

16. Jeswald W. Salacuse, "Making Global Alliances: Paying Attention to the Process," *Strategic Alliance Alert* 2 (November 1995): 6.

17. Jeffrey T. Polzer and Margaret A. Neale, "Conflict Management and Negotiation," 153.

18. I. William Zartman, and Maureen R. Berman, *The Practical Negotiator* (Hartford: Yale University Press, 1982): 27.

19. Jeffrey T. Polzer and Margaret A. Neale, "Conflict Management and Negotiation," 149–50.

20. Ibid., 152.

21. Ibid., 151.

22. Gregory P. Shea, *Managing Hospitals,* 241.

CHAPTER 14

OF CELEBRITIES AND CESAREANS

"THANKS AJAX," MILA SAID, AND IMMEDIATELY FOUND HERSELF AGAIN—STILL—BENT UNDER THE TABLE BEFORE THE NEGOTIATING SESSION. Nice shoes, folks—comfy, not too trendy. She straightened back to face level.

The physicians were still bickering, were still laying out hasty plans, were still under the apparent impression that they could get what they wanted through the sheer wanting of it, with a little dash of whining thrown in. A family doctor and a gastroenterologist started banging the table and spraying each other with expletives over who should be doing sigmoidoscopies and for how much. "Order!" said Dr. Reston into the fray. "Order!"

Just then there was a tap on the door, then a louder knock. Either nobody but Mila heard it, or everybody but Mila ignored it. The door was opened from the outside just far enough to admit the apologetic, gray-haired head of one of the insurance company's negotiating teams. "Please excuse the intrusion, but we couldn't find the secretary. We wanted you to know our team is here." This, finally, quieted the physicians. The negotiator smiled understandingly, but his eyes darted around the room. Mila was sure he was taking in every detail of what was going on. "Do you need a few minutes before we begin?"

103

"Thanks, yes," said Dr. Reston, reddening, "Just give us ten, all right?"

Mila could only imagine what intelligence the negotiator was taking back to his team. Now that she had an inkling about negotiation, she understood how much damage to the physicians' cause had already been done and how much more was coming. Her knowledge, she realized with a sinking heart, gave her a responsibility to say something, even though it would mean violating the pecking order. With a vengeance.

Better do it before I have time to chicken out, Mila thought. It was lucky that the doctors were still quiet from the insurance guy's appearance, because her voice was a little unsteady at first.

"Hey," she heard herself say. "Listen." Mila's superiors turned to her with a mixture of condescension and irritation.

Cahones, don't fail me now, thought Mila. "It seems we're going at this backward. We should delay this negotiation. We're just not ready."

There was a short silence. Someone, in a voice stiff with sarcasm, spoke from the far end of the table. "Do tell. And just what, from your vast experience, do you suggest we do?"

Ain't nothing I can do but just bully it through, thought Mila. "We should meet with the insurance company, but we should use the session as an opportunity to ask questions, and to listen. We should make them do the work of providing us with information. After that we can make a much more informed diagnosis and plot a treatment. We can't assume we already know what we need to know, and we can't just make this thing happen. Mostly, we all have to learn about negotiation. We've got to move from this distributive-type mind-set to a more collaborative model. Otherwise we'll all lose."

It was as if Mila had just stood on the table and mooned them all. Nobody moved; nobody said a word. Finally, Dr. Reston looked at Dr. Baskin, and then back at Mila. What, she wondered, is the all-time record for least days of residency before getting fired?

When Dr. Reston finally spoke, it was to the entire group. Her voice seemed to carry the weight of established medicine from the beginning of time. "This, I understand," she said, "is Mila Langston. Does everyone know this person's role here?"

Mila was pretty sure this was a rhetorical question, but there was so much loaded silence that she thought she'd better provide an answer. "I am a first-year surgical resident, Dr. Reston."

"And does everybody know what importance that has in this institution?" Mila hunkered down, preparing herself for some serious public humiliation. Dr. Reston continued, "Doctors, our residents represent our future, and their importance cannot be overstated. Mila, thank you for your comments. We needed a bit of a slap on the face. I think we should do as you suggest. We should stop dissipating our energy on squabbling and start gathering information."

A surprised murmur rippled through the room. Mila tried to keep from collapsing with relief.

"She's right," Dr. Goodner said. "We should admit to having some real problems that plague us as individual physicians when we approach negotiation. And we should admit that those same problems plague the medical profession as a whole in its dealings with insurers, employers, and MCOs. I mean, think about it, because we refused to negotiate the position that medical outcomes could be quantified, insurers did it without us."

"True," someone said, grudgingly. "Damn them."

Dr. Reston agreed. "Yes, and because providers refused to negotiate regarding fee-for-service, employers and insurers constructed our current capitated system. So now physicians face the problem of inaccurate data being used in medical policy-making that has resulted in a payer system that promotes underutilization. And the worst part of it is that we have ourselves to blame."

There was another silence, and Mila geared herself up again. "It, um, seems to me that much of the stalemate in the health care debate could be avoided if all parties understood the power of the collaborative model of negotiation. Instead of the AMA agenda, the insurance agenda, and the patient-care agenda, the emphasis should be on the shared interests of all concerned to provide broad access, cost oversight, quality controls, fair compensation, and adequate training for, well, people like me."

"And how do you propose we get to this promised land?" Baskin was throwing the full force of his skepticism at her.

"That's not fair, Ron," Dr. Reston said. "Collaborative negotiation is a difficult question for *all* of us to consider between now and the negotiating session we're so intelligently rescheduling. And I've heard theories that the very roots of our education and training may make it even harder to learn collaboration. But Mila represents the young physicians for whom we're the stewards. She's completely correct that we need to adapt to new, collaborative, relationship-oriented models of behavior. That's the only way her generation is going to retain a place at the health care bargaining table, let alone at the head of that table."

The walk to the resident's lounge ended up taking forever. Docs who'd been at the meeting kept stopping her to congratulate her on the contribution she had made and to ask if she'd had management training. The instant celebrityhood was exhilarating, but it made her feel a little nervous for the future of medicine. Why, among all of these distinguished clinicians, was what seemed like common sense so rare? Why was she, a first-year resident who had just been introduced to the fundamentals of negotiation, a relative expert? And what was the story with these rhetorical questions? Stop that, Mila, she told herself. She snorted softly.

When you got right down to it, this new medicine was difficult not because it was complex, but because it was *different* from what all of them—especially docs—were accustomed to. It was the shock of change that engendered so much insecurity. For the first time Mila thought that her fifteen-year jump might really give her an advantage. Missing that formative period might allow her to see things more clearly, without the distorting lens of habit.

Dr. Goodner was in back of Mila in line in the gift shop. Mila was getting a *Times* and Dr. Goodner was getting a couple candy bars, one of which he'd already torn into. He motioned with his Milky Way at her newspaper. "Well, you did a good job in that meeting, but if you can figure out how to deal with these patient groups, we'll be ready to saint you."

Mila looked at the headline: "Patient Advocate Group Proposes Patient Bill of Rights, Suggests Three-Step Process Before Accepting Medical Advice." "What do they want?" Mila asked.

"That's exactly the point," Goodner replied, fishing his money out to pay. "They have no idea what they want. They would rather trust some guy with no credentials, who spends a thousand bucks to start the 'Patients' Medical Society,' than the physicians who are responsible for their health." They walked out the revolving doors and past a phalanx of hospital employees smoking furiously in the sunlight.

"It's gotten to an absurd level," Dr. Goodner continued, starting in on a Mars Bar. "I got two letters the other day. The first was from WACS, Women Against Cesarean Section. It said, 'too many C-sections are being performed; other methods should be used.'"

Mila knew that even in 1985 that had been a problem, but there was no way to insert that little nugget into the conversation. Dr. Goodner continued,

"As an example of a frivolous indication for C-section, the letter cited failure of the baby's head to descend. OK, I thought, that deserves consideration. Then I opened the other letter. This was from WAF, Women Against Forceps. 'Forceps delivery is anachronistic,' it said. 'Other methods should be used when the baby's head will not descend into the birth canal.'" Dr. Goodner gave a rueful laugh. "I had fantasies of calling an emergency joint meeting of WACS and WAF: 'O.K.,' I'd tell them, 'the baby's head is here, and the introitus is a variable distance away. You tell me how to deliver it.'"

"But I thought if you were a good physician, your patients would take care of you." Mila thought she sounded more sure of herself than she really was.

Dr. Goodner stopped chewing and faced her. "Mila, that's surprisingly naive, especially from someone who sounded like you did at the meeting today. Didn't you learn in med school that patients expect a perfect outcome, and that the rest is in the marketing? You need to give the customers what they want. Just being a good doctor isn't enough anymore. I thought you understood that we need to think like business people so that we can perform like doctors. We need to secure referral patterns through network ties; we need to manage costs; *and* we need to provide good service."

"But good medicine *is* good service. Always has been, always will be."

"Always? Good service used to be getting to the patient's home and knowing a little more than he or she did. Good medicine counts. But so do shorter waiting times, ease of reimbursement, and personalized care through complete and responsive information systems."

"Good God, Bob," Dr. Baskin was sitting on the wall behind them smoking a small cigar. "You sound like an administrator. Worse yet, you sound like a salesman or—what's the buzzword—oh, a marketer! Spend your time on medicine and clear your head of that other nonsense."

Mila was just about to agree with Dr. Baskin—and maybe start repairing any rupture she might have caused with her attending, when she was back in the White.

Here we go again, thought Mila. *"Ajax, this one isn't consensual. I have some fences to mend."*

"Yes, but you were about to do so out of ignorance and defensiveness. You seem resistant to the idea that you should understand marketing, but understand it you must. Where would you like to receive this data? From a faculty member who specializes in consumerism?"

"Well, gee, Ajax, if you're going to try to convince me that in this new medicine I have to become like one of the 4 out of 5 dentists who recommend Crest, I'm not sure I want to 'receive data' about it anywhere. But if I must, maybe the toothpaste aisle of a supermarket would be most appropriate. I definitely don't want to hear about it in this prestigious hospital. Look, since you've rifled through this professor's no doubt well-functioning mind, I'll listen. But it's under objection. And I want it kept at a distance. Even with the cataclysmic changes in medicine as a profession, I will not become a used-car salesman . . . or saleswoman for that matter. Let's see, have I missed any genders, Ajax?"

"I believe you will feel differently after you have learned something of the subject, Mila. But if that is what you want, the toothpaste aisle it is."

Mila was suddenly standing on the buffed, linoleum floor of a supermarket. Soft, familiar music wafted through the air, as did in-store bakery smells. Both, Mila knew, were minutely calibrated to encourage sales. The snazzy packages stacked high on the shelves seemed to flash out at her: Sexier! Newer! Cheaper! Mila reached up for one particularly high-concept bottle of mouthwash. Sometimes she found a kind of chagrined pleasure out of reading the ingredients on these expensive concoctions. What inert substance will it be this time, wondered Mila, checking the label. The text was odd, though: 'Even the most casual economic analysis reveals that medicine is not just another industry,' it began. Suddenly the label seemed to expand in her hands. She read on.

CHAPTER 15

MARKETING AND STRATEGIC PLANNING IN HEALTH CARE

EVEN THE MOST CASUAL economic analysis reveals that medicine is not just another industry. Charles Phelps in *Health Economics* claims that it is different from most businesses in so many regards that one wonders whether anything known about other markets is applicable to the health care industry at all.

Almost everyone encounters the health care system at some time and almost always in moments of personal crisis or significance. The question, according to Phelps, is whether or not anybody behaves as a "rational economic actor" in these circumstances.[1] Health care contrasts profoundly with most markets, but this is hardly the only way in which it differs. Phelps explains further distinctions. There are few industries in which there is such a huge gap in knowledge between "seller" and "buyer"—doctor and patient. Nor are there many industries in which government involves itself so thoroughly. Additionally, there is the all-persuasiveness of uncertainty. From the randomness of individuals' illnesses to the unpredictability of how well a medical treatment will work on a patient, the workings of chance are always present, always reminding the economist that medicine is different. Finally, there are externalities to consider; in other words, one person's actions create costs and/or benefits for another.[2]

One cannot, however, leave it at that. The health care industry "represents a collection of services, products, institutions, regulations and people that accounted for more than 15 percent of our gross national product (GNP) in 1995, or almost $1 out of every $7 spent in our country."[3] In 1995, it was estimated that aggregate spending on medical care would be more than $1 trillion, out of which over $0.9 trillion went to "personal" health care costs and the remainder to research, construction, and administration. Also in 1995, about $3,300 in personal health care was paid by each of the 275 million people living in the United States.[4] No industry that size can be exempt from economic laws, can it?

Indeed, not. Although there are aspects of the health care industry that are sui generis, economics directs many of the decisions doctors make. Economics influences how doctors interact with their patients; it guides them in choosing where to practice, what to practice, and even to go to medical school in the first place. Beyond the differences, there is a world of similarity between health care and other industries, and great insight can be drawn by applying economic language and analysis to medicine.

MARKETING AND THE CONSUMER

As if one could forget, the doctor isn't a god anymore, nor is s/he the only source of information for patients. There is a profusion of information in books and on the internet. Insurance companies capture data and send out health news according to subscriber need and interest. Patients are—or at least feel—far better informed than ever before and better prepared for a visit to the physician. This makes them more demanding, more needful of treatment as customers.

Treating patients—or key stakeholders such as insurance companies —as customers means recognizing that all consumers are different and heightening one's sensitivity to the needs and wants of the particular consumer at hand. For example, throat cancer in a singer is not the same as throat cancer in a non-singer. It means increasing respect for the personal choices of patients. Whereas a surgeon's goal may invariably be to maximize patient survival, the patient may put greater weight on the quality of life. Treating your patients as customers also means acknowledging that there may be ways some patients work against your efficiency. Many patients, guided by misinformation or bias, now consume medical services that are either useless or risky. You must help them do what's best, for their sake and your own. Finally, treating patients as customers means taking in and using information like satisfaction ratings, and knowing what your product or service really is. It's not just the shot—it's the wait, the paper, the follow-up.

As labor becomes more and more divided, jobs break up. The farther downstream the physician is, the more other people market to the consumer and control or influence that interface, the more vulnerable the physician becomes. For example, consider the situation of whether a physician wants to provide bells and whistles or concentrate on cost. The segment of the consumer market being served will determine the success of either choice; the crucial question is whether the physician will define the segment he or she will serve or if s/he will abdicate that decision and the power that goes with it. Who will influence who receives a physician's name for consideration as a provider of medical care? Who will decide how that presentation occurs? Who will consider satisfaction ratings and have the power of displaying them to consumers—and deciding which consumers? Those public satisfaction ratings are very powerful and often tend to be self-reinforcing. All of these are questions of who will market physicians. In the end, doctors must market themselves. If they don't, others—like insurance companies—will. Marketing is not a simple matter of picking a medium and placing an ad. It's marketing in a universe of marketing.

PHYSICIANS IN THE MARKETPLACE

Physicians, according to Phelps, control most of the resources in the U.S. health care system, and they do so in two distinct roles. They act both as the entrepreneurs of physician-firms and as labor input into the production function of physician-firms. As entrepreneurs, physicians make the same types of decisions as those in any business, such as which input to use, how much to produce, and how to price the product. As workers, physicians behave similarly to other skilled laborers. They make rational investments in education, for example, after weighing the economic returns from specialization. The relevant labor supply affects physicians-as-workers just as it does workers in any field; soon, physicians may even, unless legal protections are formed, "face competition from foreign sources of supply."[5]

PRICE SETTING AND INFLUENCING DEMAND

How are prices set in the health care industry? Phelps answers that by suggesting that a "model of monopolistic competition with incomplete search seems to fit this market well."[6] Rather than one single price, there is a wide variety of prices. Search is usually incomplete since only a certain number of patients are willing to change doctors. As a result, each doctor has some influence over price.

Phelps claims that the price-setting power of doctors also affects the limited, but existing ability of doctors to "induce demand" in their patients, thereby increasing economic opportunities.[7] Many studies of demand inducement exist, but statistical difficulties or flaws have occurred. There has been, however, a controlled trial in a pediatric clinic that clearly demonstrates that "the mechanism of payment alters the number of visits both recommended to patients and the number . . . actually undertaken by the patient."[8] Further, claims Phelps, numerous studies have shown that physician ownership of medical services (X-ray, lab tests, physical therapy, etc.) greatly increases the use of these services for their patients. In addition, this ownership sometimes increases the price and lowers the quality of care. Phelps explains that market forces seem to limit actual demand inducement, so that many observable phenomena, such as a physician's location, relate closely to occurrences without inducement. "As with other

matters in health economics," Phelps continues, "this seems a case in which consumer information could play an increasingly important role."[9]

The concept of induced demand comes from the providers changing their medical recommendations because of financial gain. Phelps utilized the example of scheduled well-care visits for children recommended by the American Academy of Pediatrics to further express this. The belief that salary-paid doctors provide too little care was supported when they missed scheduling these well-check visits for their patients 9 percent of the time when compared to the fee-for-service doctors who only missed scheduling any of these recommended visits 4 percent of the time. On the other hand, the belief that fee-for-service doctors provide too much care was also supported when they scheduled more than the recommended number of visits 22 percent of the time, as opposed to the salaried doctors only doing this for 4 percent of their patients.[10]

HOSPITALS IN THE MARKETPLACE

Most hospitals in the United States are legally not-for-profit which "eliminates the usual corporate shareholder as a residual claimant. As a result, the hospital's profits must necessarily go somewhere else."[11] Phelps explains that various models exist which assume that some person or group receives (captures) the profits and uses them to further their own ends.

The two most common models are first the doctor-capture model in which the doctors indirectly receive the hospital's profits. Second, in the manager-utility function model, a central decision maker receives the profits and guides the hospital in a "utility-maximizing way."[12] Two other models—employee-capture and patient-capture—may seem possible but are not usually considered.

In general, Phelps summarizes that the demand curves for a hospital shift upward (outward) in the following situations:

A competing hospital's price increases.

A competing hospital's quality falls.

The extent of hospital insurance held by patients increases.[13]

The interactions between doctors and hospitals are partly determined by the hospital's decisions about the scope of services to provide. When hospitals want to attract more patients, they provide special facilities that assist the doctors' practices, thereby attracting more doctors. As a result, a hospital's success is greatly influenced by scope of services decisions.

Phelps gives the following explanation using economic terms:

We can think of hospitals as confronting a family of demand curves, with a different curve for each quality of care that the hospital might produce. Each level of quality also has associated with it a different cost curve, so there is a family of average cost curves just as there is a family of demand curves. The not-for-profit rules of the hospital require that the hospital set a price so that revenue just covers costs, which means that it must operate where demand curves intersect average cost curves. . . . The hospital can select which of these feasible choices is best by comparing the preferences of the fictitious "director" of the hospital (using a utility function) with the available choices. One choice will provide the highest utility, and this becomes the point actually chosen by the hospital.[14]

HEALTH INSURANCE IN THE MARKETPLACE

For a patient, health insurance provides a way to limit the financial risks inherent in illness. The markets for such insurance plans, however, have become quite complicated. Some firms sell group insurance; others sell individual insurance. According to Phelps, nongroup plans run a much higher risk of adverse selection than group plans, especially when the "group" is a work group.

Another important distinction among insurers is their tax status. Phelps explains that some plans (Blue Cross, Blue Shield, and Delta Dental) are not-for-profit and receive tax benefits that their for-profit commercial competitors do not. However, the "importance of these and other benefits of the Blues remains uncertain in the light of various empirical studies of the issue."[15]

A potentially important consideration in the insurance market, especially for those over age sixty-five, is the issue of self-selection. No research has found direct self-selection of HMOs, but several studies of persons in Medicare HMOs "found relatively low prior-year use by new enrollees, suggesting favorable self-selection for HMOs."[16]

Health insurance has become a popular fringe benefit because of the positive tax treatment for employer-paid premiums that accompany group insurance. An increasing number of people are uninsured through either conventional insurance or government programs. Many of these people are employed but earn around the minimum wage. Proposals for universal insurance in the United States usually center on "mandated coverage for workers and their families as a cornerstone of these universal insurance plans."[17]

MEDICARE

Medicare's structure has changed significantly since its beginnings in 1966. The most recent change concerns physician payments. In January 1992, Medicare implemented a new fee-schedule type of payment, a system based on a study of "work effort." Under this system, formally called the resource-based relative value system (RBRVS), the payment for services such as thinking and talking with patients would drastically increase, while fees for procedures would decrease. Private insurance carriers have become increasingly interested in the "new value relationships for developing benefit levels based on RBRVS. The challenge, however, has been to determine the conversion factors to be used with the RBRVS values."[18] Then, on January 22, 1997, the Health Care Financing Administration revealed possible ways to calculate the resource-based practice expense (45 percent of the physician's payment). "The implementation of any of these options could mean cuts of up to 44% [in] specialist reimbursement."[19]

STRATEGIC PLANNING

According to Schendel and Hofer, strategic planning is a business fundamental as essential to organizational growth and renewal in health care as in any other sector. Strategic planning can be looked at as six distinct processes:

1. goal formation
2. environmental analysis
3. strategy formulation
4. strategy evaluation
5. strategy implementation
6. strategic control.[20]

Strategy, of course, means different things to different people. A definition by Michael Porter quoted by Roice D. Luke and James W. Begun in *Essentials of Health Care Management* represents the most common viewpoint: "'[strategy is the] positioning [of] a business to maximize the value of the capabilities that distinguish it from its competitors.'"[21] This definition appropriately draws attention to achieving competitive advantage which is considered the central focus of strategy. Competitive advantage is relative and only has meaning when compared to the advantage of rivals. As concrete as one's rivals may be, however, one's strategy is conceptual—it is "not a plan, policy or specific intended investment. It is an expression of those highly proprietary concepts and ideas that an organization hopes will help it achieve advantage."[22]

According to Porter, the most important principle of competitive advantage is positioning—creating goods and services which are more valued than those of the competitor. Other writings about strategy give many fundamental principles that are necessary sources for competitive advantage. Luke and Begun grouped them in three categories separated by their primary underlying logic. They refer to them as the three Ps of strategy, and they are position, pace, and power. Complete explanations follow.

Position: competitive advantage gained by achieving distinctive value in the minds of consumers.[23]

Pace: competitive advantage gained through managing the timing and intensity of actions.[24]

Power: competitive advantage gained by control and influence in a specific arena.

Position

According to Luke and Begun, value can be found in position in one of three ways: low cost, high differentiation, and distinctive niche.

Positioning with low costs. The advantages of having lower costs than rivals are familiar but potent nonetheless. The competitor with lower costs can price its goods and services so as to destroy rivals' market shares and distract potential entrants to the market. In the 1970s and 1980s, the pursuit of low-cost positions led many hospitals to join multi-hospital systems (a power strategy as well). Although this did ensure survival for many hospitals and increased profits for others, it is unclear whether the tactic actually cut costs.

Positioning with differentiation. Positions of high differentiation are achieved by changing a products' characteristics—such as quality, service support, technological sophistication—to reflect distinctive value to consumers. Opportunities for this are prevalent in health care and in other service industries since production and consumption occur at the same time. These occurrences mean that consumers deal with organizations at every point and level of use, providing differentiation opportunity at every pass. "A recognition of the relationship between consumption and production may, in general, account for the ground swell of interest within health care in total quality improvement concepts and approaches."[25]

Positioning with distinctive niche. Niching positions are achieved by choosing specific arenas in the market to focus one's attention on. Such strategies are often very effective in health care, which is marked by a variety of product, services, and client preferences. Even though they require a high level of specialization, comment Luke and Begun, those who occupy such niches have come under attack from the competition during the last decade. As an example, they refer to major teaching centers whose specialty niches are being threatened by other hospitals (even those smaller and less technologically advanced) that have entered their specific market.

Pace

Hospitals may gain competitive advantage by managing the timing and intensity of their actions. Some hospitals are always on the search for new market opportunities and for competitor vulnerability. These institutions, with their "prospector-like" strategic orientations are more profitable and have larger market share than those that take a "defender" orientation.

Many hospitals will change their strategies when faced with strong environmental pressures, although "these changes are more likely to result in improved performance when they are made within the organization's 'strategic comfort zones'—that is, they are not too dissimilar in terms of accustomed patterns of action."[26]

Power

Power is the most important source of competitive advantage that an organization is able to amass in the competitive arena. Luke and Begun suggest that the greatest example of the use of power to achieve competitive advantage in the health care field is found in the increase, since the 1970s, in the many hospitals joining multi-hospital systems, contracting with management services, joining hospital consortia, or expanding into various health care and insurance businesses.

The advantage of power strategies comes from either the size (whether scale or scope) or the synergy that surrounds businesses when they combine into larger organizational entities, or both. The transformation of "synergies" into meaningful strategic advantage can be difficult in the health care field; "there are so many institutionalized autonomies and organizational complexities" that interfere with interorganizational coordination.[27] Porter identifies four power strategies—horizontal integration, vertical integration, horizontal expansion, and portfolio.[28]

The "hybrid" organization, a new form in which entities are combined without change of ownership, has gained favor in health care and many other fields. In a hybrid, long-held autonomies can be preserved, and the arrangements between the entities can be both arranged and canceled with little difficulty. While there are obvious advantages, Luke and Begun suggest that the loose connections between the cooperating organizations hold disadvantages, too. Hybrids seldom have a decisive and powerful strategic head or strong interorganizational linkages and integrative mechanisms—both critical to effective strategic performance.[29]

Endnotes

1. Charles E. Phelps *Health Economics* (Reading, Mass.: Addison-Wesley, 1997): 2.
2. Ibid.
3. Ibid., 1.
4. Ibid.
5. Ibid., 215.
6. Ibid., 255.
7. Ibid., 256.
8. Ibid.
9. Ibid.
10. Ibid., 254–55.
11. Ibid., 288.
12. Ibid.
13. Ibid., 323.
14. Ibid., 323–24.
15. Ibid., 400
16. Ibid.
17. Ibid.
18. Source: http://www.aaos.org/word-html/97news/medi.htm.
19. Source: http://www.hiaa.org/health-care/index.html#RBRVSD.
20. Roice D. Luke and James W. Begun, "Strategy Making in Health Care Organizations," *Essentials of Health Care*

Management, eds. Stephen M. Shortell and Arnold D. Kaluzny (Albany: Delmar Publishers, 1997): 437.

21. Ibid., 442.
22. Ibid., 443.
23. Ibid., 445–46.
24. Ibid., 446.
25. Ibid., 447.
26. Ibid., 449.
27. Ibid., 452.
28. Ibid., 452.
29. Ibid., 454–55.

OF SUITS AND COATS

"SO DID YOUR INTRODUCTION TO MARKETING BELONG IN THE TOOTHPASTE AISLE, MILA?"

"All right, Ajax, I was wrong, and I now understand how important this will be in the future for physicians, you smug pain in the rear. But I wish it didn't belong in my life either. You'd better put me back in reality now so I can contradict my direct superior yet again."

"Of course, Mila. Perhaps a limited rewind would help?"

Mila once again squinted against nice, normal, yellow sunlight. She smelled Dr. Baskin's cigar smoke. "Good God, Bob," he was again saying from the wall behind where she and Dr. Goodner stood, "you sound like an administrator. Worse yet, you sound like a salesman or—what's the buzzword—oh, a marketer! Spend your time on medicine and clear your head of that other nonsense."

I'm getting to be an expert at this no-parachute routine, thought Mila, and spoke: "I hate to say it, Dr. Baskin, but Dr. Goodner has a point. There's more to marketing than slick ads. I don't like it; I know you don't like it; and I'll bet no doc likes it. But that nonsense really does determine who we see, what we can do for them, and how much we get paid after it's all done. Being a doctor isn't what it used to be, but then neither is anything else."

"Here, here, Mila!" said Dr. Goodner. "Let me buy you a Yoo-hoo."

"Kids today," said Dr. Baskin and shook his head.

The next two weeks were an exhausting and stressful confusion of clinical work and surgery. Her eyes stung most of the time from way too little sleep, and her stomach was sour all of the time from way, way too much Diet Coke. And yet, she had to admit, she was pretty darn happy. It didn't hurt that politics—and Ajax—had been completely absent from her life since her IPA negotiation outburst.

She walked over to her mail bin, told Penny "nice cardigan," and finished off a granola bar, all the while completely engrossed in the puzzle of why Mr. Proctor's amylase wasn't falling as rapidly as it should have been since his pancreatitis was improving. In the mail: two policy change notices (pocket), a schedule change (pocket), three take-out menus (recycle), and one—*what*?

"OK, whose joke is this?" Mila waved the official-looking note at the other two residents in the mail room. They shrugged at her and left. Once, in med school, Tom had sent her a trumped-up note from the dean saying she wouldn't be able to graduate because of "behavior problems." She'd actually fallen for it for a moment and had vowed never again to give a practical joke-ster that satisfaction. At the time, Tom had been behind the mail bin snickering while she sweated, and she figured today's comic genius would be around for the performance, too. "Come on. Who done it, guys? 'Fess up and the sentence will be light." She was speaking to an empty mail room.

She rechecked the note, its format, and the signature. It did look authentic, and her new group of coresidents and friends were not nearly as juvenile as her medical student gang. So that meant she really had been elected to represent the residents on the education committee of the PHO.

Mila's chief resident, Susanne Wu, came in to get her mail as Mila was rereading the letter. Susanne "congratulated" her, shaking her head. "It's a waste of time, obviously," Susanne said, "but it'll look good on your transcript."

But, thought Mila, I know diddly. How am I supposed to hold a position of influence in this system? Mila didn't understand it. She still couldn't grasp why health care had evolved to this point. She understood the money changes; she understood the managed care changes; but she just didn't get why, on a day-to-day basis, providers were so confused and unhappy. What had happened over the past fifteen years to create all these divisions: Patients vs. Doctors; Specialists vs. Primary Care Docs? In a long-ago geology course, Mila had learned about the origin of earthquake faults. What cataclysmic event had caused these philosophic faults in health care? Dr. Baskin would call her idealistic and naive, but whatever *did* happen to the care-of-the-community model that had attracted her into medicine in the first place? If the Climarans really wanted to help, they would help explain *that* $64,000 question.

"Why is my first-year resident in the mail room instead of upstairs pre-rounding?" It was Dr. Baskin, who hadn't given up the fight for Mila's medical soul. She handed him the letter; he read it and whistled sarcastically. "Quite an honor." He handed it back and started rifling through his own mail. "Look—just skip the meetings when you can and get beeped out early when you can't skip 'em."

"That's truly your advice?" said Mila, who hadn't quite given up the fight for Dr. Baskin's soul either. She kept hoping to inject him with a bit of optimism about the physician's role in the system. "You sincerely see no value in having a say in the structure of our profession?"

Dr. Baskin threw a pile of junk mail into the bin and headed for the door. "You know, Mila, we joke about this subject a lot, and maybe some of it isn't joking. But I do have some advice for you, and I hope you take it seriously." Dr. Baskin folded a notice into his pocket, then looked back at her. "Don't turn into one of them."

"*Them*, Dr. Baskin?"

Dr. Baskin spoke each syllable slowly and distinctly, "A suit, Mila. You are a coat. Don't forget it." He looked at her significantly and left.

Mila sank onto a pile of "lost cat" notices on the bench. Suddenly, her head was splitting. In other words, she thought, if docs ignore the business of medicine, everything gets decided without us. If we pay attention to the business of medicine, we're traitors. Why am I being put in this position? Why does this have to be? What am I supposed to do about it? She rubbed the spot between her eyebrows and saw White.

"Don't tell, me, Ajax. There's some simple answer to all this that can be delivered in a perfectly apt little virtual environment. Well, go ahead, cram it

into my brain. If it's full, just dump some medical knowledge. That doesn't seem to be the important stuff after all."

"You're upset."

"Ajax. It's too late to try working on your sympathy skills. Just bring me the expert."

Mila was suddenly back on the mail room bench, though the White just outside the door let her know it was a virtual mail room, a virtual bench. She prepared herself for another lecture, another official world expert who'd tell her what to do.

Just then Mila noticed that she was not alone on the bench. Sitting next to her, and smiling warmly at her, was a woman Mila'd never seen before. She looked like a successful professional of some sort, confident and knowledgeable, but, somehow, not at all buttoned-down or severe. Her most striking feature was her eyes—deep, brown, and radiating empathy. She was clearly someone who had learned to let herself be herself, and Mila suddenly felt that for the first time in her recent history she was with a friend, someone she could trust. But just like all of Ajax's images, there was something not quite right with her. It was what she was wearing over her dress. Half of it was a suit and then the other half was a white coat.

"You're in a tough spot," said the woman, "but you're definitely going to get through it."

"No offense," said Mila, "but how do you know that? And why are you wearing both a business suit and a clinical coat?"

"Well, to answer your first question, Ajax has told me about you, and when you know what you need to know, you do well. Better then well. Mila, my name is Beulah Trey. I've spent the better part of my academic career investigating what makes physicians and administrators click, and I'm here to teach you some of what I've found out."

Mila didn't know why, but something in this Beulah Trey's manner made the problems seem less overwhelming. "Why don't you just relax," said Beulah, "and let me tell you about what we're facing. Oh, and by the way, by the end of our discussion, you'll understand how someone can wear both a coat and a suit."

THE CHALLENGE OF BUILDING PRODUCTIVE ALLIANCES BETWEEN PHYSICIANS AND ADMINISTRATORS

UNTIL RECENTLY, IT WAS acceptable for physicians to "collaborate" with administrators by dropping in on hospital CEOs and laying out, by fiat, what needed to happen. Because physicians brought in the patients—and, as such, the revenue—to hospitals, physicians held a great deal of the institutional power. It was part of a CEO's job description to keep physicians happy.

Today, however, it is managed care companies that control patients, and physicians are left with far less sway. If doctors want to influence hospital decision making, they must do so within existing organizational structures and protocols. In most health care systems today, physicians who want to have their voice heard can no longer drop in on the CEO. A physician now has to make an appointment to see a CEO—and usually has to do it through the CEO's secretary. And during the meeting, the physician is likely to be steered to a more appropriate administrator. The message is clear: Dr. Physician, if you want to influence something here, you play by our rules.

This means that to champion the physicians' perspective, a doctor has to learn how to work within organizations, and that is a skill that physicians historically have demeaned and still actively discourage. A physician who begins to "collaborate" with administration excites, among other physicians, tremendous suspicion and a presumption of betrayal. The physician is portrayed as betraying "coats" and in danger of becoming a "suit."

In a private interview, a physician summed up this common attitude: "[A physician who collaborates with administration] really is no longer seen as one of us, and we all know that [. . . administration is] just using him. He doesn't have any power to do anything. I actually feel sorry for him."[1]

This view promotes as an ideal a strict boundary between clinical and administrative domains. That boundary used to serve physicians well. Now, however, health care is a corporate enterprise. It can no longer afford to isolate quality from cost, and efforts to preserve a clinical/administrative split serve only to keep doctors out of decisions in which their influence is sorely needed.

Health care needs physicians who are effective in organizations, and it needs physicians who are willing to brave disapproval from their colleagues. Unfortunately, physicians who attempt to be effective in organizations by collaborating with administrators are often still groundbreakers, forced to operate in bivouac conditions. In the end, they must depend on an independent sense of where they, as physicians, can best contribute. They must find like-minded colleagues, and take comfort in the robustness of their profession. Above all, they must trust that the physician culture will, in time, adapt to changing economic realities (and vice versa), and that their efforts in breaking down the rigid physician/administration boundaries will not forever be lonely.

Unfortunately, nothing in the history of physician/administrator relations, and nothing in the socialization, education, or culture of either profession, has prepared physicians or administrators to collaborate. In fact, the past economics of health care resulted in a system of separate domains in which both parties prospered—physicians had sufficient influence to maintain the autonomy of their clinical enterprises, and administrators focused on hospital-wide endeavors. This separation of the two groups, and the inevitable tensions between them, has limited opportunities for the professions to resolve their competing agendas or understand their shared interests.

Further, the considerable differences between physician and administrator culture mean that even when members of the two groups try to work together, mutual misinterpretation abounds. Neither group questions the universality of its views nor recognizes its views are culturally based. Each group, then, judges the behavior of individuals—even of individuals from other groups—by its own norms.

The destructive potential of the dynamics that have arisen over cultural differences can be demonstrated with a scenario based on the difference between physicians' and administrators' assumptions about timing and decision making. Physicians, who must make emergency decisions at the bedside, value autonomy; administrators, who must rely on each other to manage hospitals, value the interdependence of bureaucratic structures. When a physician asks an administrator to purchase a new piece of equipment, the physician assuredly expects a timely response. To the physician, whose experience is of needing to make lifesaving decisions in an instant, "timely response" probably means immediate response—within twenty-four hours, and certainly within the week. The administrator, however, values the systems put in place for equipment purchasing. From this perspective, a timely response might be one given within the month. In this interaction, the physician and administrator each believes his or her estimation of timeliness is the correct—and only possible—one, and each is either unaware or dismissive of the other's assumptions.

A month later, when the administrator returns with the response the doctor wanted, the physicians' comment is not "thank you," but "what took you so long?" From the administrator's perspective, the doctor is unrealistic, ungrateful, and maybe even arrogant. To the physician, the administrator is non-responsive, uninterested, and perhaps evasive. Each judges the other's actions by his/her own worldview and values. There are a multitude of differences in the values and norms of the two groups, and many of those differences can lead to conflict.

DIFFERENCES IN VALUES

Physicians and administrators represent two different social realities, with contrasting worldviews, knowledge bases, and rules of evidence. Each group sees itself as advocating for patients, but each has a very different idea of what that means. The physician, for example, is concerned with the individual patient's survival and values scientific research: experimentation is the basis of his/her knowledge. The administrator, concerned with larger numbers of patients, focuses on the survival of the institution. S/he is used to fairly long time lines in which to make decisions and places value on planning and forecasting.[2] In terms of finances, physicians focus on their own areas, while administrators focus on the hospital as a whole.

DIFFERENCES IN SOCIALIZATION

Physicians pay primary loyalty to the practice of medicine in general and to the treatment of their patients in particular. Administrators, on the other hand, are loyal to their organizations. They are motivated to keep their institutions solvent and are comfortable being part of a bureaucracy.[3] These differing attitudes towards bureaucratic rules and standards (physicians' resistance vs. administrators' reliance) are sources of conflict, as are the unequal organizational loyalties (physicians' low vs. administrators' high).

DIFFERENCES IN LEADERSHIP, ORGANIZATIONAL FORM, AND COLLECTIVE DECISION MAKING

The differences between the two groups' norms concerning leadership, organizational form, and collective decision making are especially troublesome. Hospital administration is a profession suffused with hierarchy and bureaucracy. An agent authorized on behalf of hospital administration is fairly certain to be representing his/her colleagues, and a leader can be certain to be speaking for subordinates.

Doctors' relationships with colleagues and inside hospitals have never fit a hierarchical or representational model. The physicians' work model provides for individuals to act autonomously and swiftly at the bedside; implicit in this model is clinical and financial autonomy and a high valuation of individuality.[4] Historically, physicians were independent business people who contracted with hospitals for privileges and services. As doctors moved into hospital staff positions, a medical staff leadership structure did indeed evolve. It worked as a function of academic achievement and clinical expertise and was never meant to authorize spokespeople. This is in sharp contrast with the leadership arrangement in administration, which, in its structure, provides for the quick authorization of representatives and the formulation of strategy.

The result of the medical staff leadership structure is that few groups of physicians have agreed-upon methods for authorizing each other to stand or act on their behalf. Most physicians are used to speaking only for themselves individually, and physician leaders neither assume they have, nor have in fact, a mandate to speak for other doctors. Consistent with this, physicians often do not consider themselves obligated by decisions made in their absence, no matter who was present.

Administrators, then, may not know who their physician counterparts are. If they do, they may not be able to determine whom the physicians represent. Viewed as a cultural difference, this issue distinguishes between the hierarchical bureaucratic culture of administrators, where representation is a requirement, and the long-standing independence of physicians. It would seem that a structure effective for managing a hospital is not effective for treating patients, and vice versa.

From the cultural differences between physicians and administrators spring stereotypes and prejudice. Stereotypes, usually based on cultural differences, are defined as prejudices if they are derogatory and allow the person holding them to feel superior. A prejudiced person is unaware that the issue is not one of superiority and inferiority, but of difference. Although physicians and administrators have worked side by side for most of this century, they have not learned to respect the differences in their cultures; indeed, in some cases, they do not even recognize they exist. Each expects the other to behave according to his own cultural expectations and resorts to prejudiced judgments when the other inevitably does not. The tragedy is that because of their profound lack of experience with each other, physicians and administrators lack the requisite skills needed to transcend these prejudices and build productive working alliances.

What is to be done? Against this backdrop of culture clash and, for physicians, disrespect for cooperation with administration, what can a physician, administrator, or hospital do?

Before anything else, it is essential that all parties understand that industry-level economic forces are inescapable. As managed care companies gain market share, they and the federal government increasingly demand that physicians and hospitals contract as a single entity. Inside hospitals, most cost savings result from physician-controlled decision making. This means that for physicians and administrators to be successful, they must learn to collaborate more effectively; at the hospital level, structural and strategic initiatives conducive to more productive alliances must be instituted. They must avoid ineffective strategies, such as including physicians in hospital benefits programs or selectively eliminating high-cost providers, and must pursue effective strategies that emphasize quality-of-care issues. Expanding hospital amenities to medical staff members, enhancing the hospital's image in the community, including physicians in hospital governance and policy-making, and steadily improving the hospital's facilities and equipment have all been found to be highly effective.[5]

Physicians and administrators must accept that it is the group level that contains most of the hostility, antagonism, and prejudice that may stand between them. When interactions are difficult, which they are a lot of the time, it may seem easier to blame the difficulty on the professional's group identity—"oh, he's a Doc," or "she has to because she's administration"—than to fault the individual in question. When a misunderstanding occurs, even administrators and physicians who have productive working alliances blame the other's group identity rather than the trusted individual.[6]

As a short-term container for the frustration of working across cultural differences, group-to-group antagonism may actually support individual physicians and administrators in building alliances. However, as physicians and administrators become more skilled in working together, it is essential that they recognize the propensity to blame misunderstandings on the group identity, and shift to speaking directly with each other about the subject of their misunderstanding. After all, interaction between individuals is at the root of any alliance. And it is this level, between individuals, that holds the best hope for improving alliances between physicians and administrators.

The impulse that leads a physician and/or administrator to collaborate is the recognition of the

mutuality of their self interests under the current economic conditions. The intended consequence is trust. Once trust is established and maintained, a pair is much more likely to be successful. So how do a physician and administrator build a productive alliance? Build trust. Know what kind of partnership you are entering, understand effective ways to develop an effective working alliance in that kind of partnership, and develop the necessary skills.

STEP ONE: WHAT KIND OF PARTNERSHIP ARE YOU ENTERING?

The first step in building a productive alliance with a specific administrator or physician is to identify the purpose of the relationship. There are three common reasons physicians and administrators form alliances. First, they may have functionally interdependent organizational roles, as with the chair and the manager of cardiac services; theirs is a long-term alliance. Second, physicians and administrators might collaborate to meet a specific common goal; a radiology practice and a hospital, for instance, might negotiate to open an outpatient MRI clinic. Theirs is a *joint venture alliance*. Finally, as might be the case in forming a contract with a managed care company, the two may work together toward an immediate goal on the same *negotiating team*.

STEP TWO: UNDERSTAND THE TRUST DYNAMICS

Trust greatly facilitates the success of a collaboration. Since the goal is to develop productive working alliances, it is useful to know that trust develops in different ways, and in ways that vary with the purpose of the partnership at hand. It is intuitive that people gauge the situation they are in and develop trust accordingly; examining the different types of trust most frequently needed between physicians and administrators can provide a kind of road map of how to build productive alliances.

Long-Term Alliances

For collaborations like those between department chairs and department managers, long-term alliances must be cultivated. The type of trust that develops in these situations is quite durable. It is born of experience and consists of a belief in one's partner's honesty and reliability, and a faith that the partner will cause no embarrassment—even that s/he will protect one as much as possible. If the physician and administrator are effective, they will be able to implement plans that will

serve both their interests. Forging this kind of trust depends on an ability to communicate and meet expectations, both key relationship-building skills.

Physicians and administrators in long-term collaborations seem to go through two stages: the formation stage and the established phase. When forming trust, each measures the other's trustworthiness on the basis of the partner's handling of matters of mutual interest as they come up. These matters—developing a new operating room policy might be an example—tend to grow out of areas of ambiguity and are opportunities for clarification. Success in meeting these opportunities provides reason to continue building trust.

Physicians and administrators enter the establishment phase of trust when they begin to take each other's interests into account, and no longer regard critical incidents as tests of trust. This kind of trust, which includes a sense of how and when each party can trust the other, develops with time, from successful experiences and the proven ability to learn from errors.

Joint-Venture Alliances

By definition, physicians and administrators involved in joint-venture negotiations are on opposite sides of a negotiating table—a positioning that is highly likely to be adversarial. Trust can develop in this situation, but only if both parties believe the best result will be achieved if they collaborate to serve both of their interests and if the negotiation and venture is structured appropriately. An "appropriate" structure features parity between each party's valuation of the deal and the risk involved, a solid business plan that does not revolve exclusively around financial considerations, and provisions for how each party can sever the collaboration.[7] The process needs to be collaborative, and parties must meet regularly during the joint-venture negotiation. Each party needs to believe that the other's representative is authorized to make the deal. This is especially true for the physicians; their belief that the administrator has the authority to make a deal is key to the administrator being seen as an equal partner.[8]

Negotiating Team Alliances

Physicians and administrators who find themselves on the same side on a negotiating team have the easiest time establishing trust. In these temporary situations, trust seems to develop "swiftly."[9] The initial decision to trust seems to be made based on the other's reputation, first impression, and how the person who establishes the team introduces the members on the team to each other. Subsequent experiences then confirm earlier conclusions—a

physician, reported to have been appointed for her reputation for being consistent and influential, proves to be consistent and influential. An administrator, known for his expertise, proves competent. Individuals collaborating with this purpose do not hesitate to trust, and usually do not talk about needing experience with each other.

In this context, trust seems to develop as a direct result of the characteristics of the situation. The life span of the collaboration is short, and the success of the venture very much depends on the physicians' and administrators' ability to craft a consensus that reflects both perspectives. Because of the transitory nature of the relationship, there is no time to develop experience with each other. Trust seems to be present from the inception of the temporary system; for that reason this type of trust has been referred to as "swift trust," highlighting the temporary nature of the collaboration,[10] or "shared adversary trust," highlighting the power of joint adversarial positioning.[11]

One caveat about these short-term alliances: the ease with which trust is developed is situation specific. If the parties find themselves in other situations, their past experience may produce a halo, but they will probably need to reestablish more durable forms of trust befitting to their new enterprise.

STEP THREE: SKILLS THAT ARE CONDUCIVE TO DEVELOPING TRUST

Attempts to change the way health care is delivered, it has been said, "will fail because of [the] inability of hospitals and physicians to set aside historic suspicions and because of the poor interpersonal skills of the participants."[12] To put it more optimistically, interpersonal skills are essential for the development of effective physician-administrator alliances; recognition of the specific skills needed may be useful in the development of effective collaboration.

For long-term alliances, two skills are essential. The first is the ability to process critical incidents. When events occur which threaten the alliance, both parties must establish the habit of raising concerns, solving the problems, and changing behavior accordingly. Second is the ability to recognize and elicit open discussions about the expectations of the other group. This skill, of making invisible expectations visible, appears to be a foundation for how people think about, and develop, trust.[13] This implies that a key trust-building skill is the ability to communicate about expectations, negotiate what is meant by a met expectation, and establish a process for problem solving when the inevitable disappointments arise. The most needed skill, then, is not only the ability, but the courage, to respond to difficulties with discussion rather than avoidance. Since expectations change over time, continual attention to negotiating expectations is necessary.

For joint-venture alliances, several skills are relevant. First, the negotiations between the physician and administrator need to be structured from inception. Building trust in these settings takes time and experiences with each other. Regular meetings, formal and informal, are key. Negotiations need to occur directly with the main parties—not through intermediaries. The physician must perceive the administrator as having the organizational authority to champion the enterprise successfully.

Much of the work of Fisher and Ury on negotiations applies to these situations.[14] Especially important is their advice to develop a win/win attitude and to concentrate on small wins before tackling the more loaded issues.

Structuring the negotiation appropriately is highly linked to effective joint-venture collaborations. One signal that the structure may be ineffective is either party showing a propensity to blame difficulties on the personality of the other, physician or administrator. This tendency to "make assumptions about a person, while failing to appreciate the impact of situations"[15]—situations such as a lack of structure in a negotiation—is known to social psychologists as the fundamental attribution error. The fundamental attribution error implies that when someone blames a difficult situation on the other person's personality, there is a high likelihood that their conclusion is flawed. Situational variables are more likely to be the cause of the problem. If during a negotiation, personalities are blamed for difficulties, one should consider whether the structure of the joint venture itself is faulty. It is in joint-venture situations that physicians and administrators seem most likely to stereotype each other. When one of the pair labels the other in a way consistent with a known cultural difference, especially if it is demeaning, there is a high likelihood that prejudice is at play. When this is evident, no meaningful dialogue is possible.

One model for dealing with prejudice involves three steps. First, each individual needs to develop a level of self-knowledge about his or her filters and biases. Second, each needs to understand the other's culture. Finally each person must have the capacity to empathize with the other's perspective.[16]

For the negotiating team purpose, in which trust develops swiftly, trust-linked skills pertain to the launch of the venture and the transformation, if there

is one, of the alliance. The person most responsible for creating a climate of trust in this situation is the convener. It is up to this person to highlight publicly the appropriate professional characteristics and reputation of the physicians and administrators involved. The players need to be aware that first impressions are crucial: key characteristics may be an administrator's professional competence, a physician's reputation for consistency, and a physician-administrator's character.[17]

At the close of the work, physicians and administrators need to be aware of the only partial transferability of this kind of trust. In most cases, this "swift" trust, which allows the parties to function collaboratively on the negotiating team, occurs as a result of physicians and administrators elevating points of agreement and minimizing points of tension. In this way they are able to function collaboratively on the negotiating team. If and when the purpose of their alliance changes, the points of tension that have been minimized may need to be resolved if trust is to be sustained.

To illustrate the importance of this issue, imagine a physician and administrator who developed their alliance while on a negotiating team developing a contract with a managed care company. During negotiations, the physician will, in all likelihood, have experienced the administrator as highly respectful of the autonomy of physicians. Should the contract be implemented, however, administration might well try to influence the physicians' clinical decision making, since that decision making will be essential to the hospital's ability to make money on the contract. The physician may experience this as a break in the trust established.

For this reason, physicians and administrators involved in temporary alliances should be especially mindful of changes in their collaboration's purpose. Only by understanding the nature of the change and how it affects the suppressed tensions can the alliance continue to evolve and be effective. In other words, both parties must be proactive in anticipating the challenges that this change might bring and be willing to deal with them in a frank and honest manner. Otherwise, these changes could translate into a lack of trust.

Implicit in many of these skill sets is the ability to raise concerns directly. The direct talk muscle is extremely underused in physician-administrator alliances. When working with physicians and administrators, administrators frequently express frustration with physicians whom they have assumed to be representing peers but who end up to be speaking only for themselves personally. When asked whom they represent, the physicians inevitably

believe they only represent themselves. They do not feel authorized, and indeed are not authorized, to speak for their colleagues; they are often unaware that the administrator expects anything different. To talk about this issue directly, administrators would have to communicate exactly whom they expect the physicians to represent. The conversation would probably lead to a difficulty with most hospitals' implementation of physician representation—namely, that most physician representatives are appointed by administrators and have not been authorized by other physicians as representative.

At the heart of this tension over physician representation are differences between the two professions' cultural and historical traditions, physicians' rage at being put in the position of having to represent each other, and administrators' insecurity that if physicians do empower each other, they might overpower administrators. Direct talk about physician representation could result in a physician representational system in which physicians develop their ability to authorize and represent each other, in which case they might be more influential in the debates they care most about.

One way physicians and/or administrators can raise issues like representation, especially in the early stages of working together, is to use the

134   The Phantom Stethoscope

"skeptical friend" technique. Tough issues can be easier to broach if framed with the question, "What would a skeptical friend say about our effort?"

At this time in the history of physician-administrator alliances, change needs to be promoted on two levels. Organizationally, hospitals and health care systems need to develop structures and strategies that promote the alliances. At the individual and interpersonal level, however, it is the responsibility of each physician and administrator to work for improved partnerships. And only through the development of trust and alliances between physicians and administrators can a difficult compromise between concerns of cost control and quality in health care be made more palatable.

Suddenly the White disappeared from the mail room door, and Mila was back in reality. The virtual Beulah was gone, but Mila still felt her presence. She knew it would be a source of comfort and perspective for a long, long time. She instinctively looked in the mail room mirror to make sure that her white coat was clean and unstained.

Endnotes

1. Private interview with a physician by Beulah Trey.

2. S. M. Shortell, *Effective Hospital-Physician Relationships* (Ann Arbor, Mich.: Health Administration Press Perspectives, 1991).

3. M. McCollum, "What Explanations about Physicians-Manager Relationships Are Offered in the Literature" (1993).

4. Stevens, R., *In Sickness and in Wealth: American Hospitals in the Twentieth Century* (United States: Basic Books, 1989).

5. H. L. Smith, R. A. Reid, and N. F. Piland, "Managing hospital-physician relations: A strategy scorecard," *Health Care Management Review* 15, no. 4 (1990): 23–33. See also S. M. Shortell, *Effective Hospital-Physician Relationships*.

6. B. Trey, "Trust in the workplace: Taking the pulse of trust between physicians

and hospital administrators" (Ph.D. diss., 1999), abstract in *Dissertation Abstracts International*.

7. S. M. Shortell, *Effective Hospital-Physician Relationships*.

8. B. Trey, "Trust in the workplace."

9. D. Meyerson, K. E. Weick, and R. M. Kramer, "Swift trust and temporary groups," *Trusts in Organizations: Frontiers of Theory and Research*, eds. R. M. Kramer and T. R. Tyler (Thousand Oaks, Calif.: Sage Publications, 1996): 166–95.

10. Ibid.

11. B. Trey, "Trust in the workplace."

12. J. C. Goldsmith, "Hospital/physician relationships: A constraint to health reform," *Health Affairs* 12, no. 3 (1993): 160–69.

13. Y. M. Agazarian, "Glossary of systems-centered therapy terms," *The SCT*

Journal: Systems-centered Theory and Practice 2 (1997b): 3–10.

14.   R. Fisher and W. Ury, *Getting to Yes* (Boston: Houghton Mifflin, 1981).

15.   S. S. Brehm and S. M. Kassin, *Social Psychology* (Boston: Houghton Mifflin, 1990).

16.   A. McKee and S. Schor, "Confronting prejudice and stereotypes: A teaching model," *Performance Improvement Quarterly, Special Edition Embracing Diversity to Improve Performance* (January 1999).

17.   B. Trey, "Trust in the workplace."

CHAPTER 18

OF CAT SCANS AND
CUSTOMER DISSERVICE

IT WAS MILA'S DAY FOR CLINIC, HER DAY TO CARE FOR THE UNDERSERVED. Residents griped about clinic, but Mila was rather looking forward to being with people who'd never read the patient "bill of rights" and whose interest in the financial implications of managed care was zilch. She could pretend it was 1985 again, Mila thought. Yipee! Break out the Bowie! She was momentarily jarred by her schedule—she had thirty-six patients to see before 6:00. But Susanna Wu, her chief resident, peeked over Mila's shoulder and told her it was actually not bad at all: "Don't worry," she said, "half of the patients'll be late, the other half won't show. You'll be fine."

It *was* fine. Mila saw to pre-surgical problems, took out sutures, reassured patients that they were recovering appropriately. In fact, it was such a long, easy coast that at 5:30 she really did have only one patient left. "No show," Mila hoped. "Be a no show. That would make it a perfect day."

Perfection was not attained. Mrs. Bizzell showed up and did so on time. She was a forty-two-year-old caucasian woman with diabetes, hypertension, and obesity. She had with her in the tiny examination room three children, who appropriated all available tongue depressors, cotton swabs, and the scale as their rightful toys. They were nice, though. Mila took a rubber glove and made

136

a smiling face on it for each of them; they beamed. The thought crossed Mila's mind, however, that in making the puppets she was laying herself open for some serious charges by the managed care police. "Dr. Langston," they'd say. "First it was the suture in the OR, now wasting gloves. There will be no mercy for the likes of you." Mila smiled to herself.

Lillie Bizzell, however, was not smiling. "Doc, my stomach feels like it's exploding inside. At first, I thought it was too much McDonalds from last night. Sometimes I get a little carried away. But it just ain't let up."

Mila mulled over the differential diagnosis of abdominal pain in a patient of this age. She asked all the appropriate questions and got all the appropriate answers. Until they reached the subject of sex. "Is the pain," Mila inquired, with a glance at the children, "exacerbated by sex?"

"Exacer . . . what?" Mila was embarrassed for having talked in a way the patient couldn't understand. She probably sounded like an alien. She rephrased, happy the kids were intent on drawing in the margins of some Flu Shot Information pamphlets. "Have you had sex over the past few days?"

The patient grimaced, then spoke. "Micky D's ain't the only thing I get carried away on. Sex over the last few days? Of course. Just not last night. Not with this pain."

As clear an answer as any, Mila thought. Mrs. Bizzell might have her problems, but her social life sure beat Mila's own since her return from Climara.

Mila called a nurse into the room and began the physical examination, not expecting to find anything dramatic. When she began the abdominal exam, however, there was an egg-shaped movable mass palpable in the abdomen. Mila's diagnostic wheels started turning. She excused herself from the patient and got the radiology extension from a nurse.

On the way to her dictating station, Mila saw the sign for radiology and decided just to walk over herself. She passed Dr. Goodner rummaging behind the desk. "Someone brought in great brownies, Mila," he said as she passed. "Have one?"

She considered, but the fitness part of her overactive conscience prevailed. "Maybe later, Dr. Goodner," Mila said, and quickened her pace a bit.

The Samuel Harrington Center for Radiologic Imaging was in a beautiful and plush suite. Mila allowed herself a moment of pride in her profession. Even in this age of confused medical care, she thought, my patient will get the latest in technology only a hundred feet from the clinic. Maybe I've been a tad harsh on this future medicine.

"Hello," she said to the radiology receptionist, and waited, smiling, for her to finish her phone call. When she hung up, however, the receptionist ignored Mila and started entering something into the computer. Mila's smile became a little forced, but it remained. It was never a good idea, she knew, to alienate staff. They rule the world.

"I have a patient over in clinic with an abdominal mass," Mila began, "She needs a—"

"What she needs is a referral," the receptionist said, moving her mouse.

"Excuse me, I haven't been clear. I am Dr. Mila Langston, and I have a sick patient who needs a CT scan." She slid the chart to the receptionist who barely glanced at it.

"This person has LifeHealth Insurance. We don't take that. Where were you during orientation, outer space?" She returned the chart to Mila, who realized her mouth was literally hanging open. She didn't expect special treatment as a doctor, but she did expect at least a token effort to be made on behalf of her patient. Besides, she thought, during orientation I *was* back from outer space. So, there.

"Well, Ms. Hardy," she said, reading from Ms. Hardy's name plate, "how do you suggest I proceed with my patient, who is now down the hall, writhing in pain? Shall I tell her that the department of radiology sends its regards and suggests she take two aspirins and quit whining?"

Ms. Hardy gave her a thin smile, then reached under the desk. With both hands she hefted a frayed and dog-eared Manhattan Yellow Pages, and plunked the tome down in front of Mila. "You can tell your patient that Ms. Hardy said she should get a doctor who's ready to grow up and understand the radiology department at Eastside. And let her fingers do the walking. I'm sure somewhere there's a radiology department hard up enough to take LifeHealth."

Having recovered from radiology's warm reception, Mila started going through the yellow pages and tried the closest facility: "Is this the radiology center? I would like to send a patient for a—"

The voice on the other end sounded bored. "Call back tomorrow. We close at 6:00."

"It's only 5:55," Mila pleaded, but the line was already dead. Click.

Mila sat at her station, flummoxed. Luckily, Susanna Wu was going down the hall, and Mila was able to flag her. "Susanna," she said, and told the whole story. If she had expected sympathy, however, it was absent. Susanna just nodded briskly. "I think Sisters of Mercy takes that lousy insurance. But, Mila, I'm surprised you don't already seem to know what I'm about to tell you."

Mila snapped into focus, preparing for a reprimand about her clinical response to the abdominal mass.

"Mila, you should know that the only way the hospital will do this is if it is an emergency. You have to buff the chart. 'Acute abdomen,' 'impending shock,' that kind of thing usually works. No hospital lawyer wants to see those on a deposition."

"But," Mila burst, "all I want is a CT scan on this poor lady in room six. Why is that so difficult?"

"It's not difficult," said Susanna. "It's just managed care. Call it an emergency and don't worry about it. That's the only way the test will get done within the next two weeks."

Mila was not in the least surprised to be engulfed by White.

"I'm glad you're here, Ajax," she said angrily. "I've been wondering about the exact definition of Managed Care. But first I'd better warn you—I'm mad, confused, and tired. I can't be held responsible for the safety of anyone in my non-corporeal reality."

"'Managed care,'" responded Ajax, obviously reading an official definition. "'Managed care is the means by which medical care is delivered in a quality, cost effective, efficient manner.'" Ajax paused, and Mila heard a telepathic rustling of pages. "Bullshit, Ajax." Whoops, Mila thought, I guess I let that one slip. Ajax continued, briefly acknowledging the interruption, "No, I don't see the word 'bullshit' in this connection. Shall we move on?"

"Sure, Ajax," she said. But then, all of a sudden, she was thoroughly confused. Dr. Jill Reston, the family doc from the IPA meeting, was standing before her in the White. "What are you doing in here?"

As rapidly, Dr. Reston vanished and was replaced by Ajax, shaking both of his heads. "Don't you recognize a holographic image yet? My, my, Mila."

So today I've been called naive in both realities, thought Mila. Peachy.

The image of Dr. Reston reappeared, but frozen. "Mila," Ajax said, "this holographic image has the knowledge of a finance guru; it is programmed to teach you about the financial aspects of managed care. Family doctors are responsible for administering the financial aspects of the capitated system, so

I took the liberty of shaping the holograph in the image of a family doctor. I thought it would make your lesson more . . . piquant."

"When I want piquant I'll—oh, never mind." Mila was tired of wasting her best sarcasm on Ajax. "Go ahead, Ajax, wind her up."

CHAPTER 19

MARKET FORCES AND THE SHAPE OF HEALTH CARE INSTITUTIONS

SIX MARKET DRIVERS

THE AMERICAN HEALTH care delivery system has reinvented itself in recent years. Power has moved from individual to group providers due to the pressure to manage the cost of care more effectively. Doctors, insurance providers, and patients are having to function together and share goals and incentives. Many reasons exist for these dramatic changes; however, according to Roger Taylor and Leeba Lessin in an article in *Journal of Health Care Finance*, the most significant of these causes are economic in nature and specifically attributable to free market competition. Taylor and Lessin suggest six major

causes of these changes which are described in the following pages.[1]

Aggregation of Financial Accountability

Capitation, the system by which the provider receives a set payment per plan-holder per month, gives providers financial stake in their clinical outcomes. Often, Taylor and Lessin explain, the capitation is paid to an organized group of physicians and represents prepayment for much of a plan-holder's potential health care needs. In those cases, capitation rewards groups able to organize and manage care effectively—and then gives them the capital to improve even more.

141

In systems that use capitation, the primary care physician (PCP) usually acts as the central coordinator, weighing the relative values of each therapy or component of care. According to Taylor and Lessin, the decision to use a certain therapy, medical service, or procedure is based on each patient's condition, history, and the desired outcome. However, capitation discourages isolated decisions. It gives incentives for providers to consider "the spectrum of their assigned population's health care and prevention needs, and [to] allocate resources to maximize the value delivered."[2]

Competition from Other Delivery Systems and Health Plans

In pursuit of administrative efficiency, product diversity, and market share, many insurers and health plans have recently consolidated. Mergers and acquisitions "have increased the number of giant plans, many of which may have millions of members nationally."[3]

Taylor and Lessin explain that this consolidation has resulted in the development of IPAs, large medical groups, and other systems of care which can serve—or defend themselves against—these huge clusters with great purchasing power. In California, "there are a number of 'mega' medical groups, each serving between 100,000 and 300,000

managed care members under capitated arrangements."[4]

These networks, as they have grown, have created competition among medical groups and not just the plans themselves. Taylor and Lessin suggest that the resources and capabilities of both the providers and the plans are needed to succeed in this market. The groups gaining the market share are those who have understood that and have joined the health plan and delivery system components of managed care.

"In more mature markets, consolidation has resulted in a relatively small number of health plans holding the majority of managed care market share."[5] In those markets, cost is no longer the major differentiation between providers and plans. Instead, choices are based on delivery systems, service, and quality, and the focus must be on the same in order to be successful in the market.

Purchasers, or patients, now evaluate such values as quality, satisfaction, and efficiency. This fact, claims Taylor and Lessin, forces health plans and delivery systems to "prove their own worth by these new and evolving criteria"; the cost and effort of doing so has increased even further the attractiveness of consolidation.[6]

Providers, spurred on by competition, try to be more efficient in the delivery of care while still meeting or exceeding the quality criteria of other groups. Taylor and Lessin report that studies show wide differences in the levels of utilization and cost between top- and lower-performing medical groups but little difference in the outcomes. The top-performing groups, then, can provide care at less cost with higher member satisfaction and equivalent outcomes.

> As consolidation continues, it is these high performers that will be best able to absorb isolated medical practices, weak IPAs, and other medical groups—both because of their ability to bring capital and valuable know-how to these practices, and because health plans will be more comfortable moving members into these successful structures.[7]

Focus on Membership and Profitability Versus Revenue

With the prepayment system, it is in everyone's best interest to keep patients healthy and happy longer. Without appropriate care, a sick patient would cost more long-term, and an unhappy patient would find another provider, taking the capitation along. Additionally, according to Taylor and Lessin, new members bring high costs—either with initial need for services or preventive education—and if they leave early, that money is wasted.

Taylor and Lessin contend that the success of a capitated medical group depends on its revenue and cost, its number of members, and the longevity of its membership. It must provide service economically and in a way that satisfies and retains members.

This demands a very different delivery system than that of the fee-for-service system. The old system focused on units of service delivered and the fee-for-service value of those units. It required groups to base distinctions between specialty groups, partners, or departments on their relative levels of revenue generation.

That thinking must be abandoned if a group is to flourish in the capitated system. Says Taylor and Lessin, "capitated medical groups must focus on meeting the market's demand for customer service, prevention, and quality health care, while still generating a profit (or reasonable income) from their capitation payments."[8]

Requirements for Capital

It is the unpredictable market that determines the value of health care services and, therefore, the financial destiny of the provider. The delivery system of the late nineties must be much more flexible and market-driven than in the past, ready to increase or decrease either costs (including physician pay) or any of a range of services, as the market demands. It must be prepared to position and package its services in ways that will attract and hold market share. All of this, explains Taylor and Lessin, requires leadership and capital.

"Zeroing down," that is, distributing annual profits rather than reinvesting them in the practice, has long been common practice for physicians in partnerships, group practices, and IPAs. "Today's market, however, demands investment in both infrastructure and capacity."[9] Physicians can no longer focus only on their short-term interests as individuals; they must now consider how the practice as a whole will be affected long-term.

No longer can individual patient visits be considered just that. Instead, they are one event in a continuum that has long-lasting effects for both the physician and the group. Accordingly, capitated payments for presently low-cost members must be treated as both revenue and a reserve against future costs.

Further, Taylor and Lessin give some areas in which it is crucial to invest: the upgrading of information systems and electronic data for greater efficiencies and decision support in both administration and health care; the expansion of capacity to serve more patients; and, "depending on the medical group, the ability to capitalize expenditures on satellite offices, medical equipment, and other acquisitions or consolidations to position the organization for future growth."[10]

Most health plans make multi-year investment decisions. They also try to form partnerships with medical groups who will invest in market share and service improvement. "Fortunately for medical groups, good long-term capitated contracts with a growing managed care organization can not only help increase the value of the group, they can improve their access to the capital needed to prepare for the future."[11]

Consolidation of Purchasers

Purchasers, both employer groups and individual consumers, have also increased their influence through aggregation. Many states, for example, have Health Insurance Purchasing Cooperatives (HIPCs) that provide private insurance for guaranteed rates to small employers and the self-employed. In California, the Pacific Business Group on Health represents twenty-one large employers; CalPERS, a giant pension conglomerate of public employees, has forced plans to reduce premiums significantly.[12]

Large numbers of purchasers have propelled the development of "mega" medical groups, and it is on these groups that the purchasers now depend. According to Taylor and Lessin, mega groups expand rapidly, provide service to new members and in new locations, and promote efficiency. This results in lower premium levels, improved administrative capabilities and service, and higher expectations by consumers, leading to continuing competition and consolidation.

Supply and Demand Issues Related to the Provider Pool

"Estimates regarding the oversupply of specialists vary; that there is an oversupply is uncontested."[13] Market forces dictate, then, that health care dollars be drawn from hospital and specialty care and invested in primary care. Taylor and Lessin claim that the long-term success of delivery systems will depend on such measures.

It will be to no one's surprise then that this redistribution has generated a struggle amongst physicians, hospitals, health plans, and payer-led groups. In capitation arrangements, the central managers of health care costs are (usually) PCPs, and it is around these providers that medical groups, hospitals, and staff model HMOs must align. Indeed, in the areas of both cash compensation and decision-making power, the bidding up for primary physicians is well underway.

While it is understandable that efforts would be made to keep traditional methods in the areas of money and services, it will not work. Taylor and Lessin claim that it is crucial for traditional hospital and specialty leadership to recognize that they should "take advantage of these supply and demand changes [and use] current revenue to fund early restructuring for future success . . ."[14]

SIX ADDITIONAL FACTORS

There are six factors that help shape the response of delivery systems to the six drivers previously mentioned.[15]

Change from Single Patient Encounter to Customer Service Approach

In today's health care system, doctors must be concerned about the impression they make and how and who that impression affects and not just the clinical quality of an appointment with an individual patient. Members evaluate their providers on more topics than competency—range of services, cost issues, and even their length of wait for an appointment. As a result, in this competitive market, the patient's opinion must be respected. Taylor and Lessin suggest that programs to promote prevention, visible efforts to keep patients happy, and genuine concern for their well-being are successful in retaining members.

Purchaser Demand for Cost Control, Data, and Accountability

Taylor and Lessin contend that providers who decline to be accountable for clinical or financial outcomes, or who are unable to measure their medical value compromise their chances to prosper. Such providers are unlikely to be given their desired clinical autonomy or opportunities to grow.

> The increasing demands from purchasers for report cards on quality, the growth in the number of clinical practice guidelines, and the availability of sophisticated information systems to measure quality of care and service levels, are forcing physicians and hospitals to share both administrative and clinical data for the greater good of the integrated system and, not incidentally, the patient population as a whole.[16]

The provider delivery systems, then, that will be successful are those that will be both accountable and able to demonstrate it.

Health Plan Requirements and Needs

The health of a health plan depends on its ability to deliver what its customers want, to differentiate their network and services from competitors, and to lower overall costs. In a number of ways, health plans depend on their providers to help accomplish these ends for their mutual good.

Most health plans, for example, require providers to assume some financial risk. This gives physicians economic stake in keeping costs low, in dispensing resources appropriately, and in maintaining the good health of members.

Health plans need to know that their PCPs and medical groups support managed care views, in general, and are willing to reduce medical costs and supply information needed to improve the delivery system as a whole. Additionally, plans expect their medical groups to be flexible and willing to expand quickly as needed to serve new members.

Most of all, plans need physicians and hospitals to practice quality care and provide good service to members. As educated consumers, members are likely to change plans if they don't get what they perceive is their due.[17]

Provider Demand for a Level of Autonomy

Physicians have been accustomed to their independence when it comes to their practice, and they object to losing the control of decisions for patient care. There has been, in the recent past, then, tension between health care providers and plans, which at times try to "micromanage clinical decisions from afar . . ."[18]

In mature managed care markets, however, Taylor and Lessin explain that a more business-like arrangement seems to be arising. Individual providers are learning that health plans can provide important medical management support, and plans are recognizing that patient satisfaction as well as long-term relationships are improved when they listen to physicians' concerns and allow them to direct patient care.

It is the joining of financial and service incentives that eventually encourage the move from confrontation to collaboration. In other words, in these situations, when the plan is successful so are the providers, and vice-versa.

Taylor and Lessin further explain that this alignment of incentives requires individual providers to "participate in large medical delivery systems that can assume accountability for managing a capitated population of members."[19] Clinical decisions, therefore, are partially made by the physician leadership and the medical care committees of the network or group.

Technological Change

As medical technology has boomed, there has been an overuse of some diagnostic and other procedures that are not always necessary. A thoughtful approach to technology may lead some groups to no longer depend on their expensive medical equipment. When an expensive new technology would clearly add value to the clinical setting, Taylor and Lessin explain that providers might consider outsourcing the service or even joining with competing groups to share purchase.

"Information systems are one of the most important technological facilitators of change, enabling the dream of integrated and accountable systems to become a reality."[20] When these systems are used, and emerging technology focuses on cost-effective results, patients will benefit. The delivery systems that result will be "accountable for the care they deliver, and laboratories for tomorrow's improved health care protocols and technology."[21]

Regulatory Environment

State and federal regulations can greatly impact the changes in health care. Legislation, for example, that limits health plan benefits, physician pay, and the ability of the purchasers to consolidate can slow the changes in delivery systems. "Likewise, competition between providers will be reduced by strong certificate-of-need controls over capacity expansion, all-payer pricing systems, or a lack of anti-trust enforcement in provider consolidation."[22]

Regardless however of regulations or ownership, all is in place for health care to become accountable delivery systems. The most successful health plans, claim Taylor and Lessin, will probably be "consolidators and facilitators of multiple accountable delivery systems over broad geographic areas."[23] All developing delivery systems should prepare for that eventuality despite mission or ownership.

SUMMARY OF DRIVERS AND FACTORS

The major factors producing change in the American health care delivery system have operated as a distinct sequence of events.

> Each factor—whether it is capitation, controls on unit pricing, high levels of purchaser and plan expectation, or emerging capabilities of information technology—has a domino effect, toppling long-held convictions about the traditional way to deliver care and allowing much more elastic, and interconnected, delivery systems to emerge.[24]

These changes have affected different geographic areas and different components of health care at varying speeds. The response in the delivery system design has also differed greatly. The underlying catalysts, however, must be considered.

ADVANTAGED TACTICS FOR PHYSICIAN COMPENSATION

Primary Care Physicians

Compensating PCPs for maximum efficiencies within a delivery system can be achieved in several ways. According to Taylor and Lessin, some protection may be required when capitated membership is small and when access to reinsurance is limited. "In all these models, incentives could partially lead to quality and service indicators in addition to the strong financial incentives inherent in the models."[25] The models are provided by The Advisory Board.

> Full personal capitation model: Individual PCPs receive capitated payments to cover all professional service (including specialist) costs. To mitigate the possibility of PCPs underusing specialists and to lessen risk exposure, this model must include particularly strong quality controls and a higher level of stop-loss protection than group capitation models.
>
> Entrepreneurial medical group model: Physicians receive a

modest salary supplemented by a large annual bonus (as much as two-fifths to two-thirds of their total cash compensation) based on group profits and personal productivity.

Pod-level risk pool model: A number of PCPs receive a collective risk pool based on a budget for the population assigned to them. The risk pool covers professional costs and may also include capitation or risk-sharing for other downstream costs (hospital stays, mental health care, pharmacy, etc.).

Fee schedule indexing model: Fee schedules are fixed according to an individual physician's cost performance as compared to his or her peers; PCPs with relatively high downstream costs experience fee reduction, and the entire group is reduced if budget is exceeded. Some might call this thinly disguised fee-for-service medicine—it is certainly the least efficient of these advantaged models.[26]

Specialists

Specialty services can receive capitation in several ways. The specialty capitation or prepayment usually applies to professional services within that specialty for a certain length of time. It may also cover many affiliated costs. Taylor and Lessin explain that an orthopedist, for example, might receive capitation for physical therapy, prescription drugs, and rehabilitation services for a six-month period. The actual dollars capitated can be determined by experience, other similar practices, or by the number of full-time specialists required to care for the patient base, regardless of how many specialists are on the staff of the capitated group.[27]

Contact capitation: A capitated budget for a particular specialty is divided among the specialists within a group (or a limited network of groups) for each referral received.

Department capitation, Equal Distribution: Each specialist of a particular specialty within a group receives an equal share of a capitated budget for that specialty, assuming that they will also share the responsibility equally.

Department capitation, production-determined distribution: A capitated budget for a given specialty is divided among individual specialists in proportion to billings submitted. This is again fee-for-service medicine disguised as a form of managed care.[28]

Endnotes

1. Roger Taylor, and Leeba Lessin, "Restructuring the health care delivery system in the United States," *Journal of Health Care Finance* 22 (Summer 1996): 33–60.

2. Ibid., 34.

3. Ibid.

4. Ibid.

5. Ibid.

6. Ibid.

7. Ibid., 35.

8. Ibid.

9. Ibid., 36.

10. Ibid.

11. Ibid.

12. Ibid.

13. Ibid., 37.

14. Ibid., 38.

15. Ibid., 38–41.

16. Ibid., 38–39.

17. Ibid., 39.

18. Ibid.

19. Ibid., 40.

20. Ibid.

21. Ibid., 41.

22. Ibid.

23. Ibid.

24. Ibid., 42.

25. Ibid., 56.

26. The Advisory Board, *To the Greater Good: Recovering the American Physician Enterprise* (Washington, D.C.: The Governance Committee, 1995): 132; and Roger Taylor and Leeba Lessin, 56–57.

27. Roger Taylor and Leeba Lessin, 57.

28. The Advisory Board, 133; and Roger Taylor and Leeba Lessin, 57.

CHAPTER 20

OF CARIBBEAN VACATIONS AND CONTINGENCY FEES

IT WAS A CRISP, AUTUMN-IN-NEW YORK DAY. The sky was deep blue; the leaves crunched on the sidewalk underfoot; and Mila had never felt blearier in her life. Her head always ached from fatigue, her limbs were always heavy-feeling from lack of exercise, and she'd gotten zits again for the first time in, well, six years by one count, more than twenty by the other. She took great gulps of the chilly air. There were twenty minutes until her next case in the OR, and if this walk was going to clear her head, it had to start working now.

Mila headed down Avenue A. A waist-high witch was walking with her mother, eating a donut with orange icing and candy corn on top. It's almost Halloween, Mila realized with a shock. While she was existing in the closed universe of residency, there was a real world out here, with seasons marching along and life progressing normally. She found that incredibly depressing.

"*Hey, Ajax!*" she called telepathically. "*You around? Feel like shedding those six hands and gills, and taking me out for a little virtual-reality, holographic Caribbean vacation?*" Wow, she thought, this time to herself, I could be gone for a month and still be back in for sign out rounds in the emergency room! I don't know why I didn't think of this before!"

151

No White appeared, but Ajax's voice filled Mila's head. *"Mila, it almost sounds like you are beginning to tolerate me. Maybe even like me."*

"Don't get too excited," Mila grinned. "My dating history might not be stellar, but I do insist on single heads and human genitalia. Let's go."

Nothing happened. No white sand, no palm trees, no drinks bristling with paper umbrellas. *"Hey Ajax, for once I'm ready. Teach me something and I'll buy you a piña colada. Come on!"*

"Mila." She didn't know how she knew, but she knew Ajax was feeling uncomfortable. *"I can't do it. I've just consulted Quam, and he's told me that such things are clearly forbidden by Section 33.9, Clause 88, Paragraph 9 of the—"*

"—'Never Cut Mila a Break' Code? Go away, Ajax," Mila thought acidly. "Shit!" she said aloud and kicked a flattened paper cup into the gutter.

"Mila, I'd do it if I could," Ajax thought into her.

"Go away," she ordered, then muttered to herself, "Now I'm getting rejected by alien abductors. Is this rock bottom, or what?"

It was time to turn around when she saw she'd made it all the way to the playground at Thompkins Square Park. There was a sign that said the playground was only for children and their guardians, so she stayed out but looked in through the gate. If Ajax were going to abandon her in her time of need, she would have to resort to human means, like getting a dose of normal, healthy life.

There was the little witch she'd seen before, sliding down a molded plastic slide. Her mother stood and watched, just on the other side of the bars from Mila.

"Cute costume," Mila said. "It's nice to see them all dressed up."

The mother looked over her shoulder at Mila, decided she wasn't a psychopath, and replied. "Thanks," she said. "Yeah, Brittany's cute. She's got her problems, though, believe me. Gets hyper cause she's sort of ADD."

"Oh," said Mila, a little startled by this confidence. "Uh, sorry."

"It's OK," said the mother. "Actually it's fine. It's not that big a deal, but it's enough so we can sue my OB's ass and pay for Brittany's college, or whatever."

Mila asked carefully, "I don't know much about that, but how do you know it's your OB's fault?"

"Well," the mother said, watching Brittany tear around, "when they tested her for kindergarten they told me she had this slight learning disability, right?

I was upset, right? Crying. Then there was this ad on for a law firm with free consultations. You know, 'if your child is less than perfect, YOU may be in for a huge cash reward!' I called and the lawyer saw me the next day. He got the records, and it turns out the case is so tight that he isn't even going to charge me unless he wins the case."

"Yes," said Mila, although she didn't really know why she was pursuing this. "But what did the doctor do wrong?"

"I'm not sure, but it must have been something really bad if the lawyer's willing to not charge me. He's even going to talk to our whole learning disability support group."

Mila's stomach turned at the thought of a plaintiff's attorney foaming at the mouth before a group of "less than perfect" children and their parents. She opened her mouth to tell this mother that she'd been duped when all was White.

"If this has nothing to do with St. Thomas you'd better get out of here, Ajax."

"Mila, I'm sorry again. But this is more important. Trust me. First, I must show you this." Mila's shoulders suddenly sagged under the weight of a large, heavy bar.

"What the hell is this, Ajax, some Climaran torture device? Get it off."

"That," said Ajax, "is the yoke of malpractice for physicians in the twenty-first century. Although I'm now making you aware of it, I did not put it there and I cannot remove it."

"You've never been at a loss for solutions before, Ajax. Come on, what's my move here?"

"The best I can do is to help make it more manageable. Have a seat."

All at once Mila was sunk deeply in a leather chair in a tastefully appointed office with Berber carpet and fresh flowers. Across a desk, facing Mila, sat a well-tended, serious-looking woman in her fifties, dressed in a dark suit. "You need some legal advice, I understand," she said.

CHAPTER 21

LAW AND MEDICINE

IF A PHYSICIAN, WITH acts not concordant with professional standards, causes injury or death in a patient, it is considered medical malpractice.

Both withholding appropriate treatment and giving inappropriate treatment comprise a defiance of standards—"standards" being those generally used by teaching institutions, professional associations, and state licensing boards to determine negligence[1] (medical experts are usually deferred to regarding specifics). Plaintiffs in medical malpractice suits must prove that there was a "duty of care," that there was a breach of that duty, that there was injury, and "proximate cause."[2]

Medical malpractice cases often have their roots in miscommunication—not just between doctor and patient but also among consulting physicians, health care providers, and even office staff. Questions of documentation, confidentiality, telemedicine, informed consent, modification of biomedical equipment, managed care, and ethics[3] also frequently arise.

High-risk specialists such as obstetricians, surgeons, and anesthesiologists are confronted more frequently with medical malpractice lawsuits than their lower-risk colleagues, but 40 percent of all physicians have been sued at least once.[4] Malpractice claims have risen steadily over the last decade. This has affected

154

both the cost of malpractice insurance and the style of care physicians deliver.

The practice of defensive medicine is no longer the exception but the rule. The pervasive threat of malpractice suits has pushed most doctors into a preference for erring on the side of caution; to protect themselves, they order unnecessary tests, procedures, and medications. This, in turn, drives up medical costs overall and feeds the growth in claims and insurance premiums.[5]

Seventy percent of malpractice claims are dismissed or dropped before they get to court, but even a case that doesn't reach court costs the insurance carrier an average of $10,900. A case that goes to trial averages a cost of $100,000.[6]

The differential in cost between trying a case and settling is so sharp that many malpractice insurance companies push for settlement regardless of case specifics—it is more efficient to settle than to mount a defense. The resulting settlements may cut costs for the insurance companies, but can prove very costly to physicians. The damage to a doctor's reputation and career can be severe even if a case goes to trial and the doctor wins—much less if s/he's perceived to have admitted fault by settling.

Further, the insurance companies take a managed care approach to the situation and capitate the amount they spend on legal defense. This creates a conflict of interest; it makes lawyers responsible to the insurance companies that pay the bills rather than to the physicians whom the lawyers defend.[7] This approach keeps lawyers from providing physicians with the best representation.

LEGAL IMPLICATIONS OF ALTERNATIVE MEDICINE

A relatively new source of medical malpractice claims is alternative medicine. Alternative medicine is defined as "those treatments and health care practices not taught widely in medical schools, not generally used in hospitals, and not usually reimbursed by medical insurance companies."[8] Alternative therapy is that which takes the place of mainstream care, and "complementary" therapies are those which are administered in conjunction with a doctor's treatment. Complementary therapies run the risk of becoming alternative when they replace traditional therapies completely.[9]

The growth in importance of alternative medicine has been spurred, in part, by managed care and its stringent limits on patients, institutions, and providers. It is sometimes in order to avoid such limits and to regain a sense of control of their health care, that patients turn to homeopathy, acupuncture, massage therapy, mind-body treatments, and a plethora of other practices.

Many primary care providers are uncomfortable recommending such treatments to their patients and find themselves in the precarious position of mediating between their own medical opinions and the patient's prerogatives. The practices that are considered "alternative" are loosely regulated, and the providers, such as chiropractors, acupuncturists, nutritionists, and massage therapists, are often not licensed according to the same rigorous standards as physicians. This is a source of worry to primary care providers, as is the real possibility that they will not be provided with complete information if their patients do undergo such therapies.

This caution is well placed. Direct or vicarious liability can be applied to a clinic which employs a negligent provider or a physician who refers a patient to one.[10] A patient can seek alternative care regardless of medical advice, but the primary care provider may be held responsible for a neglected medical condition—if, for instance, a patient foregoes traditional treatment while receiving alternative therapy. Ultimately, it is the doctor's responsibility to inform the patient about the validity of alternative treatments and to follow up on existing conditions.[11]

The increase in the popularity of such treatments, especially among patients with chronic illness, has brought the American Medical Association to the conclusion that doctors are obliged to inquire whether patients are using alternative medicine therapies.[12] A physician is well advised to follow the AMA's recommendation. Inquire whether a patient has been treated by an alternative practitioner and take that information into account when prescribing a course of treatment. Take seriously the effect that alternative therapy can have on a patient and keep meticulous records in cases where medical advice is not being followed.

MANAGED CARE

As physicians and insurers incorporate under managed care organizations, cost and quality concerns are often brought into conflict: financial considerations have come to limit the variety of technology and treatments available to patients. Although reports of lawsuits against providers on the basis of rationing access (for example to specific drugs) are, as yet, few; there are important considerations to make when consciously limiting a patient's treatment for the purpose of limiting costs.[13]

The problems stemming from conflict of interest between quality and cost can originate not only with practitioners but also with the hospitals and integrated health care delivery systems with which the practitioners may be affiliated. These organizations often control the type and variety of treatment available, which complicates the issues of responsibility and liability. A doctor may or may not be partially responsible for neglect resulting from such externally imposed limits.

The AMA Council on Ethical and Judicial Affairs, in 1995, published an ethics standard for physicians who find themselves in rationing situations. They recommend that physicians take the advocacy role for their patients and abstain from making actual allocation decisions. Patients should be informed of the allocation criteria, as well as the degree of possibility of receiving access to scarce resources. According to the AMA, the patient-doctor relationship should take precedence over any responsibility the doctor has to his/her management organization.[14] This has become a rallying issue for many physician groups, especially as it relates to hold harmless clauses. These and other regulations often force physicians to make choices that pit patient care against financial reality. In making such choices, however, the physician runs the risk of being deselected by the management organization.[15]

Although the insurers' domination of health care delivery is on the increase, the ultimate decision making remains a matter of ethical judgment on the part of the physician alone. Informed consent laws do provide some guidance about the information that must be disclosed to the patient, but ultimate liability resulting from rationing has yet to be determined.

INFORMED CONSENT

Another legal issue facing physicians is that of informed consent. Legal action can be taken if a patient feels s/he was not properly informed about the prescribed treatment—its risks or its alternatives. Informed consent has a clear legal definition, but at its core are ethical issues that become complicated when applied to doctor-patient interaction.[16] Issues of informed consent can be particularly important in cases where alternative therapy has been sought despite the physician's advice.[17]

The precaution against such cases is requiring patients to sign informed consent forms upon arrival at the hospital, emergency room, surgery, or even the doctor's office. Such forms verify that the patient is fully informed and consents to treatment, accepting full responsibility for the decision.

It is a myth, however, that a signed form—especially a generic one—always protects a physician from liability. In reality, there are situations in which the form provides only the illusion of protection. The law calls for a "reasonable" amount of information to be disclosed. Although this is an arbitrary definition determinable only in context of the medical profession as a whole, an individual doctor's judgment, brought to bear on a specific case, usually suffices to determine an appropriate amount of information to disclose.

A further complication is that patients often resist discussions about potential, rare complications. They ask dismissive questions: "but everything will be OK, right?"; "I know you have to say those things, but that doesn't really happen very often, does it?" Consumers are as ambivalent about informed consent as they are about managed care in general. Most people want managed care for everyone but themselves and their families—similarly, although patients as a consumer group speak of the need for complete informed consent, a scared individual about to undergo surgery often is looking for some old-fashioned reassurance.

Some consent forms are self-defeating in their complexity. A Penn State College of Medicine study found that most hospital forms require at least a high school education, and approximately 25 percent require several years of a college education to ensure proper comprehension. These forms also often lacked enough specific information about individual patients.

The best forms in this and other regards were found to be ones customized by the physician.[18] A customized consent form that describes possible complications and alternatives can absolve a physician of liability in the event of a bad outcome—it shows the individual patient was carefully prepared for the possibility and consented regardless.[19] Not only that, but the very act of customizing may force the physician to consider the individual patient just enough to prevent a bad outcome in the first place.

Standards of informed consent have been challenged recently by limitations imposed by managed care. There are situations in which economic factors influence the types of treatment from which a patient can choose and do so in a way that goes against the physician's best judgment. "Clinical path models" implemented by managed care consortia to streamline care can contradict the idea of voluntariness implicit in the doctrine of informed consent.[20]

Informed consent is a process of shared decision making and should be carried out as such to avoid miscommunication. In judging the amount of information a patient needs to make an autonomous decision, the doctor must take the patient's lead. Doctors run into trouble when they presume their patients are intellectually or emotionally unprepared to handle information; in such situations, doctors may dictate a decision an informed patient might not have made. In the end, informed consent comes down to the kind of respect for the patient's autonomy and the doctor's expertise that develops from a close doctor-patient relationship.

ADVANCE DIRECTIVES AND MEDICAL FUTILITY

Advance directives, which can have a drastic effect on the course of treatment a physician follows, are issued most often by terminally ill patients. The directives can involve everything from Do Not Resuscitate orders to powers of attorney.

The legal issues underlying advance directives are similar to those of informed consent—both are intended to give the patient the power of determining his or her own course of treatment. Two Supreme Court decisions, *In re: Quinlan* and *Cruzan v. Director, Missouri Department of Health*, have outlined the right of patients to refuse treatment, even in life or death circumstances.[21]

This has created tension between physicians' traditional responsibility

to preserve lives (beneficence) and patients' rights to limit their own care (autonomy). In order to reconcile these contradictions in judgment, Death and Dignity Acts have been enacted to legalize and formalize the use of advance directives. These measures usually require the patient to design a document which instructs the doctor regarding which measures are to be taken and which avoided, if the patient cannot be consulted. These documents also must authorize a specific person who may make decisions for the patient under such circumstances. In order to validate such a document, the patient must meet a variety of criteria, including age and competency.[22]

The main responsibility of the physician in these cases is to carry out the wishes of his or her patient. If there are ethical dilemmas preventing the provider from carrying out the advance directives, they should be discussed with the patient or his/her next of kin. Blatant disregard of advance directives can be construed as malpractice in itself. A doctor treating a terminally ill patient should initiate a conversation about the end-of-life decision-making process in order to avoid providing excessive or inadequate care when the patient can no longer make decisions regarding his/her treatment.[23]

Parallel to the issues of informed consent and advance directives is the issue of medical futility—the use of technology to prolong a patient's life without his or her awareness. These cases occur most often in cases where the patient's prognosis is Persistent Vegetative State (PVS) with no possibility of recovery. In this case, family members usually consent to keeping the patient on life support. Doctors in such situations can be blamed for inaccurate prognoses that encourage family members to maintain hope while the doctors experiment with new life-prolonging technologies.[24]

SOME GENERAL PRECAUTIONS

Too often, doctors suffer devastating consequences from a case dropped shortly after having been filed. These problems usually result from the doctor discussing the case with colleagues and even with acquaintances. It is then quickly apparent how fast word travels and how damaging a public accusation can be.[25] A doctor served with a complaint should keep the matter to himself, his liability carrier, and his attorney.

Other precautions against malpractice claims can be taken with the help of information systems. Integrated records and databases can cut down on diagnostic errors and can reduce instances of inappropriate medical treatment or administration of medications due to incomplete medical histories, missed appointments, or administrative errors.[26]

Being prepared for a malpractice suit is important. Unfamiliarity with proper procedures often leads doctors to make damaging mistakes in the first days after they have been notified of a claim. Having a relationship established with an attorney ahead of time can prevent an unwanted settlement by the insurance company.

Endnotes

1. Alan Dumoff, *Malpractice Liability of Alternative/ Complementary Health Care Providers: A View from the Trenches* (www.healthy.net/public/legal—lg/medmalpr/dumoff.htm).

2. Ruslan Novik, and Ryan Waite, *Medical Malpractice* (http://www.bus./med.htm).

3. Robert F. Pendrak, "Top Ten Issues in Medical Malpractice," *Medical Practice Communicator* (1997) (www.medscape.com/HMI/MPCommunicator/1997/v04.n05/mpc0405.10.pend.html).

4. Evelyn Bradford, "Just Got Hit with a Malpractice Threat? Cool It!" *Medical Economics* (11 May 1998): 99.

5. Ruslan Novik and Ryan Waite, *Medical Malpractice*.

6. 1995 Statistics according to Berkley Rice, "Will Your Malpractice

Insurer Stifle Your Defense?" *Medical Economics* (12 January 1998).

7. Ibid.

8. Robyn A. Meinhardt, Clare Richardson, and Paula Ohliger, "Alternative Medicine and Pharmacist's Counseling Obligations," *Drug Benefit Trends* 10, no. 2 (1998): 24, 28.

9. Barrie R. Cassileth, "Complementary and Alternative Medicine: Separating the Wheat from the Chaff," *Medical Practice Communicator* 5, no. 1 (1998): 3.

10. Alan Dumoff, *Malpractice Liability of Alternative/ Complementary Health Care Providers.*

11. Lee Johnson, "Malpractice Consult," *Medical Economics* (11 May 1998).

12. Robyn A. Meinhardt, et al., "Alternative Medicine and Pharmacist's Counseling Obligations," 24, 28.

13. Nancy E. Cahill, "Cost Effectiveness Analyses: Legal and Ethical Issues," *Drug Benefit Trends* 10, no. 2 (1998): 31–36.

14. Ibid.

15. Richard Liner, "Physician Deselection: The Dynamics of a New Threat to the Physician-Patient Relationship," *American Journal of Law and Medicine* (22 December 1997).

16. Alan Meisel and Mark Kuczewski, "Legal and Ethical Myths about Informed Consent," *Archives of Internal Medicine* (9–23 December 1996).

17. Alan Dumoff, *Malpractice Liability of Alternative/ Complementary Health Care Providers.*

18. *Hospital Consent Forms Found to Be Too Complicated* (www. medscape. com/ Medscape Wire/ 1999/06.98/news.0610.hospital.html).

19. Alan Meisel and Mark Kuczewski, "Legal and Ethical Myths about Informed Consent."

20. Kimberly Strom-Gottfried, "Informed Consent Meets Managed Care," *Health and Social Work* (1 February 1998).

21. Steven R. Permut, "Advance Directives: Physicians' Rights and Responsibilities," *Hospital Medicine* 34, no. 3 (1998): 21–22, 24, 29–30.

22. Ibid.

23. Ibid.

24. James Reitman, "The Dilemma of Medical Futility," *Issues in Law and Medicine* (1 December 1996).

25. Evelyn Bradford, "Just Got Hit with a Malpractice Threat? Cool It!" 99.

26. Ruslan Novik and Ryan Waite, *Medical Malpractice.*

Additional Sources

Feista, Janine. "Legal Aspects of Medication Administration." *Nursing Management* (1 January 1998).

Haron, David. "Waste and Neglect: Fraud and Abuse in the Healthcare Industry." *Health Care Supervisor* (1 June 1998).

Johnson, Lee J. "Avoiding Liability When Closing a Practice." *Medical Economics* (15 June 1998).

Kane, Leslie. "Are There Gaps in Your Malpractice Insurance?" *Medical Economics* (March 23, 1998).

Lown, Bernard. "Physicians Need to Fight the Business Model of Medicine." *Hippocrates*, 12, no. 5 (1998): 25–28.

"Medical Malpractice Awards Double between 1985 and 1995." *Healthcare Financial Management* (October 11, 1997).

Pretzer, Michael. "Will the Big Bad Antitrust Wolf Blow Your IPA Down?" *Medical Economics* (April 7, 1997).

Rice, Berkeley. "Will Your Malpractice Insurer Stifle Your Defense?" *Medical Economics* (January 12, 1998).

Rose, Joan. "A Safe Harbor for Doctors Who Are Falsely Accused?" *Medical Economics* (May 26, 1998).

CHAPTER 22

OF PUMPKINS AND PRIVILEGE

OVER THE RIVER AND THROUGH THE WOODS, MILA WAS DRIVING TO A RITZY RURAL SUBURB OF BOSTON FOR THANKSGIVING. She had always loved this holiday and would love seeing her parents and her brother and—for the first time—her brother's ten-year-old son. How time does fly when you've flown through time, thought Mila, and caught a glimpse of a deer bounding away from her headlights.

New England, though, had always annoyed her. Boston was the hub of the universe in medicine—just ask anyone who trained in Boston. She had to admit, though, that it was a little comforting that something, even in this new world, was stable. She knew the pilgrims landed in Massachusetts. And she knew that, at least academically and on the snob-o-meter, Boston medicine hadn't changed. She had read about the merger of Brigham & Women's with Mass General, and she was comforted to think that culture clash was probably as complex as a Climaran/human intermarriage.

She squinted in the dark at the numbers on the mailboxes. Ah, finally: Number 24, the Hargroves.

The Hargroves were her brother Matt's in-laws, and boy, did they have money. Old money. Matt used to joke that even a two-doctor salary would never support the style of life Liza had grown up with. But it was only in jest; Liza had somehow acquired an easy way of dealing with money. It didn't impress her, and she didn't talk about it.

Mr. Hargrove, Liza's father, talked about it plenty, and seemed to relish confrontation. Mila had spoken with him only once. It was when she was in med school, and the recently engaged Matt and Liza wanted the two families to meet. Mr. Hargrove was not possessed of the famous Yankee reserve, and, although he was in business, he didn't hesitate to share his opinions about medicine. "Hospitals," he had said in 1982, "are the richest, sloppiest wastes of money I've ever seen. Every neighborhood clinic is drooling over having its own CT Scan, even if it will be used once a year. Someone is going to make a fortune snapping these guys out of their dream world." The "kids," Matt, Liza, and Mila, had hung out after the event for hours, dissecting every judgmental comment Mr. Hargrove had spouted. Even Matt, Doctor MBA, thought Mr. Hargrove went too far in using his business principles to condemn medicine. "Some things are sacred," said Matt, and they'd all agreed.

Thanksgiving dinner was predictably fabulous—sparkling antique chandelier, three wines, two maids. To Mila's relief, the Climaran curiosity dampener performed admirably, and she could concentrate on enjoying her family and her "new" nephew, Adam.

"A toast," Mr. Hargrove raised his champagne glass over dessert, "to my son-in-law Matt, and to the Heath Center Multispecialty Group to which he now has brought his considerable talents. Long may he reign!"

"Way to go, Dad," said Adam, a little too vigorously for the dinner table. "Hey, Grandpa Langston, are you going to start being a boss like Grampa Hargrove and Dad? Are you, Aunt Mila?"

Mila's dad chuckled. "We're all very proud of your Dad, Adam, but I think I'll just keep doing what I've always done, seeing patients. I work with some other people, now, but I'm a little old to start being a boss. And as for Aunt Mila, well, I suspect she'll find a way to hold out, too, right honey?"

Before Mila could open her mouth, Hargrove the Meek spoke up, "Adam, your Grandpa Langston is a terrific doctor, and there's no reason he should change his ways. But your Aunt Mila's just starting out, and she's too smart to be one of those whiney, the-world-is-against-us '90's docs." I guess Mr. Hargrove couldn't bear to see everyone agreeing so much, Mila thought.

"*Dad*," said Liza, "why don't you let Mila answer for herself?"

Everyone at the table looked at Mila, who didn't really know what to say. Fifteen years ago she would have taken the bait. She would have said that if business big shots had to deal with what doctors were putting up with today, they would roll over and die. She would have said she hadn't trained to be a business person and didn't want to be one. She would have demanded of Mr. Hargrove, whether, when he was sick, he wanted to see a doctor or an MBA. Mila looked down the table at her family's faces. Her dad looked happily expectant of a mighty defense; her mother, brother, and Liza were bracing themselves for a fight. Adam had lost interest and was molding his pumpkin pie and whipped cream into a volcano.

Mila still thought some things were sacred. But, for the life of her, she was not quite sure *which* things.

She took a long, diplomatic breath. "Look. Practicing medicine is not like selling widgets. We don't need every doctor to be an MD-MBA. But I understand that it frustrates business people that doctors run large practices and refuse to acknowledge that they are really running small businesses. We do have to take the responsibility for totally ignoring the business side of medicine and for allowing third parties to fill the void."

Mila was almost afraid to look at her dad. She didn't want him to take that as a betrayal. She was relieved, however, to see him smiling, as was her mother. "Smart people," said Mila's mother, "know how to make rule changes work in their favor."

"It seems to me," said Mr. Hargrove, who seemed bent on inciting an argument, "that what business people have over physicians has nothing to do with their flexibility or intelligence. It has to do with information systems. If I understand Matt, it took the insurance companies slamming data down your throats and interpreting it poorly for you to realize that you had to get into the data and outcomes game. Bone up on your I.S."

"Well, Dad Hargrove, I don't know that anyone's ready to concede that business people have anything over physicians. But I have to agree with you about I.S. Of course, information systems, in business and medicine, are only as good as the individuals that drive them."

"And physicians have either been too blind or too stupid to do the process reengineering and clinical pathways necessary to make use of the data now available."

"*Dad*." Liza was embarrassed.

Mrs. Hargrove came to her husband's defense. "Liza, dear, your father was smart enough to increase his I.S. budget in the eighties. It's a legitimate point of pride."

"But I have also been proactive enough to see the new paradigms that would be needed as we interpreted that data for the new millennium."

Proactive, paradigm, and millennium in the same sentence, thought Mila. Ladies and gentlemen, it's a world record!

That night at the bed and breakfast that Mila chose to stay at rather than having to tiptoe through the Hargrove's house, she had a quiet conference with Ajax. *"Can I get some info about information systems,"* thought Mila, *"and, while we're at it, about medical process reengineering? I'd like to be prepared for the Hargrove love-fest tomorrow at lunch."*

"Of course, Mila," replied Ajax. *"These are two of the most important subjects you can learn. I give you two experts, one who will speak on the strategic importance of information systems in today's medical environment, and the other who will address you about medical process reengineering and clinical path development."*

CHAPTER 23

INFORMATION SYSTEMS IN THE MEDICAL ENVIRONMENT

REFERENCE INFORMATION

INFORMATION TECHnology has been gradually infiltrating the health care industry throughout the past decade and will surely transform everything from patient records, to reference information, to writing prescriptions in the years to come. Much of the progress so far has been at hospitals, but private clinicians are also beginning to use networks. The decreasing cost of computers has conquered many physicians who were resisting technological advances and has prompted them to invest in information systems.

Electronic access to reference information has been the path of least resistance. Medline and other databases of journal abstracts make it possible for physicians to conduct research from computer terminals in their own offices. Such readily available information allows doctors with busy schedules to keep up with research that might otherwise fall by the wayside in a busy practice. Now, not only medical journals but full medical textbooks are also available on-line.[1]

Sites such as *MD Consult* enhance the internet's application as a reference tool. These sites pool information from a variety of sources, including medical texts, Medline, pharmacological databases, and major research centers. Many of these sites are peer-reviewed to ensure accuracy and legitimacy.[2] A number of the sites are interactive, allowing physicians to customize data quickly to their—or their patients'—needs.

The internet can link together physicians as easily as databases. The University of Washington Medical Center designed the MINDscape information system to provide physicians instant access both to crucial clinical information and to other physicians. This system links over nine thousand clinicians across five states and promotes shared information and decision support.[3]

Access to such vital information has proven useful outside the hospital setting as well. Arranging for patients to use information technology can improve the quality of care in private practice. Primary care physicians often find that the information they impart during an office visit is too extensive and unfocused for a patient to process immediately. It is after the patient has left the office that most questions arise, and it is then that questions can most easily go unanswered. Even a patient sent home with a brochure rarely gets all the answers she needs—published material is static and not tailored to specific individuals. A patient sent home with personalized information, customized to her own needs, however, is in an entirely better situation. Such material is extraordinarily easy to produce with up-to-date information technology. Practitioners can even provide their patients with access to the internet in the office and help patients customize their own information. This can, in some cases, be preferable to bombarding patients with information before they leave the office.[4] For patients with regularly scheduled visits, physicians can prepare information before a scheduled visit to make the discussion more productive.

Customized subspecialty software, such as the Animated Dissection of Anatomy for Medicine (A.D.A.M.), can also be extremely useful in helping physicians explain procedures and diagnoses to their patients. Clear explanations can promote patient cooperation and, some think, deepen the patient's trust in the practitioner.[5] Walking the patient through a treatment plan with the help of virtual animation acts also as a checking mechanism for the doctor, and gives the patient some control over treatment.

COMPUTERIZED PATIENT RECORDS

Many serious injuries stem from patient records not being available quickly enough; in an emergency, the time to pull necessary information from the records department simply does not exist. Nor do patients' medical records always follow them from physician to physician, even in the same hospital. Complications and fatalities result from lack of information about a patient's drug allergies and relevant medical history. It is now possible, however, to make vital patient information immediately available to all the physicians a patient might encounter.

Computerized patient records (CPRs) can put all the necessary information at the physician's fingertips the moment the patient enters the ER. The same service can drastically reduce the time devoted to collecting a patient medical history at the office of every specialist or subspecialist to whom s/he may be referred. Computerized records would also alleviate problems caused by incomplete or erroneous information supplied by the patient.

Several hospital systems across the country are implementing digital entry systems. Most are centered on devices such as the pocket-size PalmPilot which lets the physician enter all the relevant information, including the patient's history, diagnosis, and prescriptions, regardless of where the examination takes place. After the examination, all the patient information is quickly downloaded into the database, where it becomes instantly available to all medical personnel.[6] The benefits of such a system also include the ability to integrate various branches involved in health care delivery: billing, laboratory records, and pharmaceutical records. The ultimate result may be increased efficiency in delivery of care and the administrative tasks behind it.

The opposition to computerized records is centered on the issue of compromised confidentiality. Despite the availability of a variety of security precautions such as passwords and encryption, there is widespread reluctance to allow private information to pass across the internet, and many patients and physicians share the concern over confidentiality in general.

The real threat, however, may lie not in the method of gaining access to this information but rather in who needs—and is allowed—access. Logically, any health care professional may need access to a computerized patient record in an emergency. In a practice setting, a doctor may find it more efficient to give access to his support staff rather than to search the databases him/herself. The threat of passwords being sold or otherwise distributed becomes more real as more people gain the privileges to view the records.[7]

The Kennedy-Kassebaum Health Insurance Portability and Accountability Act of 1996 mandates the development of standards for electronic exchanges of health information. It calls, too, for Congress to enact privacy rules with regard to electronic exchanges by 1999.[8]

There exist extremely sophisticated security systems, such as biometric technology, which screens users' unique anatomical traits—fingerprints, voice, and retina—rather than relying on passwords.[9] Such security measures prevent unauthorized personnel from viewing records, but browsing by even authorized personnel can result in material falling into the wrong hands. Browsing transcends most security measures, and is difficult to control. Once sensitive information has been accessed, no technology can regulate its distribution.

One of the greatest problems with the threat, and any perception of threat, to confidentiality is that it might keep patients from reporting information. Patients might withhold sensitive information if they fear disclosure. This would result, obviously, in diminished quality of care.

MANAGEMENT AIDS

Information systems dedicated to easing the management of private practices and hospitals have also been developed in recent years. Everything from billing to scheduling can be performed electronically, and various divisions of patient care can be easily integrated. By combining databases of patient and administrative records, physicians can instantly assess a patient's situation with regard to past history of laboratory work, insurance payments, and pharmaceuticals.

Seemingly small details like getting the right piece of equipment and the right person to the right place can hold up procedures for hours in a large hospital. Software that facilitates scheduling can ease such problems. It can allow private practitioners, directly from their offices, to schedule outpatient procedures for their patients. This "enterprise scheduling" can help a primary care physician keep track of all procedures, lab work, and specialist visits. There are programs that evaluate individual performance and provide managers with tools to determine the best and most efficient allocation of resources. Software such as Encompass creates links with patients' insurance information, assessing the patient's ability to pay at the point of scheduling.[10] This process helps to inform a patient's decision-making process before any resources are allocated.

Office administration has been radically affected by information systems. Every aspect of administrative support in health care could be facilitated by transfer from paper to electronic form. Forms-editing software, to use one example of a multitude, allows forms for anything from record keeping to billing to be custom-made to fit the needs of a particular office. When used in conjunction with direct electronic billing, information systems can drastically reduce the time devoted to office administration.

All of these programs cut down on paperwork and the need for clerical support across the medical care enterprise.[11] They bring hospitals and private practices closer together and increase the efficiency of both.

Prescriptions have been added to the list of electronically administered health care tasks. With computerized prescribing, the many mistakes attributable to illegible handwriting and the misreading of similarly named medications can be prevented. These systems do more than simply relay information from physician to pharmacist. They cross-reference prescriptions with the patient's record and with guideline references. They can alert the physician of any allergies or drug reactions and offer various suggestions regarding CDC-recommended treatments. They also take into account the patient's age, weight, and other factors which may influence drug therapy decisions.[12] The systems can also be linked to laboratory databases and can prompt the physician to adjust drug therapy according to the lab results.[13] The aim is more standardized treatments which, at the same time, take into consideration individual data and the latest test results.

Not only can information systems be used to integrate the care and records of patients, they can be used to create profiles of physicians. Such profiles can include analyses of physicians' productivity, treatment styles, and other information which can help better match patients to doctors.

Such profiling has an obvious downside, however. Close tracking can incite in doctors the fear of being deselected from a managed care system or of being denied a position in a cost-driven hospital environment. This can discourage doctors from devoting adequate time to their patients and cause a general disintegration of morale. The term "economic credentialing" will bring forth either an angry tirade or a cold sweat for any physician in our current environment.

There is both great promise for and great concern about the use of information systems in the medical environment. Hospitals (such as Lehigh Valley Hospital in Pennsylvania) that have begun to implement some of this technology report improvements in health care delivery and efficiency, but they are still in the early stages of experimentation.[14] There is the danger that the medical industry will allow itself to be steered by available technology rather than by its own needs, and that systems may create problems to replace the ones they are trying to solve.

Endnotes

1. Erick Schonfeld, "Can Computers Cure Health Care," *Fortune* (March 30, 1998).

2. Bill Siwicki, "Applying the Internet in Health Care," *Health Data Management* (March 1998).

3. Mark Hagland, "Glimpses of a Web-Enabled Future," *Health Management Technology* (March 1998).

4. Karen Sandrick, "Teach Your Patients Well: Automated Education Tools for Health Clinicians," *Health Management Technology* (March 1998).

5. Ibid.

6. Josh McHugh, "Digital Medicine Men," *Forbes* (June 1, 1998).

7. Beverly Woodward, "The Computer Based Patient Record and Confidentiality," *New England Journal of Medicine* (November 23, 1995).

8. Janlori Goldman and Deirdre Mulligan, "Ensuring Patient Confidentiality in the Electronic Age," *Drug Benefit Trends* (1996).

9. Alain L. Sherter, "Let Your Fingers Do the Walking," *Health Data Management* (June 19, 1998).

10. Mary Carmen Caputo, "Balancing People, Places and Times: IT Tools Aid Health Care Scheduling," *Health Management Technology* (June 1998).

11. Ibid.

12. Gordon Schiff and Donald Rucker, "Computerized Prescribing: Building the Electronic Infrastructure for Better Medication Usage," *JAMA* (April 1, 1998).

13. Ibid.

14. Jennifer Gilbert, "Placing a Premium on Education," *Health Data Management* (June 1998).

Additional Sources

Chin, Tyler L. "Is Wireless Technology Ready to Roll?" *Health Data Management* (May 19, 1998).

"Corporate America Mum on Millennium Bug." *Medicine and Health* (June 15, 1998).

Goedert, Joseph. "Newest Privacy Bill Seeks Common Ground." *Health Data Management* (May 19, 1998).

Kilbridge, Peter M. "The Role of Information Systems in IDS-Physician Relationships; Integrated Delivery Systems." *Health Care Financial Management* (June 1998).

Menduno, Michael. "Software that Plays Hardball." *Hospitals and Health Networks* (May 20, 1998).

Morrissey, John. "VHA Delivers Messaging, Network Lets Physicians and Hospitals Share Clinical Data." *Modern Health Care* (May 4, 1998).

Siwicki, Bill. "Netting Clinical Data." *Health Data Management* (November 19, 1997).

Smith, Jay. "Gaining Practitioner Acceptance of Information Technology." *Information Technology Report* (March 1, 1998).

CHAPTER 24

TOTAL QUALITY MANAGEMENT AND CLINICAL PATHWAYS

AS MEDICAL ORGANI- zations undergo rapid change, the need to inte- grate activities across departments and units often gets bogged down by different (and traditional) methods of management and strategic plan- ning. Analysis of strengths, weak- nesses, opportunities, and threats (SWOT) is a useful strategic plan- ning technique that will serve as an aid in this horizontal integration. Separating elements of problems into these categories can help plan- ners identify what has a high probability of success and what needs extra attention.[1]

CLINICAL PATHWAYS

Clinical pathways, also known as clinical guidelines, or clinical advantage, are schedules of recom- mended clinical interventions, set and sequenced for use in guiding patient care from admission to discharge. Clinical guidelines make "a serious attempt to take the human tendency to act on pattern recogni- tion—the kind of 'autopilot' syndrome that can lead to medical errors—and turn it into a positive force for improvement of care. A well-designed guideline provides a template that is a starting point for improvement, not a definitive formula."[2]

Using guidelines has many advantages. Guidelines can be important case-management tools, generating valuable information about how patients are being cared for, providing information about what to expect and when, identifying critical decisions and actions during the course of care, and predicting achievable clinical outcomes. Then, if a patient is not following the pathway, a physician knows to look into the problem further and discover what is wrong.[3]

For clinical pathways to be effective, risk management, and all the data gathering it requires, is also necessary. Clinical pathways require review by many professionals. Important questions will need to be answered. "Were critical decisions made? Were actions performed according to the schedule put forth?"[4] The risk manager will want answers, and the data will provide them.

Clinical pathways also provide the opportunities to study quality, cost, and clinical outcomes for the nursing staff. Hospitals that use guidelines often gather data "as a part of the variance analysis process or for measurement of quality indicators . . . [and [multidisciplinary] teams provide input from a variety of perspectives for the interpretation of findings from the research."[5] The

findings are then evaluated in nursing research projects where the various solutions are considered and result in changes being made. The nursing development department, then, provides the direct care staff with the "research methodology, statistics, and analysis"[6] they need.

One of the greatest arguments for clinical guidelines, however, is the high cost of relying on each doctor's "instant and unaided recollection of the entire body of medical knowledge," because that cost can be in patients' lives. Michael Millenson, in his book *Demanding Medical Excellence*, refers to an example given by *JAMA* (January 8, 1997) that illustrates this point. When questioned, physicians usually agreed that beta-blocker drug therapy indeed improves survival for heart attack victims, which it does. However, in one state whose data were studied closely, only about one fifth of elderly patients with heart attacks received the therapy. Millenson also reported that an editorial in the same issue of the *Journal* commended clinical practice guidelines, especially those that are easily accessible on a computer screen to make physicians aware of "the existence of innovation."[7]

Clinical pathways are important, too, from the nonclinical standpoint. The use of clinical pathways can prevent unnecessary use of services, can reduce costs, and can decrease patients' stay in hospitals.[8] The use of clinical pathways can also reduce risk exposure for the caregiver if the patient is not improving as expected.

Clinical pathways, however, are designed both to improve care and to reduce costs, and these purposes can, at times, be in conflict. Millenson's comments on this follow.

> [. . . N]ot all guidelines meet the test of codifying best practice. Some are designed with an eye on the bottom line and threaten the flexibility that doctors need to serve each individual patient. Some good guidelines are implemented with a rigidity that threatens innovation. But the alternative to care guided by the evidence is care that relies on each doctor's memory. Or, perhaps, care that conforms to whatever the patient's insurance company believes is best.[9]

Guidelines are indeed becoming accepted as a way to protect and enhance physicians and their work. The American Medical Association, in December 1996, approved guidelines that are "based on solid scientific evidence."[10] By their approval then of certain health plans,

hospitals, and physicians, Millenson explains, the AMA hopes to encourage doctors to follow guidelines that are based on scientific evidence. In addition, by their disapproval, the AMA hopes to alert the public of health plans and hospitals whose guidelines do not adhere to the scientific evidence.

DEVELOPING PATHWAYS

Pathways, according to Bart Moore, a member of the Advisory Board, usually cause hospitals to evolve through three stages in their overall approach to clinical care. In the first, the hospital is on its own, in the second it enfranchises physicians in clinical reform, and in the third, hospital and physicians operate together with enduring clinical advantage. The transfer from the "problem of separate payments to the promise of capitation" is a component of these three stages.[11]

Moore explains that traditional hospitals, whose charter is to perfect hospital clinical operations, do so by such means as accelerating discharge rates, reducing staffing levels, consolidating units, standardizing some supplies, and speeding up test times. Physician-driven expenses, however, go largely unmanaged; the result is unsustainably high costs.

Further, he claims that it is necessary to enfranchise physicians in clinical reform. As a hospital does this, its charter becomes one of building physician commitment. In this system, physicians are rewarded for cost savings, which they can achieve by such measures as eliminating unnecessary tests and procedures, accelerating patient step-down, standardizing supplies and drugs, and active rounding. Physicians are also compensated for the time they devote to reengineering care for the sake of cost control.

When clinical advantage is an enduring reality, Moore contends that the hospital goal becomes enhancing clinical quality by tracking and managing outcomes and eliminating unnecessary variation. It also devotes itself to creating consumer convenience and capturing market share.[12]

ENFRANCHISING PHYSICIANS: A NECESSARY STEP

Moore cites Millay Hospital as an example of the entry of "for profits" into the health care market. When the surgeons approached Millay Hospital, for which they worked, and proposed a joint venture outpatient surgery center, the hospital rejected their offer. The physicians then turned to AmSurg for partnership instead. Together they built a surgery center ten miles away from Millay Hospital, and the hospital's income and revenue plummeted.[13]

The health care system has undergone a great deal of reform since that time, but global capitalization remains an unrealized vision throughout most of the United States. In fact, according to Moore, it represents only about 6 percent of aggregate revenue for leading systems.[14] Although the Advisory Board envisions a physician-led reengineering infrastructure, the partnership between doctors and hospitals seems not to be working at an optimal level. Capitation was supposed to align the interests of doctors, HMOs, and hospitals. The question is, why is it not working?

One reason is that physicians are selective in reducing utilization, and many cost saving possibilities are still not realized. Physicians struggling with issues such as declining reimbursement, have problems of their own.[15]

Another reason may have been unearthed by a study relayed in an article in *In Vivo the Business & Medicine Report*, that noted that while many recognize the need for new drugs, devices, and clinical approaches, physicians are usually slow to put them into practice. This is, they found, in part because of the physicians' suspicion both that the programs developed by suppliers are mainly for marketing existing products and that the programs favor one supplier over another.[16]

Another study of clinical pathways in Veteran Affairs, reported by Ronald Goldman, et al., in the *Western Journal of Medicine*, may be applicable to this situation. It found that quality management activities that were designed internally resulted in greater efforts to improve care than ones designed and imposed by outside groups. In addition, personnel costs were found to be lower for the internal management activities because fewer staff members were required than when the management came from the outside.[17]

All this research would imply that aligning hospital-physician interests can prove highly beneficial, and it is a process that cannot be done without the further enfranchising of physicians in clinical reform. This is done by recognizing physicians' contributions to reform, by rewarding cost savings via correcting the problem of early risk pools, and by targeting incentives and attaching rewards to individual specialists. Above all, it is done by sharing ownership—by making physicians true partners in the enterprise.[18]

TACTICS FOR ENFRANCHISING PHYSICIANS IN CLINICAL REFORM

Although they did not create them, the Advisory Board categorized and described the following tactics that may be utilized to achieve this partnership.

Cost Management Contracts

Doctors spend enormous amounts of uncompensated time on hospital committees, but when doctors do not attend meetings and remain uninformed of cost-reduction campaigns, savings shortfalls result. Under cost management contracts, participation is mandatory in cost-reduction committees, but doctors are compensated for their time in attending meetings. The committees are given specific cost targets and are physician-run. The use of cost management contracts generates campaigns with active physician involvement; it ensures that most doctors in the hospital are on the committees and that the majority of committee members are physicians, not staff. Cost management contracts work well in reducing costs, but they also have the potential to reduce some doctors' incomes.[19]

Actual Cost Risk Pools

The problem with traditional risk pools is that distribution of the risk pool money to doctors is not based on cost but on something else, like length of stay. So, physicians are rewarded for X, but the hospital wants Y, where Y is cost reduction. In actual cost risk pools, 100 percent of the reduced day savings flows to the doctors in the medical group. So, where physicians had been immune to cost overruns, in actual cost risk pools, MD's share in the cost decreases and increases.[20]

The example Moore gives of Cohen Hospital shows doctors and hospital united in risk using an Actual Cost Risk Pool.

> Under DRG payment system, the hospital [. . .] always [. . .] intended to reduce unit costs [B]ut it's physicians who control these costs. Under our new [actual cost risk pool] system, we provide the physicians with incentives to reduce costs, and assist them by providing data. If I can get all physicians to practice the same way inside the hospital, I can dramatically reduce my costs.— Chief Operating Officer of Cohen Hospital

> [Cohen Hospital's] willingness to work with us as a strategic partner to develop our concept of an ideal hospital reimbursement system is the fundamental reason behind our relationship. The [actual cost risk pool] was exactly what we were looking for. We now share risk on the cost of each case.— Administrator, Reed Medical Group[21]

Specialty Budget Gainsharing

For high revenue high expense specialties, the risk of revenue reduction may be offset by utilizing this method. The concept revolves around sharing cost savings with the members of the department that helped accomplish them. Cardiac surgery programs often represent the perfect opportunity to establish this interdepartmental gainsharing. The CABG (coronary artery bypass graft) procedure is a high volume, high revenue, high expense procedure for most tertiary hospitals. Incentivizing the specialists to increase efficiency through an operations improvement program may entail having them share in the financial savings.[22]

Case-Based Gainsharing

Physicians share in cost savings for all cases. This formula can be rolled out across many different specialties, from cardiology to orthopedics. To ensure doctors' participation, MDs receive greater share with higher savings; the greater the total savings, the more of it the physicians get as opposed to the hospital.[23]

Line-item Gainsharing

In line-item gainsharing, the hospital and physicians in partnership select very specific cost items, such as standardizing the use of balloon catheters. Moore implies that the hospital shares the savings with the physician groups that participate.[24]

Personal Gainsharing

The hospital develops MD eligibility criteria. Physicians must meet procedural volume criteria to qualify for the gainsharing program. The hospital then rewards individual physician's cost savings.[25]

Program Enhancement Funds

In program enhancement funds, the hospital designates a share of cost savings to a "program enhancement fund." Physicians then determine the fund allocation. For example, they may choose to increase staffing, buy new equipment, or support education.[26]

Quality Multipliers

Hospitals develop clinical performance standards. The hospital also increases or decreases the physician's share of savings depending on performance relative to clinical performance standards.[27]

Specialty Equity Ventures

The hospitals and physicians each take equity in a medical facility, such as a cath lab. Low-cost performance generates profits for both sides. The hope is that this standardization effort would cross over into the hospital itself.[28]

Tripartite Equity Ventures

By bringing in a general partner, the special equity ventures described above can leverage their dedicated expertise and providers.[29]

Getting Started

- **Procedures First**—There are large savings opportunities and significant physician upside to this opportunity.[30]
- **The 30 Percent Rule**—Pinpoint procedures for one line-item cost, as a percentage of total costs, is greater than 30 percent. This will help to target which medical conditions are ripe for gainsharing.[31]
- **The Problem with Medicine**— Medical opportunities (cognitive) are harder to capture than surgical (procedural) because cases tend to be scattered over a larger number of physicians such that each physician might have only a few of the cases monitored in the risk pool.[32]
- **Group, Not Individual**—Group, not individual means what it says. It focuses on areas where one can

change the way a group of care-givers deploys themselves, not the behavior of a bunch of individuals working in relative isolation. A highly leveraged cardiology group could reform cardiac surgery (CABG) care. With a new alliance, gainsharing unites cardiologists to reengineer care.[33]

•**A Rational Approach**—This approach consolidates facilities using gainsharing.[34]

•**Equity a Poor Incentive**—And a largely unnecessary one. When physician equity is divided among fifty cardiologists, it becomes too diluted to pass any savings on to the MD. Physicians receive a small return from savings.[35]

•**Stark Truths**—There are a plethora of legal issues surrounding economic partnerships with physicians, mostly related to some form of antitrust legislation.[36]

Total Quality Management

Total quality management (TQM) and continuous quality improvement (CQI) are management models. In an article in *Nursing Management*, Marie Taccetta-Chapnick and Greta Rafferty explain that both models seek to encourage health care workers to provide high quality service within budget limits and simultaneously promote client satisfaction. Both TQM and CQI work by making health care workers aware that "doing it right the first time decreases cost by eliminating rework, malpractice, lost business, damaged public image and turnover."[37]

Taccetta-Chapnick and Rafferty claim that important to this subject is the concept of cost-effectiveness analysis, a strategy that can be used to assess clinical treatments. This is done with measures of outcomes such as length of stay and readmission. Regardless of the measure utilized, the final results are expressed in dollars.[38]

They also refer to a useful check-list that addresses many aspects of achieving quality at the lowest possible cost that comes from Labowitz's article, "The Pillars of Quality."

Customer focus: Knowing who your customers are, their needs and expectations.

Total involvement: Organizing systems so that everyone is responsible for doing the right thing, the right way, the first time.

Measurement: Measuring quality and tracking quality improvement.

Systematic support: Ensuring that organization systems support quality effort.

Continuousness improvement: Making sure problem solving, prevention, and improvement are systematic.[39]

According to an article by David Bergman in the *Western Journal of Medicine*, quality management departments need to ensure adequate inpatient care in hospital settings as well as developing a "means to demonstrate 'high value' (best quality at a competitive price) for integrated delivery systems encompassing many sites and venues of care."[40]

As a result of the goal to improve quality and lower costs, new process-improvement methods have come into being. Bergman explains these methods as follows:

[T]he adequacy of care can be measured against explicit review criteria derived from evidence-based practice guidelines. The analysis of adverse events now uses new techniques of error analysis and systems improvement developed by other industries. The weeding out of "bad apples" has been supplanted by efforts to reduce unnecessary variability through the analysis and elimination of special causes of variation.[41]

These changes have stemmed from the new understanding that most lapses in quality come from dysfunctional systems and not from individual negligence. In addition, Bergman states that results of care are now evaluated in areas such as "patient satisfaction, functional state, access to care, and the appropriateness of care" and not simply "mortality, morbidity, and cost . . ."[42] The focus has also shifted from disease treatment to disease prevention—reducing health risks and promoting healthy living.

Bergman concurs that it is an enormous challenge to move quality management from ensuring adequate care to actually measuring, monitoring, and improving clinical activities. He contends that change must begin with medical student education and continue on to clinicians at all levels of care. More sophisticated information systems—ones that can provide outcomes at the sites of care—are necessary, as well as quality management professionals who are trained in both system analysis and statistical process control.[43]

INTEGRATED DELIVERY SYSTEMS

An integrated delivery system is

a patient-oriented assemblage of care elements, comprising both services and linking mechanisms, that guides and tracks patients over time through a comprehensive array of health, mental health, and social services spanning all levels of care, with formal arrangements and common financial incentives among all providers, payers, and consumers.[44]

According to Martin Merry, in an article in *Physician Executive*, no one is sure of the correct form an integrated system should take. Merry explains that even the pioneer models, such as Kaiser Permanente's, are breaking down due to the pressure from modern markets. He claims that many models, some successful and some not, will be developed in the near future, and a fluid environment will allow for trial and error and reformulation.

Merry describes the advantages to purchasers that come from linking isolated caregivers into integrated wholes. Integration reduces the costs inherent in the fragmentation of the old system and improves service. This is achieved, at least in part, by improving the coordination of various health services. Integration discourages individuals or isolated groups from pursuing their own economic benefit since the system as a whole must be considered and kept in balance, while keeping the cost acceptable to purchasers in order to succeed. Finally, integration provides

a leadership system that offers rational management and accountability for all the provider elements.

Because of these advantages, Merry explains that purchasers want to receive care from a "system that has compelling incentives to control costs and maintain high quality: that is, delivery of high value health care (value=quality/cost)."[45] While consumers are flexible in allowing different forms of systems integration, their desires are certainly influencing the structure of health care delivery.

Merry agrees that the movement from isolated provider units with little focus on value to highly accountable integrated systems is challenging for both administrative and clinical leaders. Clinical leaders, particularly physicians, however, have "an extraordinary opportunity to positively influence the structure, governance, and process of newly forming integrated systems."[46]

Health care futurist Jeff Goldsmith's new model of how integrated systems will develop focuses on stages one and two of the model—the formation of networks of physicians and the patient-system relationship. Each phase requires major changes in certain physician behaviors, and Goldsmith reminds the reader that such changes are better accepted when they come from within.

Stage one is marked by two major behavioral challenges. First, physicians must move from isolated practices into larger networks, and they must alter their practice patterns from "doing everything for everyone, hang the cost," to "doing the right things for the right people, in the most cost-effective manner."[47] These physician networks, however, do not have to become "salaried, all-under-one-roof 'medical factories.'"[48]

At the root of stage two is the desire to increase the value of health care—both to purchasers and to those served by the system. Goldsmith explains that value equals quality/cost is more than just a mathematical formula. While it is possible to increase value either by improving quality or decreasing cost, decreasing cost proves more attractive at this stage. Goldsmith describes the two basic approaches to cutting costs. The first is "downsizing," hoping that those left will not compromise quality; the second is to use modern quality management science to "'redesign the system-patient interface.'"[49]

Goldsmith, according to Merry, correctly chooses the latter. "Modern quality management science is the only approach to cost cutting that genuinely maintains quality, not just as a concern, but as a continuing, central priority."[50] Merry explains that quality legends W. Edwards Deming and Joseph Juran carried this idea to Japan in the 1950s, and it is the only approach that could be accepted by physicians.

Education, participation in change, and information feedback are the only ways to encourage physicians to reduce costs while maintaining high quality care. However, according to Merry, "there are limits to individual and collective changes in practice patterns. At some point, physicians will need to become more involved in redesigning the systems of care in which they participate."[51] It will be necessary for leaders to recognize the power held by the science of quality which combines quality improvement and outcomes research. Using this, physicians could deliver the highest value health care.[52] As integrated systems form—and, not infrequently, break up—around the United States, more and more opportunities appear for physicians willing to supplement their clinical skills with those of leadership.

WHO TAKES CARE OF PATIENTS BEST?

Carle Falk of the Advisory Board reported the rise of open access, broad specialty panels, capitation reform, and new product competitors in response to market demands for choice in 1997. All these relate to the overriding question of who it is that delivers the most appropriate care. Who has the lowest costs of care, who has the fewest complications, who has the lowest mortality rates, and who provides the highest quality of life?[53]

Only a few years back the consensus was that specialists and primary care physicians had equal outcomes. The findings of Shelden Greenfield et al., relayed by Falk, follow.

> No meaningful differences were found in the mean health outcomes from patients with hypertension or NIDDM, whether they were treated by different care systems or by different physician specialists. Although prepaid medicine relies more heavily on generalist physicians than does fee-for-service, there is no evidence from these analyses that the quality of care of moderately ill patients with these two common diseases was adversely affected.[54]

More recently, however, there has been a recognition of a specialty advantage in some areas. In particular, specialist care of asthma appears to be of benefit in large HMOs. Falk refers to William M. Vollmer's findings that patients cared for by allergists were more likely to receive treatment consistent with national expert panel guidelines and to report better quality of life. These findings should be kept in mind when structuring access to specialty referrals in the managed care environment.[55]

When generalists treat diabetes, the problem of doctors under-prescribing insulin arises.[56] In caring for strokes, neurologists are more costly, but achieve better outcomes.[57] Similarly, cardiologists have higher LOS, but the lowest rates of mortality.[58]

The Advisory Board reports findings that specialists, as a rule, are quicker to adopt new therapies than primary care physicians—one study noted a twenty-one-month lag time between the two—and have a more aggressive and more invasive treatment style. Perhaps not coincidentally, patients treated by specialists have lower mortality rates.[59]

It is important, of course, not just who is practicing, but where. An Advisory Board study shows that major teaching hospitals are more efficient in care delivery: for example, one may find greater access to neurologists at teaching hospitals and greater access to diagnostic technology as well.[60]

Events interpreted by many physicians as the end of medicine as it has been practiced in the past may usher in a new era of opportunity for physician leadership and influence. However, according to Martin Merry, there is no guarantee that the medical profession will be in control. Along with the many health care administrators, there are many talented managers from other industries making their way into the trillion-dollar health care industry. Many people are more than willing to help design the future of health care, and reap the profits inherent in a successful system.

If physicians, individually and collectively, choose either to hunker down in doomed attempts to recreate the past, or evolve simply as operatives and/or technicians of emerging health systems, they will likely find themselves not in [the driver's seat] but bumping along behind in the "rumble seat" of health care transformation.[61]

Endnotes

1.   Sandra Gaynor and Jo Ann Verdin, "Conducting unit-based research to improve the quality of care," *Journal of Nursing* 12, (December 1997): 63.

2.   Michael L. Millenson, *Demanding Medical Excellence: Doctors and Accountability in the Information Age* (Chicago: The University of Chicago Press, 1997): 136–37.

3.   Rodd Zolkos, "ASHRM: Risk Management by the Numbers: Hospital Data from Various Sources Can Help Identify Problem, Risk Manager Says," *Business Insurance* (November 10, 1997): 87.

4.   Ibid.

5.   Sandra Gaynor, and Jo Ann Verdin, "Conducting unit-based research," 63.

6.   Ibid.

7.   Michael L. Millenson, *Demanding Medical Excellence*, 137–38.

8.   Dulcelina A. Stahl, "Anatomy of a management system," *Nursing Management* 28 (December 1997): 20.

9.   Michael L. Millenson, *Demanding Medical Excellence*, 137.

10.   Ibid.

11.   Bart Moore, "In Common Enterprise: Enfranchising Physicians in Clinical Reform." Paper presented at the Advisory Board Medical Leadership Council Conference on Clinical Advantage, October 1997. (Proceedings published by Washington, D.C.: The Advisory Board, 1997): 6–7.

12.   Ibid.

13.   Ibid.

14.   Ibid., 17.

15.   Ibid.

16.   "Premieres Technology Push: To launch Premier Innovation Institute to speed the adoption of innovative products and svcs," *In Vivo the Business & Medicine Report* (November 1997): 1.

17.   Ronald L. Goldman, Galen L. Barbour, and Eileen Ciesco, "Contribution of locally and externally designed quality management activities to hospitals' efforts to improve patient care; includes related information," *The Western Journal of Medicine* 122 (February 1997): 110.

18. Bart Moore, "In Common Enterprise."

19. Ibid., 34–45.

20. Ibid., 46–53.

21. Ibid., 51.

22. Ibid., 56–59.

23. Ibid., 70–77.

24. Ibid., 78–81.

25. Ibid., 82–83.

26. Ibid., 87.

27. Ibid., 88–91.

28. Ibid., 92–97.

29. Ibid., 98–99.

30. Ibid., 102–3.

31. Ibid., 104–5.

32. Ibid., 108–9.

33. Ibid., 110–11.

34. Ibid., 113.

35. Ibid., 114–15.

36. Ibid., 119.

37. Marie Taccetta-Chapnick and Greta Rafferty, "Promoting Client Satisfaction," *Nursing Management* 28 (January 1997): 45–48.

38. Ibid.

39. G. Labowitz, "Total Quality Management Mystique," *Healthcare Executive* 6 (1991): 9–24, quoted in Marie Taccetta-Chapnick and Greta Rafferty, "Promoting Client Satisfaction."

40. David A. Bergman, "Hospital-based quality management: A program at the crossroads," *The Western Journal of Medicine* 166 (February 1997): 153.

41. Ibid.

42. Ibid.

43. Ibid.

44. Martin Merry, "The time is now: physicians, health care providers and purchasers cooperation in financial aspects of American health care delivery systems," *Physician Executive* 22 (September 1996): 4.

45. Martin Merry, "The time is now."

46. Ibid.

47. Ibid.

48. Ibid.

49. Ibid.

50. Ibid.

51. Ibid.

52. Ibid.

53. Carle Falk, "Clinical Advantage: Exceptional Practice and Acute Care Reform." Paper presented at the Advisory Board Medical Leadership Council Conference on Clinical Advantage, October 1997. (Proceedings published by Washington, D.C.: The Advisory Board, 1997).

54. Sheldon Greenfield, "Outcomes of patients with hypertension and non-insulin dependent diabetes mellitus . . ." in *JAMA* (1995), quoted in Carle Falk, "Clinical Advantage."

55. William M. Vollmer, "Specialty differences in the management of asthma . . .," *Archives of Internal Medicine*; quoted in Carle Falk, "Clinical Advantage," 9.

56. Carle Falk, "Clinical Advantage," 11.

57. Ibid., 12.

58. Ibid., 13.

59. Quoted from R. A. Hirth, "Specialist and generalist physicians' adoption of antibiotic therapy . . .," in *Med Care* (1996), quoted in Carle Falk, "Clinical Advantage."

60. G. E. Rosenthal, "Severity-adjusted mortality and length of stay in teaching and nonteaching hospitals . . ." in *JAMA* (1997), quoted in Carle Falk, "Clinical Advantage."

61. Martin Merry, "The time is now."

CHAPTER 25

OF FRENCH TOAST AND FRIENDLY INTERFACES

IT WAS A RAINY, DANK, EARLY-FEBRUARY MORNING, BUT MILA DIDN'T CARE. It was day one of her Get-A-Social-Life campaign. She was starting small, granted. She still didn't know Penny very well, but she liked her, and she liked the idea of having a pal from "her" generation—even if the pal didn't know it. Someone who remembered disliking *The Mod Squad* and disco the first time around. So here she was with Penny after an especially grueling night shift. They were having breakfast at the Odessa, Mila's present favorite of the Ukrainian diners in the neighborhood. The plate glass windows were steamy, and the waitress had just brought great thick slabs of french toast.

"Let's see," Mila said, determined to bring up a nonwork subject. "Oh, I know what's new. I've been thinking about getting a computer." Mila had been inflicted with a mild case of technology fever since her information systems tutorial; she was hankering for a machine of her own. She'd also found herself fascinated by the idea that medical systems could benefit so much by bulking up on technical components, but that those components were just expensive toys in the absence of true care management like clinical paths and process engineering. She forked a syrupy square of french toast. "Penny, where do you fall on the technophilia/phobia scale?"

189

"I like computers well enough," said Penny, drawing together her ever-present cardigan and then adjusting her napkin on her lap. "I keep up with my on-line Chat About Cats discussion group. It drives my husband crazy, but, as you know, you need a way to relax. What kind are you going to get?"

"Well," said Mila, happy to avoid the Chat About Cats subject, "the last computer I had was an Apple II. So I guess I'll get the latest of those."

Penny stopped cutting the fat off her bacon and looked at Mila, amazed. "If you hadn't once mentioned that you'd never replaced your Beta VCR, I'd think you were joking. But you're serious, aren't you? You're still using an Apple II. I can walk faster than an Apple II."

Just then Mila was in the White, and Ajax was at hand, in a holographic waitress uniform. "May I help you?"

"No," said Mila, annoyed, "you absolutely may not. This is not a crisis. I don't need brain surgery for every headache, and I don't need a full-blown lecture every time I have a question about something in this era."

"But information technology is one of the issues that I was told might be of some concern to you. I am prepared to help."

"Not this time, Ajax. No thanks. And wear something next time that covers your knees. Yech."

"Very well, Mila, but I predict you'll need me e'er long."

"I predict my breakfast will be cold e'er long. Get me back."

"I think," continued Penny, "You should look at a Pentium III or a Pentium MMX."

"Why? Isn't Apple in business anymore?" Mila hoped that wasn't a stupid question, but she really wanted to get this figured out.

Penny looked at her sideways. "Of course. And it commands a whopping 8 percent of the market."

In pre-Ajax times, Mila would not have bothered to go beyond this point. She would have seen it as something for the business page of the newspaper and of no interest. But now she wanted to pursue it. "But that must mean that other companies are making computers even better than my old Apple. Are they easier to use, more fun?"

"No, actually," said Penny, with a strange look, "I thought everyone knew Mac had a superior interface, and a funkier design, now that they come in blueberry, but that they blew it in the mass market. The masses bought Windows, and that was that."

The White was back. "Didn't we just agree," said Mila, "that we would not do this for nonmedical issues?"

"Mila, the story of Apple Computers is well-known throughout the galaxy," said Ajax. "It is used as a case study for logicians who choose to be corporate executives."

Mila wasn't getting it. "So what, Ajax? I may be getting a little interested in business, but let's not go overboard. Medical issues only. Please."

"But this has everything to do with medicine. The computer industry, like the medical industry, has become commodified. Think about it. Many people thought Apple had the best product, just as most people have always thought that physicians knew how to take care of patients. Nevertheless, Apple was not able to win market share and does not control the computer hardware market, and physicians do not control their own destiny in this new medical world. Why is that?"

Into the White stepped a holographic image, a pleasant-looking fellow with a salt-and-pepper mustache. "Let me introduce," said Ajax, "director of the Center on Leadership and Change at the Intergalactic School of Business. Now, shall we repair to an appropriate setting?"

"I can't believe I'm saying this, Ajax, but I'm getting used to the White. Let's just stay here."

"Very well," said Ajax, "Then I'll just let the lesson proceed. Professor, do you not agree about the physician/Apple parallel?"

"They do have a common theme," said the hologram. "If the players in either scenario could go back in time—"

"I'd hitch a ride," interrupted Mila. "Sorry. Go on."

"If physicians could remake the past, they would change things to make their superior product more adaptable for this changing environment. Similarly, many companies with superior products could have been more successful had they made relatively minor changes in their market approach."

Mila was getting frustrated. "Yes, but since we who have actually experienced time travel are rather few, wouldn't you say that has limited relevance?"

"The point is," the professorial image said, "that strong leadership and vision can give you the next best thing—a decent shot at predicting what will

happen and planning for it. If you wish to learn how to regain control of the medical system, you would do well to learn from successful and unsuccessful examples of leadership and vision."

CHAPTER 26

PHYSICIANS AS LEADERS:
A NON-PHYSICIAN PERSPECTIVE

TRADITIONALLY, THE doctors who had the most patients had the most power. Now that managed care controls so many patients, however, doctors need to find a different way to organize themselves. If they don't, their positions of influence—and their perspective—will be lost.

Accordingly, many doctors are struggling to devise a new physician leadership structure. One popular idea is the independent physician organization (IPO), in which doctors are external to any particular health care organization. There are also physician organizations which are created within the system. In this arrangement, management chooses doctors with whom to work with as leaders. If the doctors are willing, they join management.

Doctors who give up their clinical roles are likely to be viewed by other doctors as "splitters." There are, fortunately, some who realize that if no doctors join management, no one will benefit.

LACK OF PHYSICIAN LEADERSHIP

It will take the leadership of all parties in health care to bring about the changes required by the new environment. Physician leadership has, however, been missing from this effort so far.[1] Most physicians desire to practice medicine and do not want involvement in administrative or managerial areas. Medicine, however, is now usually practiced in complex organizations; this makes the need for physician leaders and managers inescapable.

According to Stephen Shortell, et al., in *Remaking Health Care in America*, the first generation of physicians to assume leadership had little management training. They mainly focused on individual institutions, departments, or divisions. Examples of these physician leadership positions were the hospital vice presidents for medical affairs, the directors for medical education, and the chiefs of specific service lines or divisions.

The emerging second generation of physician leadership focuses on more areas of health care delivery; they assume "systemwide responsibility for clinical integration, quality improvement, and group practice management."[2] They are receiving more systematic training, too—from short, two- to four-day intensive courses to executive M.B.A.s and degrees in health services management. These potential leaders must deal with many hurdles. For example, they will most likely be viewed by other doctors as traitors to the dark side (administration) and, inversely, as intruders by their nonclinical colleagues.

The next generation of leadership would arise and develop less painfully if all physicians in medical school and residency programs were taught some basic managerial leadership skills. Shortell, et al., claim that learning about communication, conflict management, change management, team building, and continuous improvement methodologies would prepare doctors to accept—and to contribute to—new leadership approaches. In addition, some of these physicians would choose careers that are a combination of medicine and management. This would put them in prime position to help restructure the delivery system.[3]

When people are satisfied with a status quo, they fight change. It is no wonder that getting physicians to recognize that they must alter their practices in response to new economic, technological, and social forces is difficult. According to Shortell, et al., a leader's job in this setting is to create the right amount of discomfort—to incite sufficient dissatisfaction with the status quo and get people to try new approaches.

The leader must provide a sense of security, too. S/he must reassure those s/he leads that the new approaches will be successful in reaching the desired goal. When change seems too abrupt, too radical, or too difficult, the opponents often react and become negative; this can pose a bigger threat than leaving things alone and hoping the change goes away. The key is to create a "zone of manageable discomfort."[4]

In the study of physician systems by Alexander, Burns, and Zuckerman (1995) leaders did several things to create the discomfort zone. Leaders would inform physicians about their own local market and emphasize what competitors were doing. They would take every opportunity to point to what was happening in other markets. They would bring in physician leaders from those markets to speak at staff meetings. Leaders would also arrange for key physicians to visit other systems where successful changes had taken place. A number of systems— Advocate, Baylor, Franciscan, Sharp, and Sutter, among them—created their own managed care product and shared its ownership with physicians. This allowed the physicians to see the importance of learning how to practice cost-effective care in a managed care environment, and it gave them some experience in doing so.[5]

To make change easier and more attractive for the physicians, the systems also provided programs to develop physician leadership. They helped the physicians conduct clinical outcome studies through managed care "colleges" and support units.

Most significantly, Shortell, et al., report that these systems spent tens of millions of dollars to upgrade clinical and management information systems. The data the new technology

provided showed that creating the zone of manageable discomfort had to be monitored and maintained. "This was accomplished by being very sensitive to managing the pace of change, knowing when to speed it up and, perhaps even more important, when to slow it down."[6]

Shortell, et al., refer to the example of UniHealth where a major change took place in order to involve physicians in consolidating eleven hospital labs into one more cost-effective unit that would serve the entire system. As expected, the process created considerable conflict. Fortunately, however, the change was managed by a bright executive. When he sensed too much uneasiness, he would put the issue on hold. Only when the parties had regained their emotional equilibrium, only when they, themselves, brought up the need to address the issue, did he bring it back for discussion. His able leadership maintained the right degree of creative tension.[7]

Although one of the most dominant groups in the history of any profession, physicians need to be empowered. Health care reorganization, in the first place, was the product of executives from other industries who were recruited into health care. Shortell, et al., claim that these executives, however, do not know what physicians know: which services should be offered; what conditions or diseases might justify clinical service lines; what diagnoses and conditions would work best for developing guidelines, protocols, and pathways; what clinical outcome measures are reliable and valid; and how new technology will influence treatment trends.

Management's need for this clinical knowledge, and the collective intensity of the other economic, political, and social forces at play in the health care world together strongly encourage interdependence between medicine and management. When it comes to working under the financial, managerial, and organizational circumstances of the restructured health care world, however, most physicians are inexperienced, at a relative disadvantage, and—perhaps understandably—reluctant. Under the old organization, there was a separation between medicine and management—the voluntary medical staff resolved problems. Now, however, the old patterns have been disrupted; the gap between "administrative" and "clinical" decision making has been largely abolished. The new relationships, and the issues associated with them, are now discussed in the economic units that involve practices: IPAs, PHOs, MSOs, among others. These are models that attempt to create incentives for concerted action, yet they leave physicians with the unmet need to control their own destinies. All of these factors together create the imperative for greater physician empowerment.[8]

PHYSICIAN EMPOWERMENT MODELS

There are several essential aspects of making empowerment work. Those being empowered must be motivated and, note well, capable of carrying out the tasks delegated to them. It does little good and, perhaps, even harm, to empower people who are incapable of doing their new task. Empowerment involves not only delegating tasks to doctors, but providing them with the means—the training and tools—to succeed.

A second ingredient for successful empowerment is the willingness of those in authority to completely release the responsibilities they are delegating. They must be willing to share some of their authority. This is difficult for those who need to be in control or who rely on their formal title for their leadership strengths.

Finally, physicians and executives have to learn to trust each other. More health care executives must be willing to invest in developing able physician leaders and then let go of their authority. Physicians, then, have to be willing to handle the responsibilities and learn about the finances, management, and organization of health care delivery.

Culture

Shortell, et al., suggest that most systems are trying to create more group-oriented cultures that emphasize teamwork, cooperation, sharing of information and pride in the organization.[9] However, as has been discussed in one of your previous tutorials (chapter 12), there are strong educational and selection biases that mitigate against this collaborative model.

Education

Every system studied either already had, or has since begun, a physician leadership development program. Executives at Advocate Health System (formerly EHS Health Care and Lutheran General HealthSystem) stated, "The EHS vision puts physicians in leadership roles, recognizing that they are gate-keepers and true integrators of health care."[10]

Most physicians are carefully chosen for the programs to represent different specialties, age groups, and areas of interest. Some systems include nonclinical executives in order to expose them to "clinical epidemiology, decision analysis, and protocol and pathway development."[11] The programs, to which several systems have sent as many as four hundred physicians, range from two- and three-day intensive seminars on selected topics to integrated curricula taught over a year or more. Most systems, Advocate, Sharp, and Sutter among them, conduct their programs along with local universities; a few, such as Henry Ford, use primarily internal resources.[12]

Shortell, et al., state that experience has revealed that time spent training physician leaders is well spent and results in increased physician commitment to the system. It cannot be overstated that this effort needs to begin during medical school and infused throughout a physician's continuing medical education. Trained physician managers are more willing and able to participate in shared ownership arrangements such as PHOs, as well as in overall responsibilities involving management and governance. While greater numbers of trained physician leaders will not eliminate conflict or distress, they will increase the pool of physicians able to address these difficulties more directly—with data, where it is available, and with more sophisticated skills and understanding.

Involvement

During the period studied, physicians became more involved in the management and governance of these systems. There was not only growth in the number of physicians serving on governing boards and assuming key manager positions (such as the vice president for clinical affairs or vice president for clinical integration), but also more intermingling with non-physicians throughout the system. Physicians were beginning to serve on meaningful task forces, committees, quality improvement project teams, and the like. Evidence reveals that these involvements positively influence operational performance.[13]

In addition, several systems have actually focused their strategic planning processes around physician groups instead of hospitals. Shortell, et al., report the example of Sentara, which has changed its entire management structure. It has created a management council charged with facilitating the system's overall strategic decisions. Four of the eight members on this council are physicians.

Incentives

The answer to why physicians would (or should) join with a given system is primarily economic. Due to an environment of increased financial risk, the systems that help maintain and expand physician's practices are the ones with which physicians want to join.

A recent examination by J. Shalowitz, M.D., and reported by Shortell, et al., revealed what primary care physicians want from a health care system.

Have a sufficient volume of patients to diffuse risk, or use creative payment schedules until risk targets are met.

Provide timely and accurate eligibility data, preferably through on-line computer linkages.

Set capitation based on realistic risks and allow compensation for adverse selection.

Provide appropriate stop-loss insurance and first dollar re-insurance—the latter for high-risk cases such as open heart, psych, and chemical dependency.

Help obtain favorable supplier contracts using the system's marketshare power—for example, to purchase packages and obtain aggressive specialist contracts.

Enable the physician to do his or her own benefit interpretations.

Leave the physician alone to manage his or her own business—do not micromanage care.

Share profits as befits a true partnership.[14]

Additionally, the research revealed that physicians also want help in conducting clinical outcome studies that would improve care and to be provided with outcome data for external reporting purposes.

Models that allowed physicians to become shareholders in their practices provided an added incentive for them to be concerned about the long-term growth of the practice. Many groups also use short-term financial incentives, such as bonus pay based on the group's meeting of productivity and patient satisfaction objectives. Some organizations in the study also pay physicians for taking on administrative tasks and responsibilities. Shortell, et al., refer to Advocate, Baylor, Fairview, and Sharp as examples because they all have policies of compensating physicians for involvement on behalf of the system that go beyond their regular work. "Fairview, for example, pays physicians for board participation at the rate of $3,000 per year, and for the development of protocols, guidelines, pathways, and outcome measures at $2,500 per year."[15] Baylor and Sentara pay physicians for working on process reengineering and protocol development at the rate of $100 per meeting. In addition, Sisters of Providence pays physicians for time spent beyond four hours at any one time or event.[16]

COMMENTS FROM ONE IN THE FIELD

It is vexing for a leader to be misinterpreted by followers, or to have followers respond counter to expectations (or hopes). When the follower is a physician and the leader is not, such situations sometimes arise from the sharp differences in the clinical and nonclinical cognitive frames.[17]

The primary allegiance of physicians is to their own patients for whom they must bear total personal responsibility. They prefer, and are accustomed to, working in collegial relationships where power is symmetrical, rather than in those where power flows primarily from an organizational office. Physicians daily work with illnesses that have, in general, time-limited courses. The results of their work are usually immediately apparent and concrete— the patient either improves or gets worse, lives or dies. At the risk of overreaching, one might say that this accustoms physicians to focusing on the short run and allows their tolerance for ambiguity and uncertainty to stay quite low.

Managers, on the other hand, owe allegiance to an organization rather than to any one physician or set of patients. Because of the high degree of interdependence necessary for accomplishing managerial tasks, accountability is generally diffused or shared. The power managers exercise is often defined primarily by the office they hold. Managerial time frames are long—it takes an eternity to accomplish anything significant— and feedback is often delayed and vague. As a consequence, perhaps, managers have a high degree of tolerance for ambiguity and uncertainty.

Physicians are likely to perceive and interpret a manager's leadership behavior in idiosyncratic ways that are sometimes quite different from what was intended. Remember as Beulah Trey told you: the impact registered on physicians comes not from what is intended, or even an administrator's behavior, but rather from what they perceive and attributions they make. Unmet expectations are translated into mistrust and miscommunications.

Physicians have distinctive motivational dynamics. Their expectations, instrumentalities, and valences differ considerably from those of managers. To motivate physicians, to release and focus their energy, one has to work on their terms, not your own.

Managers, because of their own distinctive cognitive frame, are prone to misinterpreting the intentions or behaviors of physicians and attributing malevolent cause to them. They tend to suspect that physicians are not working in the best interests of the organization. When a manager "just can't understand why Doctor X did that," it generally means a physician has acted differently than the manger would have done. Why, however, would the manager have expected otherwise? The causes of physician behavior must be interpreted through the perspective of the physician's experience and mentality—not the manager's.

The appropriate management style when leading physicians is marked by consistently considerate behavior, relationship orientation, and encouragement of participation. The degree of task orientation appropriate depends on the task-relevant maturity of the professional or professional group in the particular situation. If the physicians understand the goal to be achieved, accept and are motivated to undertake it, and possess the competence to do so (i.e., are highly mature), task orientation should be low. When this is not the case, a greater degree of directiveness is warranted. Professional task-relevant maturity is situational. A physician might be very mature in one situation (e.g., in performing professional work) and quite immature in another (e.g., working on a hospital committee to design an independent practice association).

Until recently, physician culture was defined by independence and autonomy. If you were a doctor, your priority was your patient. You alone were responsible for his or her care. No other doctor would contradict you or challenge your authority. No doctor would claim to speak for you, and you would decline to speak for others. The only basis for authority in your field would be academic accomplishment, publishing, and expertise. It was, clearly, not a traditional organizational hierarchy.

Now, however, physicians and hospitals need to interact, and doctors need to speak for other doctors. If a hospital requires "x," it cannot come to terms with each of its physicians separately. It needs to interact with a leader, and it needs the other physicians to honor the leader's plans. Physicians have no idea how to do this yet, but for the sakes of the system, themselves, and their patients, they must learn.

But if anything can be predicted in these times of rapid change, it's that physicians—smart, well-trained, and highly motivated—will figure it out.

Endnotes

1. E. F. X. Hughes, *New Leadership in Health Care Management: The Physician Executives II* (1994), quoted in Stephen Shortell, et al., *Remaking Health Care in America: Building Organized Delivery Systems* (San Francisco: Jossey-Bass Publishers, 1996): 109.

2. N. C. Dunham, et al., "The Value of the Physician Executive Role to Organizational Effectiveness and Performance," *Health Care Management Review* 19, no. 4 (1994): 56–63, quoted in Stephen Shortell, et al., *Remaking Health Care in America*, 109.

3. Stephen Shortell M., et al., *Remaking Health Care in America: Building Organized Delivery Systems* (San Francisco: Jossey-Bass Publishers, 1996): 110.

4. Ibid., 114.

5. Ibid.

6. Ibid.

7. Ibid., 114–15.

8. Ibid., 117.

9. Ibid., 118.

10. R. R. Risk and C. P. Francis, "Transforming a Hospital Facility Company into an Integrated Medical Care Organization," *Managed Care Quarterly* 2, no. 4 (1994): 12–23, quoted in Shortell, et al., *Remaking Health Care in America*, 119.

11. Stephen M. Shortell, et al., *Remaking Health Care in America*, 119.

12. Ibid.

13. C. Molinari, J. Alexander, L. Morlock, and C. A. Lyles, "Does the Hospital Board Need a Doctor? The Influence of Physician Board Participation on Hospital Financial Performance," *Medical Care* 33, no. 2 (1995): 170–85, quoted in Shortell, et al., *Remaking Health Care in America*, 120.

14. Shortell, et al., *Remaking Health Care in America*, 120–21.

15. Ibid, 121–22.

16. Ibid., 122.

17. The ideas in this paragraph and to the end of the chapter were expressed by Beulah Trey in conversation.

CHAPTER 27

OF GENETIC SELECTION AND
JERRY SPRINGER

BACK AT THE ODESSA, MILA AND PENNY WORKED ON THEIR BREAKFASTS. Why, thought Mila, did the most innocent conversation somehow end up having a connection to the new practice of medicine? Sometimes she felt like one of Ajax's holograms herself, with her whole life just happening to be a series of convenient examples.

A loud conversation at the next booth caught Mila's attention and, she saw, Penny's too. They followed the time-honored practice of eavesdropping while pretending to be utterly absorbed in sending their cholesterol counts to the sky.

"Didn't you know," one of the ladies behind Mila said to the other, "that black olives are more effective than birth control pills for contraception?"

"Are you serious?"

"Completely. That could definitely be why you're not getting pregnant."

Mila stole a glance over her shoulder so she could catch a glimpse at the purveyors of this misinformation. She turned toward Penny who obviously shared her incredulity. The two women were post-gym, late-thirties, seemingly affluent, and well-educated. And yet they were driveling about black olives? "Could be true," said Mila, between her teeth. "Of course it would depend on exactly where the olives go."

Penny smiled and shook her head but said in a low tone, "Women of that age—of my age—get a little desperate. It can sound pretty absurd, but can you blame them?"

"Check," called one of the women at the next table. Then, to her friend, "I can give you the name of my infertility guy. He's the one who was on Jerry Springer for artificially inseminating some woman with her aunt's new husband's sperm. You know, my aunt is my niece kind of thing."

"I'd have no problem with that, actually. I don't see the big controversy." There was a short bustle. "Do you have any ones for a tip?"

"No—a five. Let's just leave it." The ladies rose and put on their coats. "How about that new sex selection procedure, though? It's funny, of all the things that don't shock me, that seems too mechanical. Though I'm sure I'll end up with the old turkey baster."

"Actually, I've heard that vinegar douches virtually guarantee that you get a boy. Or, wait a sec, is it a girl?"

"I know this is weird, but part of me would just as soon hire some woman who has already had kids and needs some money to be a surrogate. I'd already be taking time off work to be with the baby while we bond, but it seems like a waste of risk actually to be pregnant at this age—there'd be no guarantee I'd be able to keep the business going up to the last minute . . ." The ladies left, leaving a small trail of an unidentifiable but expensive scent.

Mila and Penny were quiet for a moment as the waitress cleared their plates. "That was the most amazing conversation I ever shouldn't have heard," said Mila. "Is that degree of confusion and ethically challenged information widespread?"

Penny's face looked very middle-aged, very tired, even a little disapproving. It reminded Mila of the way Penny had seemed the first day they had met. Penny said, "I actually think they were on the informed end of the scale. There are so many options, so much information, so many opinions. A lot of people have no idea what's true."

This might well have some personal resonance for Penny, Mila realized uncomfortably.

Penny turned over the check, began checking the math, but looked up, "I think it's even more serious that so many people resort to throwing darts to decide what's the right or wrong thing to do."

"It really does seem," Mila said carefully, "that we can do much more medically than anyone has decided that we *should* do. Everyone should be thinking about these reproductive ethics."

"The ethics of reproduction," said Penny, "and the ethics of other things, too. How about the ethics of resource allocation and managed care? We get so wrapped up in medicine we barely take time to wonder what it all means. Now let's pay and go—I'm ready to take the PATH to Hoboken and get to sleep before noon."

White.

CHAPTER 28

THE ETHICS OF MEDICINE IN THE TWENTY-FIRST CENTURY

WITH THE INCREDIBLE technological advances in medicine, ethics has now become a major issue. Rick Weiss writes about these issues in an article in the *Washington Post*.[1] He begins with the situation of Tracy Veloff, who was carrying a child from the egg of a woman who had been dead for a year. The biological mother, Julie Garber, had been buried in December 1996 after having hastily produced and frozen several embryos. Neither the anonymous sperm donor nor Veloff, the surrogate mother, had any intention of raising the child.

Lawyers, then, were trying to discern who the parents would be. Not even the initiators of the pregnancy, Garber's parents, planned to raise the child themselves. They asserted that they had inherited the embryos along with their daughter's furniture and other possessions (an idea that some legal authorities found unsettling), and that it was their decision to make them into grandchildren. Many were relieved, then, when Veloff miscarried.

The Garber case, Weiss explains, is just one of a growing number of ethically difficult situations resulting from reproductive technologies that have redefined the meaning of "parent" and "child." "Of the many areas of science that today are giving rise to bioethical quandaries, this one more than any other, strikes at the heart of society's most cherished institution: the family."[2]

Today's ethical crisis in reproductive medicine, Weiss contends, is the product of social, scientific, and economic change. Many women, often in deference to their careers, have delayed childbearing to the point where technological intervention is their only hope of becoming biological mothers; recent advances in egg freezing, embryo manipulation, and other techniques have provided many options for those who are infertile. The $2 billion-a-year fertility industry, unanchored by federal financial support, has become a monstrous enterprise.

As a result of these factors, many uncontrolled experiments in new ways to make babies have taken place. Thousands who would have remained childless have received great joy through these new successful experiments. In 1995 alone, according to the American Society for Reproductive Medicine, 11,315 women gave birth to children conceived by some form of assisted reproductive technology.[3]

At the same time, however, these technologies have brought about ethical, legal, and social questions. New treatments are being used before they are fully proven to be safe or effective, resulting in some women

and children having a greater risk for physical and psychological harm. In some cases, according to Weiss, women may not be fully aware that they, their eggs, or the resulting embryos are essentially experiments.[4]

This scientific field remains, for the most part, without federal or state regulations, without which, critics warn, many people, especially children, could be harmed. Many people are calling for controls. Arthur Caplan, director of the Center for Bioethics at the University of Pennsylvania, is among them: "This field is screaming for oversight, regulation and control," he contends. "If you are going to make babies in new [. . .] ways, you have to be sure it's in the interest of the baby."[5]

Weiss goes on to explain that ethical issues concerning questions of parentage are only part of the problem. Now, courts are dealing with cases of inaccurate record keeping in fertility clinics, which have resulted in the loss of frozen embryos. Other questions include who is to blame when an egg is accidentally inseminated by a diseased sperm.

THE QUESTION OF PARENTAGE

Weiss contends that the greatest complication brought on by reproductive technology is the confusion of parentage. The courts, he explains, do not appreciate having to make such decisions. In the words of one New York court, these "are intensely personal and essentially private matters which are appropriately resolved by the prospective parents rather than the courts."[6]

Since there are now many ways to make a baby and many possible participants, the question of parentage may become difficult to answer. Nanette R. Elster, of the Chicago-Kent College of Law, found that some reproductive techniques in use today allow seven or eight people to have parental claims on a single newborn. With the newest technologies, as many as ten people could claim parenthood.[7] According to R. Alta Charo, associate professor of Law and Medicine Ethics at University of Wisconsin at Madison, "'We've now broken up the components of parenthood into so many pieces we can find ourselves in a situation where nobody has presumptive parental status.'"[8]

THE ISSUE OF POSTHUMOUS REPRODUCTION

Weiss continues that the problem can actually get worse, and does so, when the most obvious parent is dead. According to Weiss, the American Society for Reproductive Medicine recognizes the possibilities for confusion and recommends that people carefully consider the repercussions of posthumous reproduction. They do, however, concede that nothing is wrong with it when the deceased has left permission.

Courts, however, have not liked the idea of people inheriting embryos. "A man's sperm or a woman's ova or a couple's embryos are not the same as a quarter of land, a cache of cash, or a favorite limousine."[9]

In addition, Weiss contends that there may be negative psychological effects on children who learn that their parents were dead before they were conceived. Some experts, according to Weiss, have begun suggesting that the desires of potential parents, even if they're dead, are being considered before the welfare of the resulting children.

Weiss explains that similar problems arise with dead sperm donors. According to Lori B. Andrews, professor of law at Chicago-Kent College of Law, Illinois Institute of Technology, a man from Milwaukee made a deposit in a sperm bank, hoping to use it after cancer therapy. When he died, however, the hospital contacted his mother about the sperm. She advertised the sperm to women in need. Andrews commented:

> She [the man's mother] was quoted as saying she wanted to

have as many grandchildren as possible. Well, I'm a real big believer in consent before reproduction. I can't believe this man wanted his sperm spread all over Milwaukee. He donated thinking he would be a father to his [own] children.[10]

THE ISSUE OF RESPONSIBILITY

Weiss reports that fertility clinics are not legally required to screen their clients, but Jane Lessner, a Philadelphia attorney, argues that clinics have that responsibility. Lessner represented the biological mother in a case where the father, a Pennsylvania bank analyst, paid $30,000 to a clinic to inseminate a woman. Less than two months after he took his son home, he killed the baby and is now serving prison time. Of the clinics, attorney Lessner says, "They are in the business. They are the people [who] should know best about potential problems and therefore [they] have special responsibilities to the people involved."[11]

THE MAINTENANCE OF QUALITY

While fertility clinics may not have to test their clients' parental skills, Weiss claims that they, as businesses, still have the responsibility to keep secure the eggs, sperm, and embryos in their care. However, quality control standards vary widely, and stories abound about lost, damaged, or mishandled sperm, eggs, and embryos.

Weiss refers to the well-known case at a clinic in Irvine, California, where many embryos were implanted into the wrong women in the early 1990s. That clinic has since closed, but after that, many more cases of poor record keeping and quality controls have been discovered.[12]

THE REGULATION OF THE FIELD

According to Weiss, no single body can regulate the reproduction field, not even the government which gave up responsibility by no longer funding embryo research. As a result, many states have developed regulations. About half of all states require sperm to be tested for HIV. In addition, about half the states require a married woman to receive her husband's permission before receiving donor sperm. Almost every state requires paternal clarification when donor sperm is used, and five states regulate egg donation.

States also vary in regulation of the sale, purchasing, testing, and research of embryos. There is further variation in regulation of surrogacy situations. In fact, Weiss reports that over fifteen types of surrogacy laws have been passed by one or more states.[13]

A committee of the American Bar Association (ABA) has been trying to develop a model legislation for states to consider, but it is a difficult task. Ami Jaeger, cochairman of the ABA committee and principal at the BioLaw Group in Santa Fe, which provides legal and consulting services in genetics and assisted reproduction, says, "'The field is moving so quickly, you can't easily anticipate the next twist.'"[14]

Weiss reports the basic principles that the committee was hoping to receive backing for from the ABA. First, a doctor should be responsible to inform patients of possible legal and ethical complications. Second, that in some situations, posthumous reproduction should not occur, and third, a limit should be placed on the number of individuals creating a baby. The aim, states Weiss, would be to inform those seeking fertility treatment of the possible legal problems and, most importantly, to ensure that the "interests of the baby-to-be don't get lost along the way."[15]

MONEY-BACK GUARANTEES FOR PREGNANCY

According to an article by Ann Wozencraft in the *New York Times*, some fertility clinics are offering limited money-back guarantees to those desiring to have a baby. At least two companies (Pacific Fertility Center, a chain of six in vitro fertilization clinics, and Reproductive Health Associates, an in vitro clinic in St. Paul) are offering partial refunds to some patients who either do not become pregnant or who miscarry in the early stages of pregnancy.[16]

Wozencraft reports that those in favor of the guarantees suggest that doctors in other fields should try such guarantees as well, since rebate programs do not exist in most other areas of medicine. Wozencraft claims that this happening will depend on how the concept is accepted in the baby-making industry. The fertility clinics that offer refunds claim it helps relieve stress for infertile couples. Wozencraft also reports that some patients have spoken favorably of the offers, saying that the guarantee gives them more confidence in the clinic and helps reduce disappointment.[17]

There are those in the medical field, according to Wozencraft, who are concerned about such rebates.

They say the money-back guarantees are simply a marketing tool and may be a breach of medical ethics. In addition,

> they fear that such programs could encourage doctors to practice risky medicine to increase success rates and avoid having to give rebates. They don't like the idea of offering the program only to patients with the best chances of becoming pregnant. And they are appalled by the idea of basing what the patient pays on whether the treatment is successful. Finally, they fear that such offers give infertile people false hope.[18]

The American Medical Association has also spoken out against the guarantees, arguing that basing fees on outcomes violates the code of ethics: "Such publicized guarantees manipulate and unfairly attract patients."[19]

IN VITRO FERTILIZATION

Beth Frerking, in an article in the *San Diego Union-Tribune* further discusses in vitro fertilization. She reports about the situations of two women who underwent fertility treatments and became pregnant with multiple fetuses—Alice Cangialosi

with five and Dominica Poliseno with six. Instantly, Frerking contends that these women faced moral, emotional, and practical dilemmas. Of the two women, Cangialosi, like Bobby McCaughey (the Iowa woman who had septuplets) carried her fetuses to birth. Poliseno, on the other hand, had five embryos removed (selective reduction) and only delivered one baby.[20]

According to federal health statistics, these trends of multiple births (higher order deliveries) have tripled since 1980 and quadrupled since 1971. As a result of the use of fertility drugs and other assisted reproductive means, such as in vitro fertilization, many more women will have to deal with such issues.[21]

In multiple birth situations, there are other issues to consider. Multiple babies usually are premature and are therefore at higher risk for serious medical problems such as cerebral palsy, lung problems, and learning disabilities. Nanette Elster, a health policy attorney at Chicago-Kent College of Law, says, "There should be pretreatment counseling that informs a couple of all of the risks of (assisted reproduction) treatment, particularly the risks of multiples."[22]

Frerking reports that Dr. Bernard Lieberman, of Great Neck, New York, warns women of the risks of multiple births when using various technologies or drugs to increase fertility. But his patients, he says, may not consider the risks too seriously because they are so determined to get pregnant. Lieberman says, "I think it's really the desire to get pregnant, and once they get pregnant, they don't want to do anything to change things. You tell them there are risks, but they feel they can handle anything. If they can get the golden ring, they want to take it."[23]

That is why, maintains Elster, fertility specialists must inform patients of all the risks, before and after birth. Elster contends that this responsibility must be taken seriously by the doctor since there are no regulations. Elster explains that other countries do have some assisted reproductive regulations. For example, in Great Britain, only three embryos are implanted in in vitro transfers.[24]

CLONING

Another ethical issue in today's medical field is cloning. Holly J. Lebowitz in an article in *The Ledger* reports on the issue. According to Lebowitz, a five-member panel at the American Academy for the Advancement of Science (AAAS) agreed with the National Bioethic Advisory Commission in 1997 that "at this time it is morally unacceptable for anyone in the public or private sector, whether in a research or clinical setting, to attempt to create a child using somatic cell nuclear transfer cloning."[25] About two hundred scientists, ethicists, theologians were in attendance.

Following the successful cloning of Dolly, an adult sheep, President Clinton requested that the NBAC examine the full implications of such technology. They recommend that the issue of cloning be tabled for five years, until it is better understood, and then Congress should again review it.[26]

According to Peter Aldhous, in an article in *New Scientist*, cloning is a subject about which even the experts are still deciding. "I have not heard a single reason for [cloning of humans] that I find ethically acceptable," says Ian Wilmut, whose team created Dolly at Scotland's Roslin Institute. "The relationship between a child and the parent would be bound to be difficult and disturbed. How would my wife respond to a teenage copy of me?"[27]

There are others who claim that if cloning becomes safe and efficient, it may be encouraged in certain situations. For instance, Ray Spier, a bioethicist at the University of Surrey in Guildford, contends that society already deals with a huge diversity of family relationships. "I don't think that anything we can do in the cloning world sits outside the norm to a great extent," he says.[28]

PERSPECTIVES AND CRITIQUES

Following are some excerpts from a radio broadcast of *Talk of the Nation* on National Public Radio with host Ray Suarez and guests Arthur Caplan and Gladys White that shed some light on these complex issues.

> WHITE: . . . the National Advisory Board on Ethics and Reproduction . . . is now an independent, non-profit, inter-disciplinary, apolitical board designed to analyze ethical issues attendant to the use of new reproductive technologies. . . . There really is no other such board in the United States and we feel that the time has come to look at innovations in practice and analyze their implications for couples, for the next generation of . . . children, and for society at large. . . . And although NABER feels that the work of medical specialty groups in regulating themselves is necessary, that we've come to point in time where the insights of practi-

tioners alone are not sufficient to regulate or to guide practice on . . . the whole.

> CAPLAN: Absolutely. I think NABER is a great forum. I think there should be many others. It surprises me that there's no interfaith group [of] religious organizations talking about who they think should use the reproductive technolo-gies, what they think about with respect to the moral status of embryos either wanted or unwanted after someone succeeds in having a baby and doesn't want to use their [extra] embryos anymore that [might be] stored at a clinic. Issues looming on the horizon: the eugenic application of genetic knowledge and reproductive technology—not just to make healthier babies, but maybe to make better babies. We have lots and lots of opportunities in our society. Religious, secular, civic organizations, town hall meetings—we're not taking advantage of them.

> SUAREZ: It's sort of divorced from cost, at a time when we are trying to come to some wisdom as a country about what it costs to get help from medical people for all kinds of things.

WHITE: Unfortunately, this is one of the most commercialized realms of medical practice that exists right now in the United States, due to the fact that people, by and large, must pay out of pocket for infertility diagnostic and treatment services. Cost is already in the picture, and it's in the picture in a big major way. So we're not debating the moral issues apart [from] cost factors. In fact, patients, consumers of infertility services find themselves immediately faced with decisions about how much they want to spend, when they should stop, and whether or not they're going to be impoverished by a series of, for example, IVF treatments.

CAPLAN: Ray, I think that there are two reasons why our society, unlike some of the others that Doctor White has mentioned, has failed to grapple with the ethics. First, the business aspects of reproductive technology in this country. The profession, and those providing the services have an interest in keeping . . . the dialogue at a low key. I'm afraid that business ethics is often substituting for ethical reflection about reproductive technology.

WHITE: I think another feature of the cost-gut check, as you put it, is the major problem from an ethical standpoint that exists right now in terms of accessing these technologies at all.

In the [absence] of third-party reimbursement, we have a significant segment of our society that cannot even begin to consider diagnosing and treating their own infertility. These services are just beyond their ability to pay from the very . . . starting line. So while we worry on the one hand about those who can pay—are they going for too long? Are they spending too many of their resources? Will they have anything left to construct a meaningful lifestyle after they've come to terms with infertility? On the other hand, as a democratic society we have to continue to name and confront the issue of unfair access to infertility services. We are not being democratic in terms of making them available to a cross section of our society in need. And that's a terrible problem.

SUAREZ: But Dr. White, isn't there an extent to which who the IVF clients are—and clients of these other procedures—may force policy makers to respond to them in a way that they might not respond to the poor people who can't afford these services in the first place[?] You're talking about a portion of the population that is most likely to vote, most likely to have political clout in their own communities. Might this eventually result in pressure to force insurers to do things they otherwise don't want?

WHITE: Well, my . . . own response to that is it hasn't succeeded to date. And if, as you suggest, those who can carry the greatest political clout have been unsuccessful to date in achieving access or third-party reimbursement for themselves—I think that the idea that the access discrepancy can be made up in terms of political clout . . . just has not . . . borne fruit. It has not come to bear yet.[29]

CHRISTIAN CRITIQUE

Book reviews in an article by Arthur W. Frank in the *Christian Century* revealed opinions on the Judeo-Christian perspective of ethical issues in medicine. Frank explains that our society has become medicalized, which means that decisions are based more on medical grounds than on moral, theological, political, or legal concerns. Debates are considered in terms of medicine and how issues affect an individual's health whenever possible. As a result of the emphasis on medicine, biomedicine has gained much attention, and bioethics now causes much moral reflection. Contemporary biomedicine results in many medical decisions being made by many different people.

As a result, many people seek a Judeo-Christian response. However, it is unclear what to respond to. Frank explains that with difficult choices, it is unclear where a problem starts, what the results of different decisions will be, and what those actions are based on. William Reich, in his book *Religion and Medical Ethics*, focuses on the Christian critique of the enterprise of bioethics and claims it is "based on the assumption that the core truths could be expressed in a few basic concepts"—such as autonomy, nonmaleficence, beneficience, and justice.[30] Reich goes on to criticize this, claiming that these concepts were divorced from their meanings.[31] Frank explains that when these concepts or principles are separated from their meanings, they are also separated from spiritual values. He says, "We can agree on basic principles, but that does not mean they compel our moral action or guide us in making hard choices."[32]

According to Reich, physicians are too busy looking for physical ailments that they miss the patients' suffering, while ethicists are trying to discover dilemmas to which they can apply one of their few principles and miss hearing "the voice and moral language of women, or the secular person's plaintive plea for the meaning of suffering, dying, and illness—a meaning that is crucial to moral decisions."[33]

In these medicalized times, once difficult decisions have been made, they must then be justified. Christianity, claims Frank, can help people to decide on their justifications for their decisions. Frank claims that "Christianity first poses a dilemma, and then helps individuals live through their utterly particular variations of this dilemma."[34]

He reports that medicine exists to help humans control more of life, from before conception to death. Some, according to Frank, suggest that Christians have "lost the illusion of personal control."[35] As a result, Frank suggests there will be responses—those taking "principled" positions on issues and those searching for individual guidance.

From his book reviews, Frank contends that there is no such thing as Judeo-Christian bioethics but that there must be people who deal with these ethical dilemmas as thinking, religious beings. Frank suggests that religion's contribution is to develop people whose actions will reflect their virtues. The editor of *Religion and Medical Ethics* says that patients "have callings, too, after all, and the calling of Christian patients is never simply their own survival."[36] Part of their calling, according to Frank, is to teach a medicalized society to live life beyond the illusion of personal control.

This concept of living beyond the illusion of personal control, contends Frank, cannot be turned into one of institutional bioethics' principles because it requires limits. Bioethicists, reports Frank, can teach individual autonomy but not limits. Frank concludes with these final thoughts:

> The power of losing the illusion of personal control is in offering what Reich calls a contextualizing moral narrative. Its power is to give people a context to think about the particular stories of their lives and decide what are good justifications for their decisions. The goal is not that the good justification will ever present itself but that, under the

shadow of forgiveness, one justification can be accepted as better.[37]

ETHICS OF MEDICAL PATENTS

In an article in *Technology Review*, Seth Shulman explains that there are thousands of patented medical observations, surgical techniques, and other procedures, some as common as using an ultrasound to determine a baby's gender. The holders of these patents, Shulman says, argue that their procedures deserve patent protection like a new version of a catheter or x-ray machine.[38] Those who support such patents claim that they are vital for medical progress. Without them, they contend, emerging industries, such as gene therapy and medical diagnosis, would be negatively affected.

The impulse toward private ownership of medical technologies is in conflict with the tradition of freely sharing knowledge for the sake of the greater good. The Hippocratic Oath requires that every physician teach medicine "without fee or covenant."[39]

It's a philosophical clash that has profound practical implications. Mark Bogart, a researcher who did his work in 1986 at the University of San Diego, for example, patented a procedure to detect the presence of Down's syndrome in a fetus. He's begun to demand royalties in return for the procedure's use—royalties greater, in some cases, than what an insurance company will reimburse labs for conducting the test. Some labs have already threatened to discontinue the blood screen, and public health officials are concerned that fewer plans will offer it. Mark Evans, professor of obstetrics and gynecology at Hutzel Hospital in Detroit, said, "If the patent is enforced, it will have serious consequences to the health care of women in this country. I believe in capitalism and rewarding discoveries, but there has to be a point where social responsibility takes precedence over greed."[40]

While some have agreed to pay Bogart's royalty, Kaiser Permanente, the country's largest nonprofit hospital chain, has declined to pay and has challenged Bogart in court.[41] An association of other medical professional groups, including the American College of Medical Genetics, the AMA, and the American College of Obstetrics and Gynecology, have joined Kaiser Permanente.

Shulman explains that before the beginning of the knowledge-based economy, the difference between procedures and devices seemed clear and easy to accept. Jonas Salk, when asked about patenting his vaccine for polio, replied that the discovery belonged to the public. "Could you patent the sun?" he quipped.[42]

By the early nineties, however, many doctors and medical researchers were learning of the possible financial benefits from patents on procedures, techniques, and observations. In fact, according to an article in *Medical Economics* on March 11, 1996, the patent office was issuing one hundred patents per month for medical procedures—double the number of patents from the decade before.[43]

All types of patents present medical specialists with many private claims on methods, observations, and other knowledge that doctors before would freely use and share. Shulman writes that all types of specialists have dealt with patent violations.

According to Shulman, patent examiners will not alone be able to resolve the patent problems; many are not even arising from medical practitioners. Shulman explains that they determine if a procedure or treatment is "patent worthy" based on the existence of previously published reports. However, with the continued growth of medical knowledge, published works are not complete reflections of that knowledge. As a result, claims Shulman, patents are issued for many procedures that are neither novel nor

noteworthy. In fact, some patents are even issued for skills that most doctors are required to learn during their residencies.

When considering the thousands of procedures performed by doctors each day, Shulman quotes Robert Protman, a patent lawyer at the Washington, D.C., firm Jenner & Block, who says, "the proliferation of patents of medical and surgical procedures becomes a frightening prospect." It could, Protman continues, "wreak havoc on the delivery of medical services."[44]

The belief that medical procedures must be shared among practitioners was greatly supported in Congress. Rep. Greg Ganske, (R-Iowa), a plastic surgeon, sponsored a bill that would prohibit patenting medical procedures; about eighty other industrialized nations followed suit.[45] Shulman reports that Ganske claimed that if actions weren't taken, people would be afraid to perform the Heimlich maneuver for fear they might get sued for patent violation.

Congress, however, has tried to refrain from limiting the U.S. patent system. During congressional hearings in 1996, lawyers from the American Intellectual Property Law Association, the Intellectual Property Section of the American Bar Association, and the Biotechnology Industry Organization claimed that

218 The Phantom Stethoscope

the United States could eventually impede technological progress by excluding "certain types of patents on policy grounds."[46]

President Clinton signed the final legislation, in the fall of 1996, which sought a balance of the two sides. According to Shulman, the law allowed for patents on medical procedures, but the owners cannot sue to recover royalties from other doctors who use the procedure.

The congressional compromise will help retard some of the "worst incursions of private ownership claims into the shared terrain of medical education."[47] However, Shulman claims that the law may be unable to "address the emerging clash between private profit and the shared 'infostructure' of medical education."[48]

The law will also not stop all legal battles since it is not retroactive to all the existing patent claims. In addition, the law does not address new problems created by high tech biomedical research. The legislation refers only to medical procedures; it does not cover any claims that have to do with "the body's functions that researchers and companies can use to create diagnostic tests or novel treatment approaches."[49]

Endnotes

1. Rick Weiss, "Babies in Limbo: Laws Outpaced by Fertility Advances; Multiple Parties to Conception Muddle Issues of Parentage," *The Washington Post*, 8 February 1998, final edition, sec. A, p. 1.

2. Ibid.

3. Ibid.

4. Ibid.

5. Rick Weiss, "Babies in Limbo."

6. Ibid.; Maureen Kass, respondent, v. Steven Kass, appellant. Decided September 8, 1997, before Miller, J. P.; Copertino, Sullivan, Altman and Friedmann, J. J.

7. Rick Weiss, "Babies in Limbo."

8. Ibid.

9. Ibid.; statement originally made by a California court of appeals in November 1996.

10. Ibid.

11. Ibid.

12. Ibid.; Hearings were held on the alleged misconduct of fertility experts by the Senate Select Committee on Higher Education.

13. Ibid.

14. Ibid.

15. Ibid.

16. Ann Wozencraft, "It's a Baby, Or It's Your Money Back," *The New York Times*, 25 August 1996, late edition, sec. 3, p. 1.

17. Ibid.

18. Ibid.

19. Ibid.

20. Frerking, Beth, "Fertility drugs give birth to ethical dilemmas of multiples," *The San Diego Union-Tribune*, 22 November 1997, p. E-1.

21. J. A. Martin, M. F. MacDorman, and T. J. Mathews, "Triplet births: trends and outcomes, 1971–94" *National Center for Health Statistics, Vital Health Stat* 21 (1997): 55, quoted in Beth Frerking, "Fertility drugs give birth to ethical dilemmas of multiples."

22. Beth Frerking, "Fertility drugs give birth to ethical dilemmas of multiples."

23. Ibid.

24. Ibid.

25. Holly J. Lebowitz, "Theologicans Grapple with Cloning," *The Lakeland Ledger (Fla.)* 5 July 1997, p. D5.

26. Ibid.

27. Peter Aldhous, "The Fears of a Clone," *New Scientist*, 21 February 1998, p. 8.

28. Ibid.

29. Arthur Caplan and Gladys White, interview by Ray Suarez, *Talk of the Nation*, National Public Radio, Inc., 2 December 1996.

30. Arthur W. Frank, review of *Religion and Medical Ethics,* by Allen Verhey, ed. and *Bioethics and the Future of Medicine*, "Religion and Medical Ethics: Looking Back, Looking Forward," *The Christian Century* 113 (November 20, 1996): 1157.

31. Ibid.

32. Ibid.

33. Ibid.

34. Arthur W. Frank, book reviews.

35. Ibid.

36. Ibid.

37. Ibid.

38. Seth Shulman, "Cashing in on medical knowledge," *Technology Review* 101 (March 13, 1998): 38.

39. Ibid.

40. Ibid.

41. *Bio-medical Patent Management Corp. v State of California Department of Health Services et al.,* 98-cv-897. (BPMC initially had a separate case against Kaiser which was consolidated into the above case number.) BPMC dropped its claims against Kaiser on October 30, 1998, and dropped the case against the Health Services Department on November 20, 1998.

42. Seth Shulman, "Cashing in on medical knowledge."

43. Robert Lowes, "Are you stealing from doctors? Medical procedures and method patents," *Medical Economics* 5 (March 11, 1996), quoted in Seth Shulman, "Cashing in on medical knowledge."

44. Seth Shulman, "Cashing in on medical knowledge."

45. The bill is known as HR 1127 and was introduced on March 3, 1995. Sec. 2 of the bill is Limitation on Issuance of Patents and reads as follows:

On or after the date of the enactment of this Act, a patent may not be issued for any invention or discovery of a technique, method, or process for performing a surgical or medical procedure, administering a surgical or medical therapy, or making a medical diagnosis, except that if the technique, method, or process is performed by or as a necessary component of a machine, manufacture, or composition of matter or improvement thereof which is itself patentable subject matter, the patent on such machine, manufacture, or composition of matter may claim such technique, method, or process.

46.   Seth Shulman, "Cashing in on medical knowledge."

47.   Ibid.

48.   Ibid.

49.   Ibid.

CHAPTER 29

OF STRESS AND CINNAMON BUNS

SNOW CAME; SNOW WENT. Mila's life was a welter of clinical tasks, at which her confidence and competence increased on a daily basis, and the importance of her business-of-medicine duties became increasingly more apparent to her . . . almost on a daily basis. Clinical Pathway meetings. Cholecystectomies. Tumor debulkings. Bowel resections. A patient who vomited on her lab coat, then refused to let a *girl* operate on him. A man who begged her to save his wife, as if Mila would, or could, decide to do so or not on that basis. Risk management workshops. Morbidity and mortality conferences. Kidney transplants. Wound debridements. A patient who didn't die on the table of an aortic aneurysm. A patient who did. Amputations. Joint replacements. Sickness. Health. Business as usual.

When Mila looked up, spring was gone, and summer was full on. Hazy, sticky, smelly, cranky July. By the time Mila got to the hospital in the morning, the dampness from her shower was already replaced with a layer of sweat. After five minutes, she was clammy in the overchill of Eastside's air-conditioning. In the mystery-of-life department (for which Ajax is little help), the fact that hospitals are always ridiculously hot or cold must be in the top ten.

Mila's first postgraduate year was over—postgraduate both from med school and from her equally important alma mater, dear old Alien Abduction U. Ajax was in and out of her life. To her relief, mostly out. Mila's days were so overloaded that one more perspective, or piece of information, or advice . . . one more correction, or complaint, or person needing her, or asking her a question, or beeping her, or calling her . . . one more suture, or bleeder, or bodily fluid, one more moldy cinnamon bun in the back of her fridge, one more fly that somehow got in her apartment, one more crumpled piece of paper on her coffee table would send her over the edge.

This particular crumpled piece of paper said, "get a life." How typical. It was the list that she'd made in February that culminated in her first, and last, social event of the year. Her breakfast with Penny. That breakfast had been pleasant, but since then there had been no time to do it again. Or to throw out the list, for that matter. Mila crumpled up the paper again, and let it drop to the floor. Back to her presentation. Tonight, Eastside Hospital graduation, where Mila would officially move on to the next step in her training as a surgical resident. Then, the big one, tomorrow, an alumni bash at the University of Pennsylvania. Several residents (including Mila) would be presenting their research projects. It would also be her first trip back. Focus on the presentation, she admonished herself. She was crying.

"Stop," she said aloud, but she didn't. She hated showing weakness, even when she was by herself. Hell, *especially* when she was by herself. She rubbed her eyes with the heels of her hands. My life is medicine. Everyone who enters this field gives up a lot.

"When was the last time you felt like a person, not a doctor?"

"Can't you goddamn knock, Ajax? This is not your business. It's not a medical crisis, it's a human one." She pushed away the tears. "Bug off."

"On the contrary," said Ajax, "this may be THE medical crisis, one we've been expecting you to reach. You must learn to manage this kind of stress."

"No, Ajax. That's not the point. It's not the stress, it's what I'm getting in return. In my time, docs gave up a lot, but they earned respect. Autonomy. A feeling of accomplishment. Managed care chokes off all of that, and we're left with . . . with . . ." Mila didn't have the heart to finish.

"You've got to learn to balance a professional life which does not have all the previous accouterments—money, respect—with a severely compromised personal life. That combination has increased stress among physicians to an alarming level in this era."

"I guess it will be useful to know about stress management," said Mila. But it wasn't, Mila knew, the whole answer to what bothered her. After this tutorial, she needed to think.

CHAPTER 30

STRESS MANAGEMENT: THE PERSONAL AND THE PROFESSIONAL

"STRESS IS THE BASIC confusion created when [the] mind overrides the body's desire to choke the living daylights out of some jerk who desperately deserves it."— Timothy P. Brigham, Ph.D.[1]

The experience of at least a moderate amount of stress is universal, unavoidable, but, luckily, probably not detrimental. High levels of stress, however, are dangerous. They increase one's risk of a number of serious illnesses, among them cardiovascular disease, diabetes, and intestinal disorders. For their patients' sakes and for their own, then, physicians should know at least the fundamentals of stress management.

By the eighties, *Time* magazine had already dubbed stress an "epidemic," and it is still one of the most pervasive health problems in America today. A "high level [. . .] of stress" is experienced by 89 percent of all adults,[2] and stress accounts for 60 to 90 percent of visits to the doctor.[3]

STRESS AND PHYSICIANS

Stress is of special concern for physicians personally, too, particularly because health care industry changes are making life as a doctor ever more stressful. Managed care has been identified as one of the most prevalent sources of stress for physicians today, with its decreased job security, increased patient load, and decreased income.[4] One doctor in Seattle even coined a name for it: "Managed care hypertension." This after he measured significant increases in his blood pressure following phone calls with managed care providers.[5]

Even aside from managed care, medical practice is highly stressful. Too, many of the personality traits that lead people to become doctors in the first place can exacerbate the effects of these stresses. Many doctors are perfectionists, high achievers, responsibility takers, approval seekers, or self-sacrificers[6]—all characteristics that make it difficult for physicians to get help in managing the high levels of stress in their lives.

Not only are doctors under stress subject to health risks, but they have a tendency to make more mistakes professionally. "Burned-out physicians are more likely to make mistakes than their mellower colleagues."[7] They may, for instance, be less likely to obtain a complete patient history or order additional tests to confirm a diagnosis. Some malpractice insurers sponsor stress management programs for doctors, as the link between malpractice suits and doctors suffering from stress has become obvious.

Recently, too, however, there has been an increase in both physicians helping each other cope with stress and the development of special programs and services specifically designed for doctors affected by stress. The American Psychological Association reports that thirty-three states currently have colleague assistance programs for practitioners now in place or in development.[8] In Britain, there are, among others, the National Counseling Service for Sick Doctors and GP Stress Factory.[9]

STRESS MANAGEMENT TECHNIQUES

As is true when addressing any medical condition, there are two steps to stress management intervention—assessment and treatment.

Potential causes of stress are multiple and can be anything from environmental to emotional to health related; listening closely to the patient's situation is crucial. It is also important to note symptoms potentially related to stress, both physical (e.g., insomnia and headache) and psychological (e.g., poor concentration and excessive self-criticism).[10]

One of the physician's key responsibilities in treating stress is education. Foremost is simply helping the patient understand that s/he is under stress. Many people (physicians particularly) are reluctant to admit to being affected by stress; they see it as a weakness. The more information a physician can provide, the better off both s/he and the patient will be.

Perhaps the most important thing to keep in mind when treating stress is that one size does not fit all. Stress management approaches each have their own strengths and weaknesses, and it is critical to match the treatment to the patient's needs. Therefore, it is important to understand thoroughly both the different treatment options available and the individual patient's situation.

Herbert Benson, head of the Mind/Body Medical Institute in Boston, described the natural reaction to a stressful situation as a flight-or-fight response, manifested physically through increased heart rate, breathing, and blood pressure; as he has proven in medical studies, these reactions can be tempered through mental relaxation. The physiological changes achievable through relaxation—changes such as decrease in stress hormones, heart rate, and blood pressure—are called the Relaxation Response.

Techniques for achieving this response abound, but they all involve change: changing behavior, thinking, lifestyle choices, or situations.[11]

Relaxation. Subjects are taught techniques to relax their muscles progressively. This is the most commonly used intervention in job settings.

Physical fitness. The intent of this approach is to strengthen cardiorespiratory endurance, flexibility, and muscular function. Regular exercise is combined with a nutritious diet.

Cognitive restructuring. This is an application of the rational-emotive approach. It helps people identify their "style of thought," and understand how that style influences their behavior.

Meditation. This is similar to relaxation, except that the focus is on one repetitive stimulus or cue with which one's breathing is coordinated.

Assertiveness training. Assertive behavior is differentiated from both aggressive and passive behavior. Assertive behavior can then be used to better cope with stressful situations.

Stress inoculation. Subjects learn skills that make them better able to bear emotional stress prior to its occurrence.

Of these methods, physical fitness has been found to be the most effective in reaching its specific objectives. In terms of cost and length of training, relaxation is the most practical, meditation and stress inoculation the least.[12]

Other techniques can be effective, too. Decreasing caffeine intake, making time for leisure, using humor, getting adequate sleep, and relying on others for emotional support are frequently recommended.

Biofeedback involves the measurement of physiological responses and immediate feedback to the individual.[13] As a patient becomes more aware of physical changes created by stress, s/he may be better able to control them. There are also cognitive approaches which involve a problem-solving orientation; the patient is taught to deconstruct the things which are causing stress into more manageable pieces.[14]

There's no longer any doubt that the effects of stress on the health of patients and physicians are profound and intertwined. An awareness of the signs and importance of stress, and an understanding of how to ease it, is essential knowledge for physicians both in treating patients and in tending to themselves. Physicians must teach their patients and employ the same techniques on themselves. In so doing they will be helping their patients, themselves, then their patients again; a doctor whose own stress is eased may be better able to ease that of those s/he treats.

Endnotes

1. Flora Johnson Skelly, "Managing Stress," *Physician's Guide to the Internet* (http://physiciansguide.com/docstress.html).

2. "Stress—America's #1 Health Problem," *American Institute of Stress* (http://www.stress.org/ais/problem.html).

3. "The Center for Corporate Health—Executive Summary," *Mind/Body Medical Institute* http://www.med.harvard.edu/programs/mindbody/corp/summary.html).

4. John H. Wilters, "Stress, burnout and physician productivity," *Medical Group Management* 45 (May 1, 1999): 32–37.

5. Mark Crane, "Why burned-out doctors get sued more often," *Medical Economics* 75 (May 26, 1999): 210.

6. Ibid.

7. Ibid.

8. Scott Sleek, "Psychologists help one another survive today's challenging times," *APA Monitor* (October 1997) (http://www.apa.org/monitor/oct97/tough.html).

9. Jane Sims, "The evaluation of stress management strategies in general practice: an evidence-led approach," *British Journal of General Practice* 47, no. 422 (1997): 577–82.

10. Jane Turner and Beverley Raphael, "Stress management and counseling in primary care," *Medical Journal of Australia* 167, no. 10 (1997): 547–51.

11.   David B. Posen, M.D., "Stress Management for Patient and Physician," *The Canadian Journal of Continuing Medical Education* (April 1995) (http://www.mentalhealth.com/mag1/p51 -str.html).

12.   Cinzia Bellarosa and Peter Y. Chen, "The Effectiveness and Practicality of Occupational Stress Management Interventions: A Survey of Subject Matter Expert Opinions," *Journal of Occupational Health Psychology* 2, no. 3 (1997): 247–62.

13.   Jane Turner and Beverley Raphael, "Stress management and counseling in primary care," 574–51.

14.   Ibid.

Additional Sources

Gordon, James. "Role of the mind in healing." *Congressional Testimony by Federal Document Clearing House* (November 5, 1997).

Reid, James. "Stress management: does it work?" *Australian Family Physician* 25 (August 1996): 1245–8.

C H A P T E R 31

OF ROBERTA AND REVELATIONS

REALITY RETURNED IN A BITTER BLACK WAVE. It washed over Mila and overwhelmed her.

That was herself described in that lesson, that burned-out anxious doctor. It was her portrait—no real friends, no real personal life, no time, no love. Brimming with unhappiness and anxiety. After only a year. A single year. Despite all her wisdom from Ajax, all her tutorials and perspective and extraterrestrial support, despite all that, she *was* burned out. Mila's fists thumped at her head, which curled in on her knees.

If anyone deserves an indulgent misery bath, it's me, thought Mila. Fifteen years of her life had been lost. Connection to her past had been lost. Her times, lost. Her context, lost. All was gone, and for what? She'd been given a second chance, and she'd screwed it up. She'd failed. She was running as hard as she could down the road to being stalled and disappointed yet again.

Numb and unseeing, she dressed for graduation, walked to the hospital, nodded to friends.

She tried to comfort herself by concluding (OK, rationalizing) that there hadn't been a way for her to avoid this. What the hell was Quam thinking? There wasn't anyone who wasn't stalled and disappointed in this era. Look at

229

her fellow residents right now, buzzing with each other before the ceremony. Sure, they looked pretty much like residents did before. Best, brightest, and ball-broken from the difficult year; it had never been easy. But the future for these docs was one hell of a lot less conquerable now than before. Less money, less autonomy, less respect, less veneration. It was much more likely than before that their careers—and hers—would be fraught with obstacles and frustration.

Where's your answer to that, Ajax? No response.

She slumped slightly in her chair as the graduation speaker moved to the podium. He was Dr. Leonard Kimmel, a former dean who described himself as a futurist. Now why didn't she have that job? Mila thought. She wanted to ask this Kimmel how he'd trained for it. Had he been abducted by aliens, too, or was he just guessing blind?

"I am pleased," he began, "to have the privilege of addressing you today on this important occasion. As I look out on you, the first graduates of the new milennium, I cannot help but think of my own graduation some twenty years ago. I sat in the same seats that you are sitting in. I felt, perhaps, some of the same emotions that you now feel. Pride, a great sense of accomplishment, a bit of awe, and a fair amount of anxiety."

Mila chewed her finger. The futurist continued. "I felt proud to finally be a 'doctor,' something I had wanted to be since I was young. Just the word 'doctor' evoked images that were iconographic. Albert Schweitzer in Africa. Tom Dooley in Vietnam. Great medical missionaries helping those who needed the help the most.

"Society afforded physicians a unique prestige of somehow being 'special' members of society. Special in training, special in knowledge, special in traditions, special in privileges and, perhaps most important, special in responsibility. All this 'special-ness' left me feeling somewhat awestruck to be included in such an elite group."

Mila realized she was shaking her head. Nothing like a clueless speech to turn self-pity to annoyance. Dr. Futurist, she felt like saying, what the hell is so special about us now? We're just as marketed and market-driven as ad-agency hucksters. She thought about her father, about how everyone in town had loved and respected him. So much had been lost. So much was gone. What a stupid waste.

"Accomplishment," continued Dr. Kimmel. "Medical school, then as now, was difficult. The course of studies was arduous in its content and volume.

The educational process was part scientific training, part apprenticeship, and part ritual. To be awarded the title of 'doctor' felt good. It was not only a dream come true, but at least in some small way, earned.

"There was, of course, anxiety. No matter how much one studied and seemed to know, there was more. The image of Sir William Osler always loomed. Osler was the most famous physician of his time, the doctor of Walt Whitman. He taught medicine in this school from 1884 to 1889. Osler's was not a comforting image for me, but a demanding one. It conjured up visions of all that I did not know but felt I should. He seemed to hover over me, the quintessential senior attending, vaguely displeased with my work. No matter how hard I tried, how could I be good enough to follow in the tradition of Osler? How could I be knowledgeable enough to help those who desperately counted on me to help them? How possibly would I be able to fulfill the expectations of myself, let alone others? All those deep, almost existential questions were mixed in with the more plebeian concerns: how was I going to pay to move to Chicago for my internship since I was flat broke and, from my standpoint, hopelessly in debt?"

There was a polite ripple of laughter through the audience, and Mila let her mouth stretch in the semblance of a smile. Despite herself, Mila found herself pulled into what Kimmel was saying, almost as if he were speaking directly to her. *Speaking my life with his words*, the Roberta Flack song pulled itself into her semiconsciousness (or was it helped there by her intergalactic friend?).

Dr. Kimmel went on. "Now, as I thought of what useful pearls I might have to say to you today, of what I have learned over the years and what wisdom, albeit meager, I might impart on so important a day, three words came to me. 'Ancient,' 'modern,' and 'unexpected.' Linked with these words are themes that have always guided me in my own continued development as a physician, and perhaps may be of some help to you."

Help? I'll take it, thought Mila, even from a graduation speech. *I'm looking for a miracle in my life;* now it was the Moody Blues. She smiled realizing how pathetically appropriate that was.

"Modern," continued Kimmel. "This word always has a nice ring to it. Yet there is a somewhat melancholy connotation to it for me. Being 'contemporary,' being 'up-to-date' are not small challenges in medicine. When I walk through the stacks of the library (still much more fun for me, I must admit, than browsing with my computer), I am always impressed at the number of clearly anachronistic medical texts that feature the title of 'modern' or 'current.' These outdated books, some quite recently published, are now only of historical value. They are testaments to the pace of the change of medical science.

"Here again, for me, the image of Osler appears. I remember his famous remark about how he was continually surprised at how physicians who had stopped learning could practice medicine, but never at how poorly they could do it. The challenge for us as 'modern' physicians is not only to continue to learn, but to be effective as learners.

"This is no mean feat. The techniques called for are not simply the old ones of encyclopedic reading and prodigious memory, or of experience—even extensive experience—alone. An approach to learning that is both disciplined and creative is necessary. Here, new understandings of how adults learn and of new technologies that vastly enhance our ability to ask and answer questions can be profoundly helpful. New technologies offer us the ability to gain experience in a more focused and directed way, not simply to be dependent on who wanders in the office or who happens to be in the hospital.

"And our learning must not simply be limited to the science of medicine. The practice of medicine is a sociologic as well as a scientific enterprise. It is our responsibility as physicians, of whatever specialty, to understand the nature of the system of care in which we practice. And to understand the society that we serve. Hippocrates understood this well when he commented on the environment in his texts. We as 'modern' physicians are called to do no less.

"Finally, the Unexpected. The mid- to late-nineteenth century was a time of great scientific discovery and technological blossoming. Giants like the German pathologist Virchow and the French physiologist Claude Bernard were applying 'modern' scientific principles to medicine, and were thus laying the basis for the approach to clinical medicine advocated by Osler. Jules Verne, the French science fiction writer and a rough contemporary of Osler, was a visionary in this scientific age. He had fantastic visions—space travel, underwater exploration, new inventions. These were hardly imaginable at a time when railroads were still relatively new, travel by horse common, and automobiles experimental. Now, somewhat over a century later, Verne's visions have become ordinary.

"The parallels to modern medicine are easily apparent and should imbue us with a sense of humility, if nothing else. The challenges that you will face as mature physicians are being developed in the technical advances and societal changes happening today. The effects and impacts, whether in radical new approaches to the treatment of disease, redesign of health care financing, or fundamental ethical dilemmas ensuing from genetic engineering, are as likely to be as fantastic as Verne's visions. As servants of our fellow man, we will always need to be open to the new and the unexpected. To look for its useful application to alleviate suffering, to promote health, and to guard against unexpected harm.

"It is trite to say that medicine is different today than it was decades ago, not to mention centuries ago. Not only is the science of medicine different (remember CAT scans were experimental when I was a student, and the concept of the 'intensive care unit' had been invented a scant decade before), but the structure of medical practice is different as well. In the decades following 1970, we discovered that medicine was a business, and a very complex business at that. Since then, our language has changed and evolved, not only to reflect changes in scientific thought and in patterns of pathology with entities like AIDS, but also to reflect the change in organization. Hospital administrators are now CEOs. Health insurance is often 'managed care.' And, in the hospital, MBAs have become almost as ubiquitous as MDs (with an increasing number of us carrying both degrees after our names)."

Oh, no, thought Mila. He had me for a while, but now the bullshit starts. Another lecture about the business of medicine. She seriously considered getting up and leaving, but what Dr. Kimmel said next caught her by surprise, actually moved her.

"Even with all this newness," Kimmel said, "the sense of the 'ancient' remains. You can see it each time we are afforded the privilege of sitting at the bedside of a patient. This 'patient,' insured by HMOs and probed by MRIs, has the same worries and concerns that the patient of Hippocrates had thousands of years ago. This 'patient,' vulnerable and asking for our help, takes the same comfort from our touch as did Hippocrates's patient. And our responsibilities as physicians, regardless of what modern specialty we practice, is to be true to this ancient tradition of caring. It is what society wants, and what we would want for ourselves. To care in the special way a physician cares is our privilege and our responsibility.

"Through all of this inevitable and exciting change, we must continue to remember the ancient traditions of our profession: that it is our role to bring science, in the form of medicine, to serve humanity, and also to bring humanness to the practice of science. Go forth. Try to do good. And have fun! Thank you."

Mila rose and clapped with everybody else, but unlike everybody else, Mila was in an internal turmoil. Because during that last part of the speech, she had finally understood.

What was it about the current medical world that made it less likely she'd end up stalled and disappointed? Nothing. Nothing at all.

Mila thought back to the poor docs in the negotiation experiment so programmed to do only as told, so programmed to follow authority, so frozen in their hierarchy and wedded to the rules-as-stated that they refused to talk to each other, and lost everything, every single time.

Dr. Schwietzer hadn't been like that, nor Dr. Dooley nor, for that matter, Dr. Osler, the futurists' stern ghost. None of them had been mindless, white-coated trudgers, unmindful of the realities of their eras.

In the end, it was not a matter of adapting to a new reality, of learning to accept increased restrictions on her day-to-day choices, and upheaval and arguments and acrimony about the future of her profession. It was not a matter of drinking less coffee, clocking out at 5:00, relaxing, and calling it a win. That simply wasn't a solution worth trading sixteen years of her life for, and it wasn't a solution Dr. Osler would be proud of.

What, Mila thought as she clapped, was different about her now than the other doctors her age who'd lived through the rise of managed care? Mila had been formed by the same hierarchical, non-collaborative acculturation that her old peers had. But they, having gone through change after change, could see only through the lens of loss. And indeed there had been loss. Plenty of it.

But Mila *had* been taught something by Ajax and his cronies—that lens is only one of many; it's a matter of perspective, of acculturation. She really had been given a gift—a chance to step outside herself. She was no longer sealed in her own set of biases. And now she had to use that perspective. She had to stop being like those lockstep docs in the experiment. She had to stop listening to other people—including Ajax & co.—about what was right. About what was good for medicine. About what was possible. She had to consult her own conscience and her own intelligence.

In the end, it was a question of whether she could peek over the walls of the maze. Whether she could stay aware that it could be done, and that it was worth doing. And it was the realization that when the world is in chaos, the opportunities to change it for the better exponentially increase.

Quam's admonitions made sense now. She did have a second chance. She had learned a lot about the new realities. But certain things never changed—Dr. Kimmel had made that clear enough. The opportunities for optimism were not based on the external environment or the reality of the day. They were based on the processing of that reality and the available information. The learning. And the need to make things better. Indeed, all the ingredients are here, even in the year 2000.

C H A P T E R 32

OF LATTES AND LOST (?) OPPORTUNITIES

REVELATIONS AND RESOLUTIONS ARE WONDERFUL THINGS, THOUGHT MILA, BUT APPLYING THEM KIND OF SUCKS.

Mila's forehead was glued to the Amtrak train window as it sped along, Philly-bound, her first trip back since she started collecting interstellar frequent flyer miles. She had a vague optimistic twinge that perhaps this trip would represent a bridge between her old life and new life. Well, she thought, hope is the thing with feathers and absolutely no basis in reality.

All right. Time to remember her management discussions. Best case and worst case scenarios. Best case, she thought, I go back to Penn and realize that losing fifteen years didn't matter. That at least I got to make some new and interesting friends from outside this planet. Worst case scenario—I go back, realize what I've missed, feel really, really shitty, and take up a nice hobby like repetitive head-banging on hard surfaces. Either way, though, it was time to resolve things and be normal. She had to shed Ajax once and for all because normal did not mean depending on alien beings from another galaxy. And she had to figure out how she felt about everything else, too.

As she mulled, her eyes wandered. Out the window Trenton flashed by. Stone embankments. Trash. The back of the seat in front of her. The old lady snoring next to her. Aisle. A woman, forties, with a laptop. Someone next to the woman, reading. A successful-looking man, forties, really cute.

It was Bill.

It was Bill, and he was still a big, solid, strong-looking guy with a face full of dignity and compassion and fun. He was starting to get gray around the edges and was wearing glasses now, which he never had as a student. But he also had around him an aura of experience, even of wisdom. Mila could feel every inch of her body flushing, her insides jumping around. Her worst case scenario seemed awfully likely, suddenly. Psychosis, anyone?

She tried to calm herself. It's an old pal. Not a cause for an entire adrenal implosion. Take it easy. It didn't work.

All those stupid dates in the old days. All those insipid, pompous boys. She'd been so narrowly focused, so bound to the expectations she'd formed long before, that she hadn't even been able to take the tiniest chance with someone obviously great. He might be married to that woman next to him, have kids. And even if he's not, and even if, with the help of Ajax's curiosity dampeners, she could somehow explain why she was still twenty-seven, even if that were possible, Bill had gone and grown up without her. He had a hunk of life and a career. But damn, he still looked good.

Too many thoughts. Mila went to her compartmentalization mode. Possible love of my life, loss of. Debit column. Done. Move on.

She picked up her papers, but couldn't resist peeking out from behind them. The train would be pulling into 30th Street Station soon, and Bill was joining the line waiting to leave, reaching easily for his overnight bag from the overhead rack. As he turned to head down the aisle, he happened to look Mila's way, and their eyes caught. Look away, Mila, she thought, but she didn't.

Bill looked at her vaguely, seemed to start a little, and gazed more intently. He almost seemed to be about to speak, but the line in the aisle started moving. He shook his head a little, as if dismissing a silly thought, turned away and walked off.

Down to the salsa music blaring from the upstairs window, it could have been 1985, the day Mila left. She was walking down Spruce Street, revisiting the sites of her 'departure' in the interest of closing the loop.

When she got to 38th Street, there it was—the Spruce Street Deli. Only now it was called The Convenience Corner. *Convenience for the Twenty-first*

Century—Welcome to the Spruce Street Convenience Corner, read a sign in the window. Mila laughed. It wasn't just medicine. Reengineering had reached all the way down to her old haunt. She had to go in.

To her surprise, changes went beyond the sign. The place was cleaner, the old Bunn-o-matic replaced by a gleaming gourmet coffee setup. There were a fair number of customers but no feeling of jostling or impatience. A substantial professional-looking woman was giving instructions to the young man behind the counter. The woman turned and spoke.

"Well, I'll be damned. It's Dr. Mila. What skin cream you using, girl? You finally listened to me about less books, more sex?" It was Gladys, and Mila couldn't believe how good it felt to see her.

"Gladys, you look like you're doing more than slinging scrapple these days."

Gladys laughed. "Don't worry, I haven't become one of your obsessive anal types—I still know how to have a good time. But I do own about twelve of these places now. Let's just say I saw the light. The white light." Gladys winked at Mila.

Mila winked back almost reflexively. God only knew what *Gladys's* white light was—the one thing Mila knew for sure was it was a different white light than hers. "Right," Mila smiled. "White light."

"No, Dr. Mila," said Gladys. "The real White Light."

Mila kept smiling. It usually worked when she had no idea what was going on.

"The White, Mila," said the young man behind the counter, and Mila suddenly saw that it was Quam.

"Hello, Mila," she looked behind her and recognized Dr. Enos, the visionary CEO from Eastside. She started to reply when a merry voice spun her around again. From in back of the counter, "Are you surprised?!" It was Ajax, holding an enormous cake in the shape of a mortarboard, blazing with rocket-shaped candles.

The other customers in the store crowded around Mila, and she saw that they all had party hats on and were squawking party blowers. They were people she knew: Dr. Reinhold, Beulah Trey, Zorak, even Dr. Kimmel. Mila stood, weak with confusion, her disparate friends pumping her hand, hugging her, congratulating her. A champagne cork popped. Gladys stood back from them all, chuckling. "She's surprised, all right, Ajax, she's surprised. Let's have some mercy. Let's tell her now."

"Do that," said Mila, dizzily. "Is this it? Is this my long-awaited psychotic breakdown?"

"No, baby. Mila, in fact you've handled this better than most of us did. Am I right?" The bizarre group of celebrants seemed to nod in unison. "Let's put it this way, Mila. The Climarans are kind of our guardian angels. Every hundred years or so, they try to clean up some of the mess we've accumulated and try to give us a kick start into the future. I won't bother you with a long history lesson, but think back to the industrial revolution. There were a few people who were able to combine the best of the old with what future technology had to offer. Did you ever wonder how they were able to make what seemed like all the right moves? They seemed to be able to see into the future. What they really had were our friends, the Climarans.

Mila couldn't seem to form words. Gladys took a serious tone, "Take it easy, child, no need to talk. Calmly collect your thoughts. We can all read them."

Mila decided to look at this analytically, and somehow her mouth remembered how to talk. "Gladys," she asked, "Are you a—one of—them?"

Gladys threw back her head and laughed, the laugh of the 1985 Gladys. "No, honey, I wouldn't know what to do with those six arms. I must admit, though, I've had a few men that seemed like they were possessed with extra appendages. No, I'm as human as you are Mila. It's just that all of us here have had the opportunity, courtesy of the Climarans, to see into the future. Our job is to make sure that we use that knowledge wisely."

Mila felt like she'd been turned upside down and shaken. "I thought that this was all about the Climaran abduction squad. What about the brain dissection and the problems with the space-time continuum?"

Ajax thought into her brain, "Mila, I'm sorry we couldn't tell you the truth. Until we are sure that a particular human will fit in with our little group, we need to use what I guess you would call a 'cover story.' Did I use that correctly?"

"Ajax," said Gladys in a tone of warning, "you just stick to the facts. Save the lexicography for later."

"Oh, of course." He waved several arms in apology. "So if you turned out to be the wrong person, you wouldn't be able to betray the identity of the others."

Gladys rolled her eyes. "In other words, what our green friends are telling us is that over the years they have learned the fine human art of spin doctoring and bullshit."

"'Plausible deniability' would be the management term," said Ajax, obviously savoring. When you're up to your ass in blood, Dr. Baskin had always told Mila, take a deep breath, stop the bleeding, and then start thinking. If there was ever a time to tamponade the artery and get to the basics, it was now.

"All right. Let me get this straight," Mila said. Ajax had an arm around Beulah. It was just too weird. "There's a group of us in different human endeavors, and these aliens allow us to see the future. We get our own personal tour guide and some good advice from some interesting holographic images. But so what? I'm no better off than a doc who got an MBA to begin with. I'm still sitting here in 2000, and we've still screwed up the medical profession over the past fifteen years."

Finally Dr. Enos spoke. His voice was as authoritative and exacting as it had been during orientation last year. "Mila, you reason quickly. That will make you a great surgeon. It is also why we all thought you were a perfect candidate to join us in this endeavor."

"Thank you, sir," said Mila. "I think."

"Mila," Enos said, "your assessment of this situation is accurate except for one thing. Have you ever thought of what it would be like to go back to 1985?"

Mila was quiet for a long moment. "I do still think about it a lot." She bit her lip. "The idea of having to endure the painful fifteen years that medicine has gone through is not good. I wouldn't want to do that. But although I know I would have ended up, as you said, stalled and disappointed, I guess I still wish I hadn't lost all of those years." Mila blinked and swallowed. "And all of those opportunities." Gladys came over and gave Mila's shoulder a squeeze. Mila took a breath. "I'll adjust. But I can't say I don't wish I could go back. With all my present knowledge, that is."

"Bingo," grinned Gladys. "Get that girl a free cup of latte, Quam."

Ajax could, apparently, not contain his excitement. "Mila, in reality, we are not in 2000!" All six of his arms began tossing around with glee. "Oh, I always love this part the best. Isn't it marvelous? Are you surprised? Oh, look everybody, she *is* surprised."

Mila narrowed her eyes. "What are you saying here, Ajax?"

"The current date is March 16, 1985. Your experience on the spaceship and your entire surgical internship occurred over the last twenty-four hours Earth time. To all your friends and your family, that's the period of time that you have been gone." Ajax's very skin seemed to vibrate with the news. "And they're not even worried, because I left them a note in your handwriting. You did promise to call back today."

Dr. Enos took over. "What you have become, in essence, is an ambassador—an ambassador to the future. The ten of us will get together once a month to talk about how we can move the health care world forward toward a brighter tomorrow. It is in no way certain that you will be able to make all the changes in medicine you'd like to based on your new knowledge. You may not even be able to alter the direction physicians choose to take. But you will be able to argue, as will I, for a reasoned approach based on measured quality and reasonable costs. You'll be able to work for creative partnerships with our patients, employers, industry, and insurers. So when 2000 does roll around, perhaps physicians who have been willing to listen to us will be the opinion leaders and will be spread around the country. Mila, people will assume that you are somewhat of a visionary, and our friends from Climara will continue their covert existence."

Mila was still putting it together. "I'm back in 1985, nothing's changed? I've got all this business and clinical knowledge and I can go ahead and start my first year residency at Eastside?" Everyone nodded. She turned to Ajax. "What about you? Does this mean that our relationship is officially over?"

If Ajax could have smiled, Mila thought, he would have been doing it with both his faces, fit to burst. "You will always be able to summon me, but I won't whisk you away to any more virtual reality adventures. Your reality, as well as the future reality of health care, will depend on what you choose to make it."

Mila had one more question, "How will I know when it's time to meet again?"

"You will just know," said a voice, and all was White.

And then she was back.

Paul McCartney and Stevie Wonder were crooning over the loudspeaker, and Tom was leaning over the counter to Gladys. "It's just like you and me, Glads. Don't you see? Ebony and ivory! Perfect harmony! Oh, hi, Mila."

She was back. "Where's the Beef" was back on every magazine cover, the Bunn-o-matic was a'perking. Tom pointed his thumb at her facetiously. "So you leave all your friends for a night of drunken merriment by yourself, huh?" He put on his most obnoxious look, the one that he usually saved for when he was discussing his latest social escapades. He nodded his head toward the corner.

Mila hadn't noticed—over there, flipping through an *Enquirer*, was Bill. His hair was still black. When he noticed her, he put the paper down.

Tom snorted. "Bill over here had a fun night. He actually went with the sparkling spring water." When Bill smiled, little lines crinkled around his eyes. Those would grow someday, Mila remembered. Tom went on. "Man, the babes were scamming my buddy here, he just let 'em pass. Jeez. Twins, too. You can't believe how twins love docs."

"Have you had dinner yet?" Mila asked Bill quietly.

"Nah," said Tom, "I was puking up that beer until about an hour ago. God, Mila, ya' gotta wish ya were a guy doc. We get all the fun, believe you me. Hey, wait, you guys, I've just gotta get my change for the fifty. Come on, Gladys, hurry it up; they're leaving without me."

"Sorry, Dr. Tom. I guess I'm just a little slow today. Now, where was I . . . ?"

As the door closed behind Mila and Bill, the little bells jingled, and Gladys smiled.

GLOSSARY

adjusted cost per admission. The typical cost for a single hospital stay for one patient. Typically adjusted by age, sex, institutional status, Medicaid, disability, and possibly the presence of a specific disease state.

baby boomers. Generally applies to people born in the period 1945–1960, when the birthrate in the U.S. was unusually high. In health care, a group that has changed the services required based on their vocal consumerism and sheer numbers, e.g., increased marketing of geriatric services secondary to the aging of the baby boomer population.

best care. Treatment that is judged most likely to benefit the patient upon considering the available scientific evidence (measuring the general efficacy, the particular effectiveness, and the expected outcome) for various treatment options.

best practices. Practices, procedures, or systems that result in unusually strong performance or that set a standard for performance.

binding arbitration. Settlement of a dispute by a third party (arbitrator), where the disputants agree to be bound by the arbitrator's decision before beginning the arbitration process.

243

capitation. A method of payment for health services in which a practitioner or hospital is prepaid a fixed, per capita amount to cover a specific period of time for each person served, regardless of the actual number or nature of services provided to each person.[5]

care management. The comprehensive management of a member's health problems wherein the chronically ill or otherwise impaired individual may require long term and/or costly care.[1]

care panels. The group of patients for whose health care a single primary care physician or group of physicians is responsible.

carve-out benefits. Services which are managed, financed, and risked separately from other health services, primarily high-cost or specialty services such as mental health, vision, dental, or substance abuse programs.[4]

case management. A managed care technique in which a patient with a serious medical condition is assigned an individual who coordinates, manages, and monitors continuous, cost-effective treatment, sometimes outside a hospital setting.

cash flow risk. The possibility of running out of cash on hand to meet current obligations.

claims data. Data collected by an insurance company in the process of assessing and paying for health care costs (claims) for their insureds.

Climaran. Three-gendered aliens from the planet Climara responsible for revolutionizing health care in the late-twentieth century by empowering health care providers to regain control of the medical universe.

clinical pathways (critical pathways). A timed sequences of interventions in the patient's care plan to achieve desirable outcomes and reduce variations in healthcare procedures. They are designed to prevent unnecessary utilization of services, reduce costs, decrease length of stay, and optimize cost savings. In managed care, clinical pathways also serve as predictors of achievable clinical outcomes.[7]

coat. A physician, as opposed to a "suit," an administrator or manager.

collaborative bargaining. A form of negotiation in which a problem-solving approach is used to creatively find the "best" solution in which the result is the best possible for all parties.

collection risk. The possibility that an amount of money owed will not be paid.

consultant. An independent specialist who provides expert evaluations and advice to a client under the terms of a retainer or on an hourly or per diem basis.

consumerism. In medicine, the movement to change the processes of the clinical environment so as to be more patient-driven, leading the way to such entities as "medical malls," twenty-four-hour service, women's health centers, and various combinations of traditional and alternative medicine.

Continuous Quality Improvement (CQI). A systems approach to identifying problems in health care delivery in a continuous fashion. Scientific methods are often employed to improve work processes, eliminate wastes, etc. in order to meet and exceed customer needs and expectations (see TQM).[4]

coordination of benefits. A process wherein if an individual has two group-health plans, the amount payable is divided between the plans so that the combined coverage amounts to, but does not exceed, 100 percent of the charges.[1]

coordination of care. A process whereby different providers delivering health care to a single individual are coordinated to avoid repetition and harmful interactions.

copayment. A type of cost-sharing whereby insured or covered persons pay a specified flat amount per unit of service or unit of time, with the insurer paying the rest. The copayment is incurred at the time the service is used. The amount paid does not vary with the cost of the service (generally included in managed care plans).[5]

cost effectiveness. The value of a product or service in relation to its cost.

covered lives. The group of people who receive benefits from a health plan. In an HMO these are also called members.

customer differentiation. A market coverage strategy in which a hospital or group of physicians decides to operate in several segments of the market by tailoring a specific strategy for each group of customers. Patients are usually better served because products offered are specifically designed to meet the needs of specific segments.

customer service. Term that has not traditionally been used in clinical practice, but now applying to innovative processes that do not necessarily increase the quality of care but allow patients easier access to services or information.

defensive medicine. The ordering of treatments, tests, and procedures for the sole purpose of protecting the doctor from criticism or malpractice suits rather than for more carefully diagnosing or treating the patient.

direct costs. Costs incurred as a result of providing a service that can be directly linked to the provision of that service. For example, materials used during a visit are a direct cost.

disease-management programs. Programs designed to ensure that individuals with specific diseases receive a full range of appropriate diagnostic tests and treatments. Typically these programs result in lower health care costs because they substitute preventive care and early diagnosis for acute care.

distributive bargaining. Often called "a zero sum game," distributive bargaining consists primarily of concession making (buying a used car) vs. collaborative bargaining which involves a search for mutually profitable alternatives.

economic credentialing. Taking a physician's economic behavior into account (i.e., tests ordered, hospital bed days, outcomes) in deciding upon medical staff appointment or reappointment.[1]

economies of scale. The lowering of average costs per service or item as a result of delivering a larger volume of those goods or services.

epidural. A form of analgesia (preferred by many women in the United States) which affords pain relief while allowing the mother-to-be the opportunity to be awake and alert during the delivery.

Exclusive Provider Organization (EPO). A type of managed care plan in which the member must remain within the provider network to receive benefits.

experience rating. A method of setting premium rates based on the actual health care costs of a group or groups primarily used by managed care organizations and insurance companies.[4]

fee-for-service. Traditional method of paying for medical services whereby a practitioner bills for each encounter or service rendered. Also known as indemnity insurance. This system contrasts with salary, capitated, or prepayment systems, in which the payment is not changed with the number of services actually used.[4]

foundation model. A health care system which contracts with a medical group for professional services and manages all non-physician staff and facilities.[4]

full-time stiff. A derogatory term sometimes used by private practitioners to describe physicians who choose to sell their practices or be acquired by hospital entities. The term implies that these physicians will no longer be working as hard or be as productive as when they were in private practice.

gatekeeper. The primary-care physician who must authorize all medical services (e.g., hospitalizations, diagnostic work-ups, and specialty referrals) for a member.[1]

good-old-boy network. The perception of many practicing physicians that decisions at major medical organizations are made by a group that is predominantly male, predominantly over fifty years of age, and predominantly out of touch with the average practitioner.

governance. The manner in which something is regulated, often in medical administration. Usually separated from management, e.g., boards govern; administrators manage.

group model. A type of health maintenance organization (HMO) which contracts with physician groups at a negotiated fixed or capitated rate for a defined group of enrollees; in exchange, the HMO usually provides the facility, staff, and administrative support for the physician group.[4]

group practice. The application of health care service by a number of practitioners working in systematic association with the joint use of equipment and technical personnel and with centralized administration and financial organization.[5]

Health Maintenance Organization (HMO). An entity that provides, offers, or arranges for coverage of designated health services needed by plan members for a fixed, prepaid premium. There are four basic models of HMOs: group model, individual practice association, network model, and staff model.[8] Under the Federal HMO Act, an entity must have three characteristics to call itself an HMO: 1) an organized system for providing health care or otherwise assuring health care delivery in a geographic area, 2) an agreed-upon set of basic and supplemental health maintenance and treatment services, and 3) a voluntarily enrolled group of people.

hold harmless clause. A section of a contract in which a party agrees not to hold another liable for a specific risk. For managed care organizations, a controversial section of a contract with a physician that has the effect of decreasing liability to the insurer for noncovered services.

hospital admission. A single stay in a hospital by a single patient.

incentive alignment. A blueprint for inducing physicians to work or produce at a level consistent with the organization's goals by offering certain benefits or other compensation when they exceed the level specified.

incentivization for optimal utilization. A theoretic concept whereby the above benefits, monetary or otherwise, would be paid for best practices, assuming that those could be determined and quantified. This is in contrast to fee-for-service (incentivizes overutilization) or traditional capitation (promotes underutilization).

indemnification. Protection or insurance against penalties incurred by one's actions.

indemnity insurance. Insurance coverage which reimburses medical expenses traditionally in a nonmanaged environment based on procedures and encounters after they have occurred. Payments are made either directly to the provider or to the insured.[4]

indirect costs. Costs that cannot be directly linked to the provision of a specific good or service, for example, rent and receptionist salaries. Often these are linked back to a specific service by the use of a formula based on labor hours or direct costs. Also called overhead.

individual practice association (IPA). A type of HMO in which a partnership, corporation, or association of providers has entered into an arrangement for provision of their service. Practitioners provide care in their own offices and serve HMO members as part of their regular practice.[4]

information technology. A popular generality that covers many innovations in the abilities of computers, microelectronics, and telecommunications to produce, store, and transmit a wide spectrum of clinical information in ways that will revolutionize medicine, e.g., electronic medical records.

integrated delivery system. A regional health care system or network which provides a "continuum of care from acute care and outpatient ambulatory care to skilled nursing and long-term care." From a managed care perspective, an IDS may contract to provide this wide range of services to a defined population within a geographic area.[4]

Kaiser Health Plans. One of the first and one of the largest health maintenance organizations in the U.S., based in California. Kaiser is a group model HMO.

law school. A type of school that produces individuals that grow up to be the butt of ninety percent of physicians' jokes.

length of stay (LOS). The number of days that a covered person stays in an inpatient facility.[8]

liposuction. The sucking of fat through an automated mechanism, traditionally thought of in a plastic-surgery sense. Managed care organizations, however, have given the term new meaning over the past decade, e.g. "we are sucking the fat out of the system."

managed care. An organized system of managing and financing the delivery of health care services which integrates the financing and delivery of appropriate services to covered individuals by arrangements with selected providers to furnish a comprehensive set of services, explicit standards for selection of the care providers, formal programs for ongoing quality assurance and utilization review, and significant financial incentives for members to use providers and procedures associated with the plan.[5]

Managed Care Organization (MCO). See HMO above.

Management Services Organization (MSO). A management entity owned by a hospital, physician organization, or third party. The MSO contracts with payers and hospitals/physicians to provide services such as negotiating fee schedules, handling administrative functions, and billing and collections.[1]

Mandy. The subject of a song written by Barry Manilow often heard on elevators and easy-listening radio stations.

Marcus Welby, M.D. A television show which ran from 1969–1976 and was held in high esteem by various medical groups. The quintessential generalist, Dr Welby would be seen in one episode providing house calls, performing difficult surgery, and delivering babies.

market segmentation. Dividing a market into distinct groups of customers who differ in their buying behavior. Segments are typically based on demographics, or preferences (usually determined by surveys or analysis of purchasing behavior).

match. A process by which every resident's future is determined by a mainframe computer programmed by the National Resident Matching Program.

mature marketplace. A market in which sales growth is slow because the product or service has achieved acceptance and is reasonably well understood by most potential buyers. For providers, profits typically stabilize or decline because of increased marketing outlays to defend the product or service against competition.[6]

MBA. Masters of Business Administration. The graduate-level degree obtained by many business managers and an increasing number of physicians.

medical necessity. The supplies and services provided to diagnose and treat a medical condition in accordance with the standards of good medical practice and the medical community.[8]

member satisfaction. A measure of the satisfaction of insureds with their health plan. Usually determined by surveys.

morbidity rate. The incidence of disease in a population.

mortality rate. The rate of death in a population.

multispecialty group. A number of practitioners from more than one medical specialty working in systematic association with the joint use of equipment and technical personnel and with centralized administration and financial organization.

National average for marriage longevity among physicians. Less than the average for most professional groups, except for attorneys.

National Practitioner Data Bank. A database mandated by the Healthcare Quality Improvement Act of 1986 based on the perception that the increasing occurrence of medical malpractice litigation and the need to improve the quality of medical care had become nationwide problems that warranted greater efforts than those that could be undertaken by any individual state.

NCQA. The National Committee for Quality Assurance (NCQA) is a private, not-for-profit organization dedicated to assessing and reporting on the quality of managed care plans.

network. A group of providers and facilities able to contract for a defined set of healthcare services.[4]

opportunity cost. The cost of losing an opportunity, i.e., the value given up by using a resource in one way instead of in an alternative, better way.[4]

outcomes. The art and science of measuring effectiveness of patient care in terms often related to quality and efficiency, e.g., cost, mortality, health status, quality of life, or patient function and satisfaction.[4]

outcomes measures. Quantitative indicators that offer some assessment of the results for a patient after care, for example, how long it took to restore the patient's ability to walk or to work.[1]

overutilization. Promotion of more services than might be necessary for a given patient or population, e.g., fee-for-service insurance.

patient-centered care. Health care that is closely congruent with and responsive to patients' needs, wants and preferences, e.g. physicians and other caregivers shedding their paternalistic image and undertaking the more laborious process of exploring optimal outcomes with the patient.

patient satisfaction. A measure of the satisfaction of patients with the health care they've received. Often linked to a specific episode of care. Usually determined by survey.

payers. The individuals or organizations that pay for health care. Includes insurance companies, employers, and individuals.

pecking order. A pattern of behavior first observed in hens and later recognized in other groups of social animals (e.g., surgical residency programs) in which those of high rank within the group are able to attack those of lower rank without provoking an attack in return.

Peer Review Organization (PRO). A physician-sponsored organization charged with reviewing the services provided patients. The purpose of the review is to determine if the services rendered are medically necessary; provided in accordance with professional criteria, norms and standards; and provided in the appropriate setting.[8]

per member per month (pmpm). A method of payment whereby a network or provider receives a set amount of money per person every month under capitated payment arrangements.[4]

performance improvement. An area that takes into account the sum total of providing more efficient clinical care, e.g., quality, cost, work flow, materials requirements, inventory control, and labor.

personal statement. An opportunity for a resident applicant to express some of their personality on an otherwise mechanized application form, often the source of inane comments, e.g., "I knew I wanted to be a gynecologist since I was three years old," etc.

physician profiling. The practice of examining patterns or averages in a physician's practice, such as the average cost for an individual with a specific disease state.

Physician Hospital Organization (PHO). A contractual organization involving a hospital and its medical staff developed for the purpose of contracting directly with employers and managed-care organizations. This allows for the opportunity to better market hospital-physician services and achieve administrative efficiencies.[4]

point of service plan (POS). A health plan allowing the covered person to choose to receive a service from a participating or nonparticipating provider, with different benefit levels associated with the use of participating providers. Point-of-service can be provided in several ways:
- an HMO may allow members to obtain limited services from nonparticipating providers;
- an HMO may provide nonparticipating benefits through a supplemental major medical policy;
- a PPO may be used to provide both participating and nonparticipating levels of coverage and access; or various combinations of the above may be used.[8]

population based medicine. Medical care which takes as its target a population, rather than individuals. This involves a shift from the classic paradigm of an individual physician providing comprehensive, continuous, and affordable health care to patients as they present in the clinical setting to a population-based systematic approach that identifies persons at risk, intervenes, measures the outcomes, and provides continuous quality improvement.

practice guidelines. See protocol.

practice style. The favoring of certain treatment options based on a physician's preference, which may reflect peculiarities among some groups of physicians (specialist-generalist, geographic location, etc.) Treatment based on practice style may lead to care that varies with respect to appropriateness, utility, cost, and to the quality and quantity of resources utilized.

Preferred Provider Organization (PPO). A program in which contracts are established with providers of medical care. Providers under such contracts are referred to as preferred providers. Usually, the contract provides significantly better benefits (fewer copayments) for services received from preferred providers, thus encouraging covered persons to use these providers. Covered persons are generally allowed benefits for nonparticipating providers' services, usually on an indemnity basis with significant copayments. A PPO arrangement can be insured or self-funded. Providers may be, but are not necessarily, paid on a discounted fee-for-service basis.[8]

premium. A predetermined monthly membership fee that a subscriber or employer pays for their HMO coverage.[1]

primary care provider. A provider, the majority of whose practice is devoted to internal medicine, family/general practice, and pediatrics and serves as the primary access into the medical system for the patient. An obstetrician/ gynecologist may be considered a primary care provider.[8]

prostatectomy. Surgical removal of the prostate or part of it.

protocol. Statements by authoritative bodies as to the procedures appropriate for the physician to employ in making a diagnosis and treating it. The goal of guidelines is to change practice styles, reduce inappropriate and unnecessary care, and cut costs. You may hear these referred to as practice parameters, clinical practice guidelines, or protocols.[1]

quality of service. The quality of medical and nursing care. Third-party payers and agencies frequently initiate, encourage, or mandate the establishment of quality-assurance programs. Medical practices can be measured or compared to assess the level of excellence in the medical or nursing care provided.

Relative Value Scale (RVS). The compiled table of relative value units (RVUs), which is a value given to each procedure or unit of service. As payment systems, RVS is used to determine a formula which multiplies the RVU by a dollar amount, called a converter or conversion factor.[8]

Resource Based Relative Value Scale (RBRVS). A method of determining physicians' fees based on the time, training, skill, and other factors required to deliver various services, developed by the Health Care Financing Administration (HCFA) to provide a more equitable physician reimbursement system for use by Medicare recipients. Generally, this has the effect of increasing reimbursement for cognitive services and decreasing reimbursement for procedures.[1]

risk. Possibility that revenues of the insurer will not be sufficient to cover expenditures incurred in the delivery of contractual services. Often considered a four letter word (in a negative sense) by physicians, e.g., "There's no risk in this for me, is there?"[5]

risk management. A program of activities to identify, evaluate, and take corrective action against risks that may lead to patient or employee injury and/or property loss or damage with resulting financial loss or legal liability.

risk-pool allocation. The process by which any profits or losses in an at-risk capitated contract will be dispersed among the hospital and physicians. Often the trickiest part of determining a risk-pool allocation is among the different physician groups and specialties.

risk-sharing agreements. A contract through which an HMO and contracted provider each accept partial responsibility for the financial risk and rewards involved in cost effectively caring for the members enrolled in the plan and assigned to a specific provider.[1]

single-specialty networks. A group of physicians in the same medical specialty who have joined together to share the risk of providing care to their patients who are covered by a given health plan.

social life. Time spent in non-work-productive activities, e.g., dating, hobbies, athletics. Does not include watching *Star Trek* reruns while studying anatomy. Traditionally had been an unnecessary indulgence for many medical students and residents. With the advent of workload limits and kinder, gentler residencies, these activities are making a comeback for young physicians.

space time continuum. Based on Einstein's two relativity postulates, a condition in which elements of length and time are no longer invariant under a transformation from one set of axes to another set which is in uniform relative motion with respect to the first. More importantly, an excuse for Captains Kirk and Picard whenever they got the Starship Enterprise into trouble.

SSRI. A type of antidepressant. Alternatively, according to some theorists, a necessity for every human being until our biological evolution allows us to produce enough serotonin to handle modern-day stress.

staff model HMO. A type of HMO, similar to the group model, in which physicians are salaried employees who provide their services exclusively to HMO enrollees.[5]

stewardship. The act of choosing service over self-interest, e.g., to replace the traditional management tools of control and consistency, stewardship organizations will offer partnerships and choice at all levels to their employees as well as to their customers and hold themselves accountable to those over whom they exercise power.[3]

stop-loss insurance. Insurance purchased by an HMO or health insurance company to protect itself or its contracted medical groups against losses above a specified amount as a result of caring for a policy holder. Also refereed to as reinsurance.

suit. An administrator or manager, as opposed to a physician (coat).

surgical personality. When used in a kind way, one who is precise and deliberate. Most often used as someone without social graces or manners who thinks quite highly of him or herself.

systems approach. A way of thinking about events, processes, and organizations in which the economic, organizational, and social context (systems) in which they occur are seen as essential to shaping, defining, and motivating them.

third-party payment. Payment for health care by a party other than the enrollee (for example, by an insurance company).[5]

Total Quality Management (TQM). A system for integrating quality-related efforts throughout an organization so that all the functions can focus together on the efficient satisfaction of the customer's needs. Total quality management often involves participation across functions and up and down the hierarchy in an organization. (see CQI)[2]

underutilization. Promotion of the use of less services than might be optimal for a patient or a given population, often incentivized through traditional capitated contracts.

utilization. The frequency with which a benefit is used — for example 3,200 doctor's office visits per 1,000 HMO members per year. Utilization experience multiplied by the average cost per unit of service delivered equals capitated costs.[1]

utilization review. Evaluation of the necessity, appropriateness, and efficiency of the use of medical services and facilities. Helps ensure proper use of health care resources by providing for the regular review of such areas as admission of patients, length of stay, services performed, and referrals.[1]

withholds. The portion of the monthly capitation payment to physicians withheld by the HMO until the end of the year or other time period to create an incentive for efficient care. The withhold is at risk; i.e., if the physician exceeds utilization norms, he does not receive it. It often serves as a financial incentive for lower utilization, not to be confused with a bonus.[1]

Glossary References

1. American Medical Specialty Organization, Inc. AMSO "Definition of Terms."

2. Don Berwick et. al, *Curing Health Care*, (San Francisco: Jossey Bass, 1990).

3. Peter Block, *Stewardship*, (San Francisco: Berrett-Koehler Publishers, 1994).

4. The Governance Institute, "Healthcare Terms and Abbreviations for Boards and Medical Leaders."

5. Judith A. Huntington, "Glossary for Managed Care,"

6. Philip Kotler, *Marketing Management: Analysis, Planning, Implementation and Control*, (Englewood Cliffs, NY: Prentice Hall, 1991): 350.

7. Dulcelina Stahl, "Anatomy of a management system," *Nursing Management* 28 (December 1997): 20–21.

8. United Health Care, "The Language of Managed Care and Organized Health Care Systems."

ABOUT THE AUTHORS

Leaders in their respective fields of medicine and organizational science, the authors have brought together their individual experiences as medical practitioner and business consultant in *The Phantom Stehoscope—A Field Manual for Finding an Optimistic Future in Medicine.*

Stephen K. Klasko

Stephen K. Klasko, M.D., M.B.A., has bridged the art and science of medicine with business and administrative changes through a unique background consisting of private practice, academic and administrative medicine, and business training. He received a B.A. from Lehigh University in chemistry and biology and his M.D. at Hahnemann University. He then completed a nutrition externship at University of California, Davis, and began his OB-GYN residency at Health East Teaching Hospitals. Dr. Klasko practiced generalist OB-GYN in Allentown, Pennsylvania, and was involved in the transformation of a small two-person group into one of the largest private practices in the area.

Klasko later became residency program director at Lehigh Valley Hospital, Allentown, Pennsylvania, engineering the expansion of the program from eight to sixteen residents. In 1996, he completed the Wharton Executive M.B.A. program. Currently he is the chairman of the department of Obstetrics and Gynecology at Lehigh Valley Hospital, President of the Board of the Lehigh Valley Physicians Group, a 150-member multispecialty group, and professor of clinical OB-GYN at Penn State University, Hershey Medical Center.

During the past several years, Klasko's main research interests have included alignment of physician incentives with organizational goals, development of a business curriculum for physicians and students as a means of educating residents to feel optimistic about their future, and improvement of physicians' negotiation and collaboration skills. He is the recipient of first prize in a physician writing competition for his article entitled, "Mamas, Don't Let Your Babies Grow Up To Be OB-GYNs." He has written extensively on clinical issues such as "Psychological Effects of Hysterectomy," business issues such as "Biases Physicians Bring to the Negotiating Table," and social issues such as "Stress Management and Burnout Reduction for Young Physicians."

A sought-after lecturer, Klasko uses his love of science fiction and his knowledge of the business side of medicine to inform and encourage audiences with talks including "Independence Day: Educating Residents To Seize the Future," and "Crossing the Galaxy: A Hitchiker's Guide To Physicians and Administrators." He is a member of the faculty of the Governance Institute and has been involved with Wharton's Aresty Institute of Executive Education's Medical Staff Development courses.

He holds a private pilot license and has a passion for running marathons.

Gregory P. Shea

Gregory P. Shea, Ph.D., is a Phi Beta Kappa graduate of Harvard College, and holds an M.Sc. in management studies from the London School of Economics, and an M.A., M. Phil., and Ph.D. in administrative science from Yale University.

Shea consults, researches, and writes in the areas of organizational and individual change, group effectiveness, and handling conflict. He is a principal in the Coxe Group, an international consulting firm; senior fellow at the Leonard Davis Institute of Health Economics; senior consultant at the Center for Applied Research; and is on the faculty at the Wharton School of the University of Pennsylvania.

His writing has appeared in the *Sloan Management Review, Journal of Applied Management, Journal of Applied Behavior Science, Journal of Conflict Resolution, Handbook of Industrial and Organizational Psychology* (second edition), *British Journal of Social Psychology, Journal of Management Development*, and *Research in Personnel and Human Resource Management* (volume 5).

Shea has worked full-time in both industry and academia, and his awards include an Excellence in Teaching Award from Wharton. He serves as contributing editor to the *Journal of Applied Behavioral Science*, as a reviewer for *Group and Organizational Management, Journal of Applied Psychology,* and *Personnel Psychology.* Shea is a member of the Academy of Management and the American Psychological Association.

To contact the authors for consulting services or public speaking appearances:

Stephen K. Klasko
pibroch775@aol.com

Gregory P. Shea
shea@wharton.upenn.edu